CAST AWAY

Cast Away

*True Stories of Survival from
Europe's Refugee Crisis*

Charlotte McDonald-Gibson

THE NEW PRESS

NEW YORK
LONDON

For Nathaniel and Danny

Requests for permission to reproduce selections from
this book should be mailed to:
Permissions Department, The New Press, 120 Wall Street, 31st floor,
New York, NY 10005.

First published in Great Britain by Portobello Books, London, 2016
Published in the United States by The New Press, New York, 2016
Distributed by Perseus Distribution

ISBN 978-1-62097-263-2 (hc)
ISBN 978-1-62097-264-9 (e-book)
CIP data is available.

The New Press publishes books that promote and enrich public discussion and
understanding of the issues vital to our democracy and to a more equitable world.
These books are made possible by the enthusiasm of our readers; the support of
a committed group of donors, large and small; the collaboration of our many
partners in the independent media and the not-for-profit sector; booksellers,
who often hand-sell New Press books; librarians; and above all by our authors.

www.thenewpress.com

Printed in the United States of America

2   4   6   8   10   9   7   5   3   1

The Union is founded on the values of respect for human dignity, freedom, democracy, equality, the rule of law and respect for human rights, including the rights of persons belonging to minorities. These values are common to the Member States in a society in which pluralism, non-discrimination, tolerance, justice, solidarity and equality between women and men prevail.

Article 2, the Treaty of the European Union

All this killing, all this blood, I can't believe it. There is no war like the war in Syria. The people can't stay in Syria in this war. They try to come to Europe, and look at what Europe is doing. They let them pay smugglers €5,000, €6,000, €10,000 and go by the sea and die. And after, when they arrive, they say 'welcome'. Why? Why don't you try and bring these people here safely? If you arrive, they say 'welcome'; if you die in the sea, they say 'never mind'. Why?

Hanan al-Hasan, Syrian refugee

Contents

List of Country Codes

AG	Algeria	LO	Slovakia
AL	Albania	LS	Liechtenstein
AU	Austria	LU	Luxembourg
BE	Belgium	LY	Libya
BK	Bosnia and Herzegovina	MD	Moldova
BO	Belarus	MK	Macedonia
BU	Bulgaria	MO	Morocco
DA	Denmark	MT	Malta
EG	Egypt	NL	Netherlands
EI	Ireland	NO	Norway
EN	Estonia	PL	Poland
EZ	Czech Republic	PO	Portugal
FI	Finland	RO	Romania
FR	France	RI	Serbia
GG	Georgia	RS	Russia
GM	Germany	SI	Slovenia
GR	Greece	SP	Spain
HR	Croatia	SW	Sweden
HU	Hungary	SY	Syria
IC	Iceland	SZ	Switzerland
IS	Israel	TS	Tunisia
IT	Italy	TU	Turkey
JO	Jordan	UK	United Kingdom
LE	Lebanon	UP	Ukraine
LG	Latvia	WE	West Bank
LH	Lithuania		

KEY LOCATIONS ON
THE MIGRANT ROUTE

Featuring

Majid Hussain: *born in 1993 in Jos, Nigeria, to a wealthy family. A football-loving teen, Majid was brought up by his father after the death of his mother. He was forced to seek sanctuary in Libya when sectarian violence erupted in his home state.*

Nart Bajoi: *a lawyer and systems engineer, born in Syria in 1981 to a father who worked as a civil servant in Bashar al-Assad's government. His brothers followed in their father's footsteps, but when the Arab Spring brought pro-democracy protests to Syria, Nart joined the underground opposition.*

Mohammed Kazkji: *born in 1992 into a large family with a cobbling business in Damascus. Mohammed studied hard and dreamed of becoming the best electrician in the world, but then the civil war broke out and he was called to serve in Assad's army.*

— Nidar: *Mohammed's uncle, who left Syria in the 1980s and set himself up with a car repair business in Misrata, Libya. He is father to three children: a baby boy also called Mohammed, and two young daughters, Siham and Maram.*

— Omar: *Mohammed's friend, a Syrian plasterer in his early twenties forced to leave his home to avoid military conscription.*

–Yahea: *Another friend of Mohammed of a similar age and from the same neighbourhood, a confectioner who dreams of introducing Syria's sweets to Europe.*

Sina Habte: *an Eritrean born to a doctor father and a civil engineer mother in 1988. Sina excelled at school and became a chemical engineer.*

– Dani: *Sina's husband, born in 1973, a civil engineer and university lecturer.*

Hanan al-Hasan: *born in 1964 to two Palestinian refugees in the northern Syrian town of Al-Hasakah. Her father was the first Palestinian to become a judge in Syria, and Hanan devoted herself to building a safe and prosperous life for her four children in Damascus.*

–Talal Al-Hamzah: *Hanan's husband, born in 1963, a small business owner originally from the northern Syrian city of Homs.*

– Rim Hamzah: *Hanan and Talal's eldest daughter, born in 1990.*

– Izzat: *Rim's fiancé.*

– Bisan Hamzah: *Hanan and Talal's second daughter, born in 1992.*

– Ismail Hamzah: *Hanan and Talal's first son, born in 1996.*

– Riad Hamzah: *Hanan and Talal's youngest child, a son born in 2000.*

Introduction

An Impossible Choice

Istanbul, Turkey
19 April 2015

A new life was on its way. Sina could feel it. Her hand moved over
the curve of her belly, from the flatness to the swell and down
again, a wave at the very centre of her being, a life wriggling and
kicking in his own sea inside her.

Delina. Our Delina. Sina and her husband Dani had already
chosen his name. She loved the meaning. *Wanted. This is what we
want.* Sina had not always been so sure. Living with her parents in
Eritrea, bonded to the military, earning around $30 a month, and
watching friends and relatives disappear into the country's vast
underground prison system, she could hardly imagine bringing
another soul into such a world. Then suddenly she was pregnant
and all that mattered was getting this tiny speck of life to a place
where he would never know the shadow of a dictatorship, and
where his parents could see him grow up free.

Her quest was almost over. In four months Sina had taken
their unborn son over five countries and two continents. She
had made it to Istanbul, and the safe life they sought was just a
few miles away over the short stretch of sea separating Turkey
from the European Union (EU). But for the past month, Sina
had been alone. A smuggler had betrayed them, and Dani was

stuck in Uganda. Now she was fearful. Nothing felt safe any more and she didn't know what to do.

It was Sunday, 19 April 2015. Early that morning the crew of a Portuguese merchant ship in the Mediterranean had watched in horror as an old fishing vessel rammed their hull, and 800 men, women and children sank to the bottom of the sea. Sina knew that many boats had capsized, and that many refugees had drowned trying to reach the shores of the European Union. And now a smuggler was urging her to board a boat leaving that evening for Greece carrying another consignment of Syrians and Eritreans.

Two days earlier, Sina had been in a private hospital looking at her baby on an ultrasound scan. The doctor told her that her son was ready to come into the world, and handed Sina the numbers for the hospital along with a piece of paper with a few Turkish words scrawled across it.

'Help me. I am pregnant and am going to deliver my baby,' it read.

She was now four days past her due date. What use would that scrap of paper be in the middle of the Mediterranean? Sina knew that women had given birth in the dark hulls of smuggling vessels, surrounded by bodies in the grip of fear and panic, inhaling hot air saturated with the smell of human waste, diesel fumes and rotting fish. Their babies were born, only to be lost to the sea moments later, and Sina could not bear such a fate for her child.

But the smuggler was becoming agitated, his voice rising as he spoke.

'Sina, I am telling you, you have to go,' he told her. 'If you stay here it will not be good for you. It only takes one hour to reach Greece and then you can go directly to the hospital and deliver there.'

Sina was confused. Who could tell her what was best for her baby? She needed Dani more than ever, but he was nearly 3,000 miles away, just a scratchy voice at the end of a cheap Viber phone call. She was all alone. She didn't know who to trust or what she should do.

On the edges of the European Union – on the coasts of Turkey and Libya and behind the 235 kilometres of steel fences and razor wire barricading in a continent – mothers, fathers, sons and daughters were faced with similar impossible choices. A Syrian mother-of-four who spent her life trying to shield her children from harm looked down at a tiny inflatable boat and wondered if she had the strength to stand up to the smugglers and demand another vessel; a father thrown into the sea had to decide whether to try to hold on to one child or let him go to save another; a young Syrian entrusted with the lives of his uncle's family had to choose whether it was safer to take them with him across the Mediterranean or leave them behind in a country consumed by war.

The hundreds of thousands of people gathering at Europe's gates had put off this moment for as long as they could. Abandoning a home you had spent your life building or a country where you were planning a future was not a decision anyone wanted to make. So at first people had stayed, hoping the war would end, the suicide bombings would stop, the dictatorship would fall, or the West would come to their aid and defeat the Islamic State or oust President Bashar al-Assad. When people were finally forced from their homes in Syria, Afghanistan, Iraq, Eritrea or any of the other nations in the grip of war, many had stayed in neighbouring countries, keen to remain in a familiar culture and language, keeping that hope of return alive for a little longer. It was only when there was nothing else left – when there was no income, education, shelter, food or safety – that people put themselves and their families in a boat and took that last gamble.

For decades hope of a better life had pushed people to Europe's unwelcoming shores. Some considered taking the risk to escape poverty and find work, others fled wars and famine. But the real challenge for the European Union – and for the values of human rights and dignity for all which it espoused – would begin in 2011. The Arab Spring was transforming a region, and European politicians were quick to hail it as a revolution against oppressive regimes. But when it came to helping the victims of this noble pursuit of democracy, their response did not match their rhetoric.

Over the course of the next five years, Syria would descend into a terrible civil war, chaos would engulf Libya, and the number of people in the world forced from their homes would match the scale of the Second World War. The people on the move hoped that Europe would remember its own history, and would have learned the lessons from the darkest days of its past. But very quickly, the hypocrisies at the heart of the EU would be exposed by the million or so desperate souls seeking a little help from one of the richest regions in the world. Children would be tear-gassed on the soil of a union which preached human rights for all. Coils of razor wire, armed soldiers and riot police would block borders over which people, goods and capital were meant to freely flow. National leaders would refuse sanctuary on the grounds of religion on a continent which had vowed never again to persecute minorities. East and West clashed over competing values 25 years after the fall of the Berlin Wall.

But the war-weary could not simply go home, so they were compelled to attempt ever more risky voyages towards a region determined to keep them out. Among the hundreds of thousands of people forced on an odyssey to Europe were Sina and Dani, desperate to save their unborn son from a life of military service in Eritrea; Majid Hussain, a privileged Nigerian boy fleeing sectarian violence; Nart Bajoi, an idealistic lawyer who risked his life trying to oust Assad; Mohammed Kazkji, a Syrian teenager who just wanted to study hard and please his parents; and Hanan al-Hasan, who watched in horror as the safe life she had built for her children in Damascus fell apart. In the space of a few years a multi-billion-dollar underground smuggling industry stretching from sub-Saharan Africa to Scandinavia would emerge to facilitate such odysseys. It was a trade fuelled by extortion and exploitation, but its customers had no other choice when there was no legal avenue to apply for asylum in the EU. And so the illicit passage to Europe would become the most dangerous journey in the world.

Of the thousands of people who perished, less than ten per cent would be identified. Most shipwreck victims stayed at the bottom of the sea, no nation willing to pay to recover the bodies and try and find out whose son or daughter had died locked on a lower deck or slipping out of the grasp of a loved one and into the waves. Of the bodies that washed up in Europe, there was no money to search for identifying marks or test for DNA. Most would end up in unmarked graves.

The International Organization for Migration keeps a database listing every reported death on the approach to Europe since 2000. Lives are reduced to a single line, with just a hint at the chain of events which led to their deaths: 'Woman dies in childbirth on a boat set sail from Turkey. The body was abandoned at sea'; 'Rolled over by the truck he tried to hide under to leave Greece'; 'Young girl and her grandfather missing after boat overturned while crossing Evros River'. The list goes on and on, and every day another short story about an anonymous victim can be added.

While politicians have felt able to lament the nameless dead, they have shown less empathy towards the nameless living seeking refuge on European soil. It is all too easy for governments and the public to turn away, to think of them as somehow a little bit less human, and leave them to their fates. But they have names and stories to tell, and they deserve to be heard.

Dani knew the dangers of the sea voyage, and tried to convince Sina to stay where she was.

'You don't have to move anywhere at this time,' he said.

It was the voice Sina loved, but it seemed very distant, so faint that she couldn't hear the cadences in tone which would let her know what he really thought, what he really wanted her to do. 'If you don't want to stay in the smuggler's house, go to a hotel,' he told her. 'I am trying to find a passport, I will come soon.'

But he had been saying that for weeks and still he hadn't come. The smuggler in Kampala had vanished along with the money and the promised documents that would allow Dani to travel. He was trapped there until he could arrange for more papers and a plane ticket.

Sina was smart and tough: she was a chemical engineer, used to life in the field and the logic of the laboratory. But she was not used to making decisions about her life on her own. When she did, she could be impulsive, acting with the naivety of someone who had only ever known the harsh paternalism of a dictatorship. She was twenty-seven years old, but ever since she had been sent to the scrub of western Eritrea a decade ago for her military indoctrination, the state had decided everything for her: where she would live, where she would work, where she could travel. Then Dani had come into her life, promising to always be there to keep her safe and happy. He had spent hours searching the internet for advice on pregnancy and childbirth, and Sina had been glad to rely on his advice and let him take care of her. But he couldn't help her now; she was nine months pregnant and marooned in a strange country. And the smuggler was insistent, pushing her to get on a bus to the coast.

No, she thought as her hand caressed her bump, this was a choice she would have to make alone.

2011

Number of refugees and migrants entering the EU: 141,051
Number of deaths: 1,500

1

A Dictator's Revenge

Majid: Tripoli, Libya

Majid Hussain didn't know who would turn up on his doorstep first: Colonel Gaddafi's foot soldiers following orders to purge Libya of its migrant workforce, or vengeful rebels wielding Kalashnikovs and the conviction that everyone with black skin deserved to be lynched.

For months the Nigerian teenager had watched on television in Tripoli as rebels not much older than himself stormed through the desert in their cheap sunglasses and mismatching camouflage, and it had seemed inconceivable that this shabby army of the disaffected could pose a threat to Muammar Gaddafi's calm and ordered capital. He had heard rumours that all Africans from south of the Sahara were at risk of attack from rebels seeking mass punishment for the few who had colluded with the regime – but surely these were just rumours? Every day Majid still went to work and returned home every evening to his reliable air-conditioning and his satellite TV. The rebellion had remained remote from his life, and he wanted it to stay that way.

This war is none of my business, he thought. *I have already seen my own country torn apart by old hatreds – I don't need to see that again.*

Majid and his housemate Ali had laughed off reports on CNN and the BBC about fighting on the outskirts of Tripoli, and they didn't want to believe the news that Gaddafi was bombing civilians in Benghazi. It was all Western propaganda, the two

Nigerians convinced each other. Even when a spokesman for Gaddafi warned on public radio that they would flood Europe with migrants if there was any Western military action, the young men remained unconcerned.

'Come on,' Majid had said to his friend, 'of course they don't want Europe to be full of immigrants, so NATO will leave us in peace.'

Finally, on the morning of 12 August, 2011 Majid could ignore the reality no longer. The air-conditioning unit was still spluttering along and Libyan state TV continued its delusional broadcasts, but outside the ground was shaking. The French Mirages and British Typhoons were cutting through the clouds above his head as NATO bombing raids thundered closer to Gaddafi's compound, and closer to the two frightened Nigerians.

This is what an earthquake must feel like, Majid thought, as pure terror coupled with a sense of utter powerlessness overwhelmed him.

He was no longer safe in Libya. Clouds of dust and smoke rose above the minarets and cranes of the Tripoli skyline. Before the air had cleared, the order came from the top. The rebel army, supported by NATO, was closing in and Colonel Gaddafi finally made good on his threat. All migrant workers still living in Libya were to be rounded up, taken to the coast, and forced on board whatever vessels were available. There they would be sent out into the waves in the direction of Malta and Italy, a flotilla of human despair heading directly to Europe's shores.

As the Arab Spring began its eastward creep from Tunisia and protests broke out in Libya in February 2011, a voluntary exodus of the country's large migrant workforce had begun. During the first few months of fighting, the Egyptians, Pakistanis, Bangladeshis, Filipinos, Vietnamese and sub-Saharan Africans beat a relatively calm path overland to neighbouring Egypt and Tunisia, patiently queueing under the fierce desert sun to submit their papers at the crowded border posts. But soon people were fleeing with nothing more than the clothes they were wearing. Gaddafi had bolstered his military with mercenaries from nearby states, relying on Tuareg tribesmen from Mali to put down any rebellions that threatened to erupt in the Libyan hinterlands. These men became targets for vengeful rebel groups looking to vent their anger at the regime. They didn't wait to gather any evidence: anyone with black skin came under suspicion. Sub-Saharan migrants found on the street were beaten, robbed and locked up. Hundreds died in the wave of retribution. As the rebels advanced on Tripoli, thousands of foreign workers found themselves trapped and terrified in the city centre, awaiting their fate.

This wasn't the first time Majid had felt so helpless: he was only eighteen but already weary from what seemed like an eternity on the run from events beyond his control. And he was so tired of running. Life was not meant to be this way. Majid's father had prepared him for business dinners and charitable endeavours, not for a flight across continents in search of peace and security.

Majid had been one of Nigeria's luckier sons, born to an industrious family which had managed to navigate its way out of the poverty and corruption which infected so many lives there. His grandfather was one of the first police officers in independent Nigeria, and his father practised medicine before turning his hand to business and ascending the corporate ranks to become a management executive at the Nigerian National Petroleum Company.

During Majid's childhood, there was not much family around – his mother fell ill and died when he was four years old. An old passport photograph was all he had to remember her by, and other relatives had drifted away. But he felt no great emptiness in his life. He had his father, a kind and generous man who paid the school fees for the poorer children in their neighbourhood and insisted on supporting the underdog teams whenever he and Majid watched football. Majid preferred the relatively sure bet of being a Manchester United fan and used to tease his father for his soft heart. But he was stricter when it came to his son's education: first it was home schooling, then a private academy with extra English classes, before enrolment in a management studies course.

As an only child, Majid had the run of their mansion set in generous grounds in the city of Jos in Northern Nigeria. There was a housekeeper, a driver and a cook, and he had plenty of friends from the local football team. Although occasionally teased for his height – he bore the nickname 'Smallie' with equal measures of affection and annoyance – he played with a determination and agility that belied his short stature. And he was growing into a good-looking young man with a smile that quickly spread to his eyes and lit up his face, with just a glint of good-natured mischief. Most of all it exuded kindness, and only time would tell whether he was cut out for the ruthless world of Nigerian business towards which his father was steering him.

In the end Majid's wiles and athleticism proved more useful than any education.

In 2009, his steady path towards a comfortable life and lucrative career came to an abrupt halt. Near the end of the previous year, sectarian violence had erupted in Plateau State. Since Nigeria had achieved independence, religious clashes had come and gone with the inevitability of the seasons, with Jos sitting uncomfortably on the divide between the Christian south and the Muslim north. But this conflict was particularly brutal, with hundreds of people killed in Jos as gangs went from house to house, Christians attacking Muslims and Muslims attacking Christians with equal ferocity. Mosques, churches and homes were razed, as politicians from both sides fanned the flames.

At first Majid felt no fear. When you lived with your hero, what was there to be frightened of? He was fifteen and his father still towered over his life, although he was no longer the agile man who could match his son's prowess on the football field. Majid's father was 65 and had retired from the National Petroleum Company, deciding it was time to start a more low-key wholesale business and devote his dwindling energies to philanthropy.

When a Christian mob turned up at the family compound on 9 January 2009, there was little he could do to defend his son.

It was early morning when Majid's father heard a noise in front of the house and went out just in time to see a man scale the fence and open the gate to a gang of young men high on hatred and violence. The spacious grounds gave him a little time to grab Majid and race him towards the rear of the house where he kept his chickens. He only had a few minutes to think, and hoisted Majid onto the chicken coop, from where he could climb up into the coil of razor wire that topped their perimeter fence.

When the men burst in behind him he realized he had no time to escape himself, but he had done everything he could to save his child.

'Go!' was his last word for his son.

But Majid couldn't: he was frozen with fear on the top of the fence, his legs tangled and bleeding in the wire and his gaze fixated on his father as the axe hit the point where his arm met his shoulder. At first Majid was surprised by the lack of blood. Even as a second blow fell and his father crumpled, it all seemed so clean. Then the axe came down again and split his skull, finally opening up a torrent of red. Still Majid sat on the fence and watched, as if he were seeing it all through the filter of a dream. He watched silently as the life flowed out of the only family he had ever really known.

Finally the mob finished its frenzy and turned to the boy on the fence. One man picked up an iron weight and flung it high to try and dislodge him. Majid kicked his legs free and jumped down on the other side.

At that moment he started running, his life now suddenly set on a different course. First he ran away from the mob's screams.

Then he ran through the forests, finding himself alongside other men, women and children who had watched similar evils befall their homes and their families. He continued running through the region, seeing houses aflame and bodies in the road. He stayed on foot, eventually running out of the state entirely. He avoided large urban areas and trekked and hitched rides through the jungle, sleeping rough and eating whatever he could scavenge.

Nowhere felt safe any more, so he kept running.

Not once did he stop to ask himself where he was going or what he was doing. The only motive propelling him on was a deep survival instinct, a drive to make it alive from one day to the next, dimly aware that a hardness was forming within him as he ran from his country.

I am scared of no one. I have no fears, nothing, because of what I have seen.

An anger was also welling inside him. A cycle of revenge and old hatreds had robbed him of his father, and he was afraid that if he stayed in Nigeria he too would end up sucked into a life that would leech any remaining humanity out of him. So he ran to escape the desire to avenge his father and perpetuate the sectarian bloodshed.

If I stay in Nigeria, having seen what I saw, will I be a good person? he asked himself. *I don't think so. I will have this anger. I will just be waiting for the slightest opportunity to kill.*

Finally he crossed the border north into Niger, a vast desert nation and smugglers' paradise at the heart of the African continent. There, hanging out penniless in markets and bus stations among other itinerant souls, he heard about the life of plenty that could be his in oil-rich Libya. The streets may not exactly be paved with gold, but they said you could fill the tank of your car with petrol for less than ten dollars, and that was enough for Majid.

In the lawless border towns of southern Niger, you could get anything you wanted for the right price: guns, drugs, women. The thriving smuggling trades were run by nomadic Saharan tribes with a history of moving to wherever they could find the best resources. In the past those resources were water and arable land, but as nations in Europe and North Africa introduced more visa restrictions in the 1980s and 1990s, the most lucrative resource was the constant stream of human beings driven towards richer, safer nations. With their knowledge of the punishing desert climate and a history of navigating its farthest reaches, smuggling people across the Sahara was a natural vocation for the nomads.

When fifteen-year-old Majid turned up in sand-blasted Agadez – a caravan city carved from the desert by the ancient salt traders and now epicentre of the new business of hopes and dreams – he felt utterly lost and alone. He was grateful for the kindness when a local man approached and offered him food and assistance, not questioning his motives even when the man told him how to sneak aboard a smuggling truck which was heading to Libya.

'Don't worry – when other people are getting on the truck, just do it,' the man said.

Majid followed his advice, and mingled in with those who had paid for their clandestine passage north. They clambered on board the light goods vehicle with their bundles of belongings, the men hanging over the sides as the women and children settled down on top for the long drive.

It was just one cold and cramped night on the desert tracks before the fugitive passenger was discovered. When the smugglers did their morning headcount, they headed straight for the skinny boy shivering in a T-shirt and filthy jeans. They didn't even bother beating Majid or trying to extort money out of him. He clearly had nothing to give them. However, after threatening to leave him to die in the desert, they became oddly accommodating.

'OK,' the Chadian driver said with a sudden change of heart, 'come on, get in – whenever we stop, if you need food, just let me know'.

For the rest of the winding two-week journey north, Majid

happily took him up on his offer and thought how lucky he was for this small act of compassion. He failed to realize that he had become nothing more than a commodity to be traded and battered for the best deal. The smugglers had seen it all before, and had their own plans for the poorest of the poor who turned up in Agadez desperate to head north but unable to pay their way. Their agents prowled the bus stations for the most vulnerable, encouraging them to smuggle on board vessels and tipping off the driver about their illicit cargo. Everyone got a cut until they arrived at their final, dismal destination.

For Majid, that was a desert border post manned by a ragtag bunch of Libyan security forces and tribal militia. The mask of friendship fell from the Chadian driver's face as he shoved the boy out and into the hands of a kidnapping gang, who bundled him onto the floor in the back of a pick-up.

The drive seemed short compared with his journey over the desert. Majid spent a couple of hours crouched beneath the seats trying to make sense of his situation. Had the kind man in Agadez really been working with the smugglers? What fresh indignity lay in store for him when the truck stopped? As he climbed down from the pick-up, he looked around in despair. His new home was an old farmhouse crumbling to dirt, but the locks on the doors were sturdy and the dozens of people cowering on the floor had clearly been there for some time.

Majid was held in the acrid heat for days, visited once in the morning and once in the evening by a man bearing bread and water. Each time he would slap the sides of Majid's head and demand that he call his relatives for money. Each time Majid would tell him the truth.

'I have no family.'

Like the other hostages, he either had to find someone who would pay for his freedom, or work off his debt. It took a week for Majid's captors to realize there was no one to extort, so they found a job for him: tending camels at a sprawling desert farm, where the landowner had few kind words for his new charge. Majid's delicate hands and slight frame were unsuited to manual labour, and the exasperated farmer soon gave up.

'You're an idiot, you have no idea how to feed a camel!' he shouted at him one morning before taking him back to the main house.

'He's just a child, he is so little,' the farmer told his wife, asking her to put him to use as a houseboy.

And so Majid found himself trapped in a life of domestic servitude with nothing for his efforts beyond crumbs of bread and water. For a month he was forced to get up at dawn to scrub the floors, wash the dishes, clean the toilets and perform whatever task the mistress of the house dreamt up. She was not cruel exactly, but she treated Majid as worthy of nothing but a few orders barked in broken English.

With each day that passed, a little more of the humanity Majid had been desperately trying to preserve ebbed away. But his ingenuity was undiminished, and he dedicated his energy to forming a new plan to escape. One morning his captor jotted down a list of a few items and sent Majid to the market. He didn't flee straight away, but formed a mental map of the town. The next time he was sent to the market, he vowed to make his escape. Desperate for help, he ran up to every black face he could see on the street and tried to explain his situation. But the words tumbled out in English, and most of the French- and Arabic-speaking men shrugged their shoulders and turned away.

Then Majid caught sight of an older man watching from the shade of a street café. To Majid's surprise the stranger started addressing him in the local language of Plateau State.

'Calm down,' he told Majid. 'You can't be on the streets – the Libyans know each other and it will be easy for them to locate you.'

The man told him he would be safer at his house. Majid wanted to resist, wary of the older man's intentions. Twice he had trusted in people's kindness, and twice he had been betrayed. Perhaps the apparent Good Samaritan knew of Majid's father and was aware that the family once had money. But Majid had little choice: all he had in his pocket was a handful of notes for the weekly shop.

His trust in the stranger paid off: for six months the man kept him hidden at home, providing him with clothes and food and trying to engineer a way to get his new young charge to Tripoli, where he had a brother who could help him settle and find work. Eventually he heard that a friend was stopping by en route to the capital and asked him to take Majid with him. That final leg of his journey to Tripoli was a comfortable one. Majid didn't have to hide among a crowd or crouch on the floor of a car: the friend was a Libyan police officer who didn't think twice about ferrying an illegal migrant across the country to fill one of the many jobs going in the capital.

Since the 1970s Libya had been something of a promised land for people from the poorer African nations. In many countries south of the Sahara, a young man might expect to earn around a hundred dollars a month during his lifetime before dying in his fifties with nothing to hand down to his children except unrealized dreams of a better life. Libya, by contrast, was booming. The oil finds and Gaddafi's ambitious social development projects meant there was more work than the nation's six million citizens could handle, and cheap labour flooded in.

Exactly how Gaddafi dealt with this labour deficit over the years depended on which geographical pole he was gravitating towards.

At first the workers came from North Africa and the Middle East, as Gaddafi tried to position himself as a strongman of Arab nationalism. But when fellow Arab leaders refused to back him in the face of a UN arms embargo in 1992, a wounded Gaddafi had to look elsewhere to realize his geopolitical ambitions. That marked the start of his pan-Africanism policy, with the

Libyan ruler touting himself as a saviour for an entire continent. While his visions of a single African currency, one army for the continent and a pan-Africa passport failed to make any headway, he did open up his borders to sub-Saharan Africans who wanted to live and work in Libya. Hundreds of thousands took up this opportunity, and even when he tilted back towards Europe in the 2000s and agreed to requests for more border controls, the workers kept coming – they just were not all there legally. By 2011, there were estimated to be 600,000 legal migrants in the country and between 750,000 and 1.2 million people working there without official paperwork.

At first, Majid was one of the latter. But now, finally settled in Tripoli, he was beginning to feel at home. By mid-2011, as the revolution gathered pace in the east of Libya, Majid was working as a stock-taker in a supermarket, earning decent money and living almost rent free. His landlord was an army major, and often they would share a meal, and maybe a joint, and talk politics into the small hours of the morning.

The major had a very one-sided view of Libyan history, but Majid listened intently.

Libya used to be an impoverished desert backwater where people lived in mud huts, his landlord told him, and then Colonel Gaddafi staged a coup in 1969 and built a nation which shared the oil wealth and brought prosperity to all. The major and Majid did not talk about the purges of hundreds of students, academics, journalists and other 'enemies of the revolution' that happened as Gaddafi had set about building his paradise in the desert in the 1970s. Nor about the dozens who were hanged and mutilated on public television, a lesson to anyone unconvinced by his power grab. These disappearances and deaths carried on well into the 1980s and 1990s, with the Libyan regime also sponsoring terror abroad as Gaddafi fashioned himself as an anti-colonial pariah of the Western world. Tony Blair, the former British Prime Minister, may eventually have been able to bring Gaddafi in from the cold during their rapprochement in a Bedouin tent in 2003, but new business and trade ties did not mean that Gaddafi was a reformed man. Old habits die hard, and when unrest started simmering again in the eastern provinces during the Arab Spring, the Libyan strongman didn't think too long before ordering his troops to open fire on unarmed protesters.

He was also quick to remind his former Western partners that the proximity of Libya to Europe may not bode well for the future.

'If you threaten [Libya], if you seek to destabilize us, there will be chaos, Bin Laden, armed factions,' he warned as the support grew for a military campaign against him. 'You will have immigration, thousands of people will invade Europe from Libya. And there will no longer be anyone to stop them.'

With a thousand miles of Mediterranean coastline and around two million migrants living in Libya at the start of the war, Gaddafi had plenty of human capital to bargain with.

For decades, Gaddafi's regime had been profiting from people's desire to reach Europe. With the Italian island of Lampedusa less than 200 miles away, a steady trickle of people had launched off Libya's beaches on dilapidated vessels, willing to risk their lives on the gamble of reaching richer, safer lands. Most were young men heading to Europe to work; others were seeking sanctuary from conflicts, droughts and famines. Gaddafi saw only opportunity in their desperation. No criminal enterprise could operate in Libya without the dictator sharing in the loot, and people smuggling was no different. The boats left for Europe with the security forces either turning a blind eye in exchange for bribes, or actively facilitating the voyages.

Migration was just another political tool for the dictator, and the extent to which Gaddafi could exploit this bargaining chip became clear when the economic crisis took hold in Europe. Rising unemployment and stretched government budgets meant that the few thousand people arriving on EU shores in boats from North Africa became easy targets for politicians looking for someone else to blame. In 2009, Italy's President Silvio Berlusconi came up with a solution: they would intercept boats in Italian territorial waters and force them back to Libya, where his old friend Gaddafi could take care of them.

Italy had retained strong economic ties with its former colony. Libya was its largest supplier of oil, while the Libyan government also held stakes in everything from Unicredit, Italy's largest bank, to the Juventus football club. Berlusconi and Gaddafi had a close personal friendship. A persistent rumour in Italy credits Gaddafi with coming up with the phrase 'bunga bunga' to describe a harem of women – a phrase now universal shorthand for the sex parties which led to Berlusconi's downfall. So when Italy offered to invest another €5 billion in Libya, Gaddafi was happy to take the boat people off Berlusconi's hands. People had spent days at sea with no food and water making the crossing from Libya to Lampedusa, only to be beaten with clubs and cattle prods as Italian sailors forced them back onto Libyan vessels and turned them round. The Italians sent at least 1,000 people back to Libya – an effective police state with little regard for human rights – with no effort made to assess who was on board the boats or whether anyone was a legitimate asylum seeker in need of protection from war or persecution. No one really knew what happened when the men, women and children returned. Libya is not party to the United Nations' 1951 Refugee Convention which guarantees the rights of people needing international protection, and conditions in Libyan detention centres were appalling. Many people never even ended up in detention, but were transported to Libya's inhospitable southern borders and dumped in the desert.

Whatever the morality of the deal, it proved effective for Rome. Clandestine arrivals by sea fell from 10,236 in 2009 to 1,662 a year later. But while the Italian policy may have stuck a finger in the dam, it did nothing to address the underlying causes or halt the overall flow of people entering Europe illicitly. They just found another route, with an increase in arrivals along the Greek border in that period. The Italian policy was also in breach of the European Convention on Human Rights, which prohibits returning people to a country where they may face degrading and inhuman treatment. Berlusconi was eventually forced to abandon his push-backs policy in 2010 when the European Court of Human Rights started legal proceedings. Gaddafi then came back to the EU with a new plan: for the right sum, he could stop the people ever leaving Libyan soil in the first place. In summer 2010 he made the EU an offer that sounded more like a threat: give him $5 billion a year or he would flood the continent with foreigners.

'Europe might no longer be European, and even black, as there are millions who want to come in,' he warned during a visit to Rome, where he did not shy away from playing on old European racial and religious prejudice. 'We don't know what will be the reaction of the white and Christian Europeans faced with this influx of starving and ignorant Africans. We don't know if Europe will remain an advanced and united continent or if it will be destroyed, as happened with the barbarian invasions.'

European leaders were sufficiently spooked to come up with a deal. While publicly there was shock at the audacity of the offer, the European Commissioner for Home Affairs Cecilia Malmström and the European Commissioner for Enlargement and European Neighbourhood Policy Štefan Füle visited Tripoli in early October 2010. What emerged was a pledge to pay Gaddafi €60 million over three years for 'economic development'. During the same trip they came up with a deal to 'develop our co-operation on migration-related issues'. This was despite Libya's dismal human rights records and evidence compiled by human rights groups that Gaddafi's preferred method for dealing with unwanted migrants and refugees was to truck them out to the remote Saharan border outposts and leave them to die.

The migration problem was not solved. People would still flee war, famine, poverty and persecution. They were now just dying somewhere else, out of Europe's sight.

For Majid, Libya had always been a place to settle and make a life for himself, rather than a staging post on the way to Europe. He had no interest in risking his life packed in a decommissioned fishing vessel like a battery hen simply to reach a continent which didn't want him anyway. He had inherited an interest in international politics from his father, and read enough news to know that Europe was not the golden land of opportunity many people seemed to think it was.

Life in Libya was not perfect. Majid felt a wall growing around him, isolating him from everyone else. He told the few friends he had that he wasn't scared of anything, but in reality he was scared of the night. When darkness fell visions of his father's death would haunt him as he tried to sleep, the anger would return, and he felt like he was losing himself again. How could he ever be happy when he had lost the most important person in his life? But he had a job, some friends, a comfortable home – at least that was something.

Living a good life, peacefully, maybe I can be free, he thought.

The Nigerian teenager had clung on to the belief that Libya offered him the best chance of a bright future right up until the morning of 12 August, when six soldiers knocked on his door.

In the end it was Gaddafi's forces who got to Majid first. He should have known better than to stay at home. While the major who owned their house may have been amiable over a few spliffs during the good times, his allegiances were to his colonel and he didn't hesitate to act on Gaddafi's order to round up the foreign workers. The soldiers knew exactly where to find Majid and Ali. When the knock on the door came, the two young Nigerians didn't even have time to exchange words of surprise, let alone gather their belongings or their savings before they were marched at gunpoint into a waiting truck. When Majid tried to resist, he was told he had one other choice.

'You can stay and fight for Gaddafi.'

So he reluctantly climbed aboard the truck bound for the coast.

Gaddafi's spiteful expulsion of thousands of foreign workers marked the start of the mass exodus from the Libyan coastline which would over the coming years test the very principles at the heart of the European Union. Within a few months, Colonel Gaddafi would be dead. Rival rebel groups would start battling for power as Libya sank into a prolonged and chaotic civil war. The people smugglers would thrive like never before, with no functioning law enforcement to stop them. The countries which had helped oust Gaddafi would shrink from view. Scarred by military interventions in Iraq and Afghanistan, they would decide that the messy task of nation-building was best left to the victors, no matter that it wasn't even clear yet who they were.

Majid was not thinking about any of that yet. As the truck rumbled towards the Mediterranean, a sad sense of resignation washed over him as he considered his short, troubled life.

From the day of my father's death, I have been running and searching for some kind of peace, but this is so hard to find, he thought. *You just keep running until you find a safe place, but a safe place does not exist.*

2

Into the Storm

Nart: Damascus, Syria

The darkness that had started to envelop Damascus every evening irked the ruling class. For those Syrians who still believed that President Bashar al-Assad was a benevolent force bringing prosperity and security, the power cuts were an unwelcome reminder of a country on the brink.

Much of Syria's elite had been trying to continue the masquerade of a normal life in the enclave of calm that prevailed around the Old Town. They may quietly move their children to a school closer to the centre or have a discreet chat with relatives in Lebanon about taking an extended visit, but open talk of a country descending into civil war was pushed aside. They didn't want to hear about the massacres of protesters in cities across the country. As the months passed, though, it was getting harder to ignore the revolt. Trips out of Damascus to summer homes in the mountains might be disturbed by tanks blocking the roads. The art galleries remained open, but visitors dwindled; the waiters served breakfast with a smile at the boutique hotels, but the only guests were journalists; food vendors still set up shop, but their prices kept on climbing. There was an eerie absence of security forces to enforce everyday laws, their priorities now elsewhere. In a city that was once meticulously policed, traffic violations and petty crimes became common.

And then the sun set, and the nightly power cuts brought

home the uncomfortable truth: Damascus was now a city under siege. Sanctions against the oil industry by the European Union and other Western powers had started to bite, and electricity was now rationed. When an illuminated street plunged into darkness, residents stumbled over kerbs and reached in pockets for torches. Inside homes, dusty candles were pulled out of cupboards and families headed to bed early to curtail another evening in each other's dimly lit company avoiding the topic of civil war.

Then there were those who found opportunity in the disarray. Gold vendors sold out of sovereigns as people stocked up on assets which wouldn't be affected by the sanctions. Black market traders thrived as goods disappeared from the shops.

Most of all it was the disaffected who cherished the hours when their city became blanketed in darkness. When there were no street lights and the windows were black, no one knew whose voice was shouting anti-Assad slogans into the night air. Some men leaned out of suburban tower blocks and yelled, 'Allahu Akbar' – a provocative cry to the secular regime. Students who had been forced to stay silent as relatives disappeared into the jails and torture chambers of Bashar and, before him, his father Hafez now started making their way to each other's houses in the dark streets. There they would plot the furtive demonstrations which broke out in pockets of Damascus every Friday after prayers. Opposition activists used the cover of the night to break into transport depots and pile anti-Assad leaflets high on the roofs of buses, the revolutionary material falling like confetti on the public when the vehicles started their morning rounds. In the streets which crawl up the mountain slopes around Damascus, dissidents hastily scribbled 'Down With Assad' on hundreds of ping-pong balls, and then rolled them down the roads before the sun came up, revealing their night's work.

And the darkness meant a Syrian lawyer, Nart Bajoi, could evade security forces as he transported the blood needed for transfusions through the night-time streets of his city.

Nart was about to turn thirty and was on the verge of finishing his apprenticeship in criminal law. He had ten years of hard studying behind him – not only for his law qualifications, but also to become a Microsoft Certified Solutions Expert. It was hard to earn a living with only one job in Syria, so best to have two professions, he reasoned. He also understood the value of good connections, and had a vast network of friends and acquaintances across the country.

Unless you were a member of the small Alawite sect of the Assad family, everything in Syria cost money. Passports, university, schools – money disappeared into the vacuum of fees and bribes. Successfully navigating life in Syria required a certain cut-throat entrepreneurial spirit, and Nart was ready to do what it took to get ahead. A few months earlier he had been focused on the next step in his life: renting an office and opening his own legal practice. He was even thinking of proposing to a girl he had first set eyes on two years ago when she was just sixteen.

Then in February, everything changed.

It began with a handful of schoolchildren. The Arab Spring had travelled from Tunisia to Libya and Egypt, and now dissent was stirring in Syria too. President Assad wasn't taking any chances, and even a dozen rebellious boys seemed to pose a threat to the paranoid government.

'The people want to topple the regime': these words, spray-painted in Arabic on a wall in the southern city of Deraa, were enough to get fifteen teenagers thrown in jail, where they were burned and beaten and their fingernails pulled out. When relatives of the detained boys marched on the governor's house to demand their release, they were met with gunfire, and the first blood of the uprising was spilt.

Nart knew straight away that he had to help.

They came out peacefully, he thought, *and the police and intelligence just shot innocent people.*

Nart was not from a family of dissidents: his father was a civil servant, and his brothers had followed in the patriarch's footsteps. For his whole life up until that protest in Deraa, Nart had played by the rules. But despite his ambition, he now discovered a rebellious streak inside him which would not allow the regime's actions to go unchallenged. He was fed up of seeing other people acting only out of self-interest, choosing to ignore atrocities elsewhere in the country simply because they had not touched their lives yet. It had happened before, but at least in 1982, when Hafez al-Assad massacred 20,000 of his own people to crush a rebellion in the town of Hama, people could claim ignorance. Now YouTube, Facebook and other social media existed. No one could pretend they did not know what was happening, and Nart felt a moral duty to act.

First he started turning up to the clandestine Friday protests, riding the wave of euphoria as electrified crowds engaged in running street battles with regime forces. Nart was so swept up in the revolutionary fervour that he barely heard the gunfire that rang out all around him. It was the same for so many Syrians, that sense of invincibility and oblivion to danger; the release at finally being able to shout the truth about the regime obliterated all fear.

Then one day a friend called Nart.

'You were at the demonstrations,' his friend said.

Nart was astonished and asked him how he knew.

'I saw your bald head on Al-Jazeera,' the friend teased.

All the men in Nart's family went bald young, and he had never really worried about losing his hair. He was a sturdy man with the stout chest, broad shoulders and round face that suited a shaved head. But now he was involved in illicit activity he realized that this physical characteristic could be a distinguishing feature, and he had to be more careful. He also began to wonder if the protest movement could make better use of his particular set of skills. Turning up on street corners and yelling for the end of a dictator was certainly cathartic, but they had been doing that for months and Assad was as entrenched as ever.

A few of his fellow protesters were convinced they could topple the president before the end of the year. After all, when a fruit seller burned himself to death in a remote Tunisian town in December 2010, it had taken just a few weeks for President Zine el Abidine Ben Ali to fall. In Egypt, two months of protests ousted President Hosni Mubarak. Nart knew it would not be that simple here – if they gathered in central Damascus like the Egyptians in Tahrir Square, Assad's forces would mow them down. So clandestine aid networks started appearing across the country to help support a revolution for the long haul. The protesters needed places to sleep, clothes to wear and food to eat. Those injured by regime thugs needed medical care and first-aid supplies. Then there were the simple humanitarian needs of the civilians trapped in neighbourhoods besieged by Assad's forces, poor families trying to survive day to day. If there was anything Nart could do to help, he was ready.

Across the city others like him were risking their lives and doing their part with whatever resources they had. Men and women from all different backgrounds were finding ways to help bring an end to the regime. Plumbers used their vans to get past security checkpoints to outlying neighbourhoods. Enterprising mothers put their babies in the front seat when they delivered fresh food to activists forced underground, knowing they would be much less likely to get stopped by security on the lookout for dissenters. Housewives in central Damascus opened their doors to the people fleeing from regime retribution elsewhere in the country. Parlours once reserved for endless cups of tea and chatter were now strewn with sleeping bags and air mattresses and grateful families wondering what their future held.

At this point, Nart's canny networking skills really began to pay off. He had plenty of connections from attending high school in a smart Damascus suburb, from his years at law school, from his computing course, and from his university years playing semi-professional football – a career ended by a bad knee injury which would plague him for years. Nart had stayed in touch with everyone.

When he graduated in 2010 – a year before any talk of revolution – many of his peers had embarked on careers in the police or intelligence services. Most of them did so for a safe salary and a stable job, not out of an ideological love of the regime, and now that the protest movement was beginning to gather momentum they saw nothing wrong with slipping their old friend some information about which neighbourhood the security services would be raiding next, where the regime was setting up checkpoints, and which spies had infiltrated the movement.

'In Syria, the walls have ears,' Nart used to hear his relatives whisper to one another when he was younger.

For decades people had been imprisoned on barely a shred of evidence. Bashar al-Assad was following in the footsteps of his father Hafez, who had helped cement a draconian emergency law in 1968 which allowed police to arrest anyone suspected of the vaguely defined crime of threatening national security. But Nart knew how to work the system. One man he sat next to at school for twelve years joined the Shabiha, the brutal personal militia of President Assad made up only of the most loyal members of his Alawite sect. Luckily for Nart, his classmate remained even more loyal to his childhood friendship. Three times he made a clandestine visit to warn Nart that his name had appeared on a list of wanted protest organizers, and he had removed it for him.

Armed with this source of inside knowledge, Nart served as the eyes and ears of a Damascus-based protest cell of around thirty people. Their tasks were varied: rent houses and book hotels in the city for families fleeing devastated neighbourhoods; transport protest organizers wanted by the regime between safe houses in the city; courier blood for transfusions from Lebanon across the country. When the border was closed down, Nart used freezer bags and collected blood donations from the doctors and nurses who had put their skills to use in the clandestine networks. Each cell had one point person who liaised with just one other point person from another cell. The names and identities of the other cell members remained secret – that meant there were fewer people to betray when the interrogators got to work with their instruments.

It was a constant cat-and-mouse game with the authorities, and the risks were huge. Everyone knew somebody who had disappeared into the regime's vast jail network, where tens of thousands of political prisoners languished even before the Arab Spring. Those who came out were never the same. It was not only the missing teeth, the welts on the back, the arm that would never recover from the splintered bone. For some a light went out in their eyes; others were afflicted with a nervous fidget which would never leave them, a compulsion to be forever looking over their shoulders.

The torture methods deployed by the regime were infamous. Not content with depriving people of their freedom, the security forces wanted to terrorize the population into submission, and they dreamt up ever more horrifying ways to inflict mental and physical anguish.

Prisoners who made it out of the torture chambers alive spoke of the familiar techniques such as beatings and electric shocks. But it was the more elaborate tortures like suspending a person from a wall with their arms out in a crucifixion position or hanging them from a hook like meat waiting to be butchered that instilled the greatest fear. Men and women were raped within earshot of the rest of the prisoners. Some were locked in tilted metal coffins too short for their bodies for weeks on end. Another regime favourite was the 'dulab', where a tyre is forced over the victim's neck and his legs so he is folded forward. He is then tipped on his back, immobile, and beaten. For the pious, female prisoners were beaten naked in front of them along with threats that their wives, mothers and sisters would be hauled in for the same treatment.

Often it was this psychological torture which broke the prisoner, and another underground aid network or activist cell would be betrayed.

'Trust no one, not even your brother,' Nart warned comrades in his network.

He knew that the time would come when his own name would be revealed under torture, so when it became clear that the fury in Deraa would not be contained to one city, Nart had applied for a new eight-year passport and ID card. At least he now had an escape plan and this kept him going when dark thoughts started playing at the edges of his mind. With his two degrees, his modest savings and his fluency in English, he thought he would be welcome anywhere. And given his activities as an anti-regime activist, he had a well-founded fear of being persecuted if he were forced back home, so he was sure other countries would offer him sanctuary.

For now, though, Nart wasn't thinking about leaving. He was still useful to his own people, and was determined to keep going, travelling and sleeping between safe houses by night and lying to his family about his whereabouts. He tried to push aside thoughts about the pain, torture and possible death that capture would entail, and focus instead on keeping one step ahead of the regime.

When he was a teenager, he had thought that becoming the master of many trades would allow him to earn enough money to have a decent life and look after his family. Now, that entre-preneurial spirit was driving his life as a revolutionary: his work doing the computer systems for an international courier gave him the contacts he needed to ferry goods around the city with the perfect alibi. He had installed the CCTV at a market which they now used as drop-off point for supplies. When he went to the courts for his law work, he checked the books for records of activists who had been detained. He began to notice a pattern. Early in 2011, protesters were jailed for around one month. Towards June and July, the sentences seemed to increase to around three months. By the autumn, the Free Syrian Army was starting to gain traction in the country: it was no longer just an underground protest movement, and the authorities responded with greater force – by then, if someone was arrested torture was inevitable and they would be lucky to be released at all.

Some of the people arrested were given a choice: stay in jail or fight for the regime. Many of Nart's friends spoke with bitterness about Assad's foot soldiers, but Nart knew that most of them were just boys – some of them even boys he knew from his neighbourhood – who were forced into the front lines and who would die or be injured defending a regime they had little love for. Nart's knee injury had spared him from conscription, but for many others, choosing to stay in Syria meant that the call to serve Assad was fast becoming an inevitability.

Mohammed: Damascus, Syria

As the insurgency spread, the regime needed to feed its own ranks, and for the majority of teenagers and young men who did not have the wealth and connections to dodge the draft, it was just a matter of time before the papers arrived demanding they report to barracks. And while news of Assad's atrocities may have been censored, you only had to turn on the TV to see what serving for a spell as one of Assad's defenders could entail. Tales of heroic soldiers injured battling the 'terrorists' were broadcast on the state airwaves. There in the military hospitals, wounded soldiers lay in their beds repeating the regime lines, blaming MI6, the CIA and Israel's intelligence agency Mossad for the unrest spreading across the land. But there were also those who could not speak about their experiences. One man sat by the bedside of a son, his head buried in hands which held the young man's limp wrist. A bullet had shattered his spine and left him tetraplegic, and the boy was heavily sedated.

'He is just one soldier, what is his sin?' the father asked. 'Now he will not walk again for the rest of his life.'

In another room a man lay on a bed, his neck twisted to one side as his bed pan was changed. The nurse nudged him to talk, but his eyes simply rolled around in his head. There was no family by his bedside.

Mohammed Kazkji's father could not imagine such a terrible fate for his gentle, hard-working son. Mohammed was nineteen years old and had the tall, lanky physique of a basketball player – a healthy young man who would make ideal cannon fodder for the regime.

'You are a man now, but I don't want you to join the army and be a soldier,' Mohammed's father told him one evening, urging him to think about leaving Syria. 'If you stay here, I will lose you for sure.'

Being a foot soldier for Assad was not exactly Mohammed's idea of a career either. He had bigger dreams.

'I'm going to be the world's best electrician,' he told his friends.

With his rangy frame, slouched shoulders and thin face with big features, Mohammed had the look of an overgrown teenager. But his appearance hid a determined work ethic inherited from his cobbler father, whose shoes were prized throughout his Damascus neighbourhood. The word 'impossible' was not in his father's vocabulary, and Mohammed wanted to be just like him. Success meant being the absolute best you could be at everything you tried: it was the code he had decided to live by and one he hoped would make his parents proud.

Mohammed loved children and had dreamed of becoming a paediatrician, but was disappointed when he didn't get good enough grades to enter medical school. He had worked so hard, and didn't understand why he had failed. But rather than getting despondent, he threw himself into a new career path and started studying electrical engineering. Two years into his course and he was showing natural talent, so why would he want to go abroad now? And how could he leave his mother behind and lose the calm hand steering him through the labyrinth of choices daunting any young man? She had urged Mohammed to study electrical engineering, knowing her son well enough to see that the vocation would suit his endlessly questioning nature. Family meant everything to him: the middle boy of three sons and with two younger sisters to look out for as well, Mohammed had never once felt alone. Setting off by himself was unthinkable. How would they all manage without the extra help in the shop? Very soon he was hoping to bring in extra income from some practical application of his studies.

Unlike Nart, the politics of the uprising didn't interest Mohammed, but while he tried to convince himself that the war would be over before he had to learn to fire a gun, he could see that work was drying up for his father. Surely this meant they needed him more than ever? So at first he brushed off his father's suggestions that he think about escaping and tried to carry on as normal. But as the weeks passed it became clear that life was no longer normal, and everything he had once taken for granted was starting to collapse: free education, free healthcare, the sense of a secure life.

In the autumn, his school in a Damascus suburb shut down: the fighting was closing in and the only other college offering Mohammed's course was a day's travel away, and the roads were no longer safe. Thoughts of death and injury started to destroy Mohammed's peace of mind.

He tried to imagine a life in the army and the possibility that he may have to kill for his country. More likely he would be the one on the end of a bullet or bomb, he concluded. Then he started to think about the dishonesty of a system that would propel him to the front line while protecting hundreds of others.

Why was it only the sons of ordinary working people who were sent to their deaths? He knew that if his family had money and connections they could pay their way out of military service. Other young men were now thinking about leaving too. But where would they go?

All this was weighing on Mohammed's mind when the notice arrived in the post: now that he had turned twenty, it was time to report to the police station for service.

3

Welcome to Europe

Majid: Tripoli Port, Libya

Orders had been obeyed at gunpoint from the moment the soldiers arrived and marched Majid and Ali out of their home and down to Tripoli's port.

When they arrived there, Majid at first felt relief. Dwarfed by Libyan naval ships but recognizable by their jaunty blue paint, a flotilla of old fishing boats moored in the shingle and rubbish bobbed gently on the waves. These were the vessels – not the military ships – being loaded with men, women and children. When Gaddafi took to the airwaves to threaten a tide of migrants headed to Europe, Majid's mind had conjured up cruise ships. If Europe really was a few days' sailing away, then surely they would have bigger, sturdier boats?

Maybe the journey to Europe will just take an hour, he thought.

There was no reason for him to know otherwise: he had no interest in going to Europe, so he hadn't paid much attention to the stories doing the rounds in the migrant communities of other people who had attempted the treacherous trip. His confidence ebbed away, however, when he saw the fear in the eyes of the other people on the beach. It was mostly young men, but some had their families with them, and the huddles multiplied as more trucks arrived. Majid estimated that there were thousands of people at the harbour, most of them black Africans like him, but also people from Bangladesh and Pakistan, all of them looking nervously towards the vessels.

Loading people onto the trawlers was taking time and only a few boats left each day, so at night the waiting passengers had to sleep on the hard ground and try not to think too hard about the voyage ahead. On all sides twitchy regime soldiers with their fingers on the triggers of AK-47s kept watch over the crowd. These people had once built their houses, manned their tills, cleaned their homes and served their food; now they were just merchandise to be herded down a jetty and onto the boats. Those who resisted were beaten with rifle butts; those who tried to flee were stopped with bullets. Majid saw three people shot on the edges of the crowd, the gunfire an example to any others who thought that their freedom lay on the streets of Tripoli rather than on the waves of the Mediterranean.

After nearly a week of sleeping rough, it was Majid and Ali's turn. The loading was done in the bright and burning Libyan sun as midday approached. There was nothing clandestine about this voyage: for most of the last few years the smugglers had operated with the knowledge of the regime, and the exodus now had the full support of Colonel Gaddafi himself, so there was no need for the cover of darkness.

Although the boat looked unseaworthy to Majid, it was in reasonable condition compared with vessels that would attempt the journey in years to come. It was not in Gaddafi's interests for these people to drown at sea. The boats were a weapon meant to reach their target and scare Europe into a xenophobic lockdown, forcing European leaders to backtrack on a bombing campaign which was already close to unpicking his hold on the nation. That said, Gaddafi didn't mind what state his human weapon arrived in: dead or alive, as long as they arrived, the message would be the same. So there was no point in providing life jackets or the supplies needed for a sea voyage under open summer skies. Majid was handed one small bottle of water and marched onto a single-deck fishing vessel painted blue with a red strip down the side, which once may have made it look jazzy but now had faded to a tired pink.

People pushed their way on board under the supervision of the soldiers, every nook of space filled up. The soldiers packed the boat to absolute capacity by making everyone open their legs so that another person could be slotted in front of them, like the poorer families Majid had seen back home wedged on the back of a motorcycle, mother, father and three children clinging to each other in an impossible feat of balance. On the wooden deck, hundreds of people sat in a tangle of limbs. Majid became separated from Ali, but was able to secure a spot on deck by the side of the boat, where he could better his chances of survival if it sank. At least he wasn't in the hold, where there was so little light and the air was thick with the smell of engine oil and rotting fish.

When they finally cast off, Majid glanced at the man with his hand on the engine. The Ghanaian in his late twenties looked as nervous as everybody else on board. He was no captain, merely another migrant with a few hours of sailing instruction who had been given the task of keeping hundreds of people alive on a 200-mile voyage on a sea he had never navigated before. Nevertheless, Majid tried to stay calm, even as the first hour in which he thought they would make land passed and they remained at sea. Another three hours passed, the sea remaining flat under the fierce Mediterranean sun. But as the sun began to set, there was still no sign of land, and the waves began creeping higher up the side of the swaying boat.

It was then that Majid fully realized his vulnerability.

At least when he ran from the sectarian violence that killed his father he could rely on his wits and his speed to stay safe. Here, he was trapped. There was nowhere to go. He was just one of hundreds of frightened people who would probably die soon. That was the fate he resigned himself to, and somehow he began to accept it.

The conditions had deteriorated by the hour. It hadn't taken long after setting sail for the arguments among bewildered passengers to subside, replaced by the sounds of weeping and retching. No one on the boat cared any more that someone was crushing their arms or leaning on their legs. Hours earlier Majid had felt annoyed by the grumbles of 'Move... Stop it... I am suffering!' which bounced off the human bodies pressed cheek by jowl. Now moans replaced those agitated cries, but there was little point in trying to comfort the other passengers when there was no comfort to offer. High waves tossed the boat in all directions it seemed, apart from forwards, and Majid felt like his intestines were turning inside out. People were forced to go to the toilet where they sat. At least Majid was spared the vomiting which had seized many people on board.

Then there was the crying. The mothers and their children seemed to be staying quiet, drawing strength and comfort from one another. But Majid had never seen so many men in tears, gripped by a state of near-hysteria. In among the weeping and retching was the sound of whispered prayers. Glances to the captain offered little reassurance. His face was frozen in a grimace of frightened determination as he ploughed through the waves to an unknown destination. Majid felt like he was being hypnotized by the ferocious rocking of the boat, and by the endless black sea and endless black sky. The only elements of stillness were the stars above him and the seabirds sitting calmly on the swell, their guttural squawks sounding like laugher at the human calamity being played out alongside them.

Majid's throat was becoming more and more parched from the lack of water. Dehydration can cause the mind to play tricks, and soon the skies were undulating as much as the waves, and he couldn't tell which was which. Both melded into one dark mass which conspired to sap away any last trace of his humanity. He had no idea which country they were going to, or even in which direction they were headed. No matter how hard he tried, he could no longer imagine a future, and his only thought was that they were going to be at sea for ever.

It was darkest night when Majid started to think about taking his own life. A slight shift of his weight and he could be tumbling into the dark sea, the waves swallowing him up as the ship sailed on regardless. Then at least the running would stop. He thought he heard the splash of bodies hitting water, and was convinced that men were jumping overboard to escape the punishment inflicted on them for nothing other than trying to improve their lot. Who could blame them? Many had fled wars and terror and persecution, just like him, and were now in the dark with only their thoughts for company. Majid found himself lost in regrets. For the last few years he had tried to build a safe life so that he could come to terms with the events in his homeland and make it from one day to the next. Now, in his hungry, thirsty and confused state, death suddenly seemed to be the least bad option. Here he was two years after he left Nigeria and he still appeared to be running.

I have been trying to run away from death, run away from trouble, but something keeps chasing me: maybe it will be better if I jump into the sea and that will be the end of the problem.

At that moment, being swallowed by the sea seemed like a better death than starvation on the deck. But his legs were like lead beneath him, and his body refused to comply with the suicidal thoughts racing through his dazed mind. At one point Majid thought he heard voices in the water. He heard cries and splashing and was not sure if it was more people from his boat giving in to the sense of powerlessness and flinging themselves into the sea, or another vessel. Then he thought he caught sight of a boat a few hundred metres away, sinking below the waves. Could it be another one of Gaddafi's missiles, about to dump its human payload at the bottom of the sea? Or maybe it was nothing but the visions which had been plaguing him for hours. He had no idea. All he wanted was for the pain to end. If the boat sank, Majid decided, he would be glad. At least the suffering would be over. Without Ali nearby, there was no one to talk to – the only conversation on the boat happened when someone stopped moving. Then a passenger would ask for one of the few lighters on board to be passed along in the darkness so that they could hold it up to the face of their motionless neighbour to see if they were dead or alive. If they were dead, their body was tossed into the waves to prevent upsetting the children.

Majid didn't know how much time had elapsed when he finally saw the lights on the horizon. The hours had strung out into days. Later he remembered that the sun had gone down twice, so they had been at sea for at least forty-eight hours. At some point during the voyage, he was sure that a navy ship had spotted them and escorted them back out to sea. Eventually, however, the Ghanaian man who had captained the boat managed to fulfil Gaddafi's wishes: he struck land in Italy, and Majid stumbled out of the boat, ecstatic to be on dry land. He didn't know which country he was in, and he didn't care. He was alive. He could stop running. He could try and build his life again.

But, as he was about to discover, Lampedusa was ill prepared for the deluge of people the Arab Spring had spat out, and it was woefully ill equipped to welcome them.

The Italian author Giuseppe Tomasi di Lampedusa never visited the Italian island which gave him his name, but in his novel *The Leopard* he wrote about death in a way Majid could relate to.

'Dying for somebody or for something, that was perfectly normal, of course; but the person dying should know, or at least feel sure, that someone knows for whom or for what he is dying.'

Many of the people who have washed up in Lampedusa in recent years were there because of causes they were prepared to die for: Syrians who would die to defeat Bashar al-Assad; mothers who would die to protect their children. They did not want to die for Europe, but Europe forced them to take that risk to reach safety. And for many of those people, Lampedusa was their first taste of the continent's hospitality.

An arid speck of land closer to North Africa than Europe, Lampedusa had throughout its history been a staging post for people and goods, repeatedly changing hands over the centuries as competing sea powers briefly exploited it before abandoning it once again. The uninhabited island of around twenty square kilometres was neither European nor African, but always sought after as part of a grander plan. The British considered buying it when Malta fell into Napoleon's hands. The Russian tsars thought it might make a fine naval base from which to expand their powers. For pirates, it became a convenient stop-off during their exploitation of the bounty of the Mediterranean. Then, in the seventeenth century, Lampedusa came under Italian control. Attempts to colonize it, however, stumbled because of its inhospitable terrain, and in the late nineteenth century the Italian government alighted on the idea of turning it into a penal colony, and about 400 convicts were shipped out to serve their time in absolute isolation. As the years passed, however, the population of the island bulked out, and while it never quite thrived, fishing and tourism brought enough income to build nice homes and create a small slice of comfortable Italian life in the middle of the Mediterranean.

But then came the Arab Spring, and the island started to look like an overcrowded penal colony once more.

The first boatloads of people started arriving just days after the overthrow of the Tunisian president, Zine El Abidine Ben Ali, in January 2011. Unsure what the future held as anarchy gripped the nation, many Tunisians chose an eighty-kilometre trip over the sea. In one month, 5,700 people arrived on Lampedusa – just 300 short of equalling the entire population of the island. This was manageable. The men, women and children would disembark for a short stay in the migration processing centres which had always been there to deal with a steady – if modest

– flow of people chancing the waves for a better life, before being flown to mainland Italy.

But week after week the boats kept on coming, and soon there was a backlog of people waiting to be processed and sent onwards. A small detention centre designed to house 850 was quickly over capacity, with 2,000 people living in its cramped confines and 3,000 more sleeping rough on the rain-soaked docks. The boats to transport people to the mainland stopped arriving, and humanitarian supplies began to dwindle. And then Libya descended into chaos and Gaddafi pushed its migrant population out to sea. It was not the first time that the island had been on the receiving end of Gaddafi's revenge tactics. In 1986, after the United States launched air strikes on Libya in response to terrorist attacks against US citizens, the colonel attempted to lob a couple of Scud missiles over the Mediterranean in the direction of a US naval base on Lampedusa. They fell far from their mark, but this time his actions hit home.

By September 2011, at least 54,000 people had made land in Lampedusa – around half were Tunisians, the other half a mixture of nationalities forced to flee Libya. This was an influx on an unprecedented scale. The previous high had been 31,000 people arriving in all of Italy and Malta in 2008 – the year before Italy started paying Gaddafi to keep them at bay.

Italy's migration policy was in tatters, and Europe's leaders had started to turn on each other, just as Gaddafi had intended. People stumbling off boats found themselves sleeping in the foetid air of overcrowded centres with no beds, no doors separating the showers and the toilets, and limited supplies of fresh water. Tempers flared, and after a riot and arson attack at the main reception centre on 20 September, relations between the new arrivals and the authorities deteriorated. Everybody blamed someone else. The mayor of Lampedusa accused the government in Rome of leaving them to cope alone; the government in Rome accused the EU leaders in Brussels and other European capitals of abandoning the refugees to their fate.

'Europe is completely inert,' the Italian foreign minister at the time, Franco Frattini, told reporters. He urged the European Union to come up with a proposal to redistribute the new arrivals throughout the continent, but nobody responded. By the end of 2011, the EU – with its population well past 500 million – had resettled just 400 of the most vulnerable refugees created by the Arab Spring. The rest were left where they were in the Middle East and North Africa, with many of them planning to brave the seas for the misery of Italy's detention centres.

Berlusconi was quick to play his hand. He declared that he would grant all the new arrivals full papers so they could travel onwards to whichever European country they liked, prompting German politicians to accuse the Italian leader of blackmail. So some extra EU funding was approved for Italy, a sticking plaster in the hope that the wound the Arab Spring opened would soon heal and the flood of refugees would diminish back to a trickle.

The Italian government meanwhile came up with its own solution for the Tunisians. Stability was slowly returning to their homeland, so Italy decided to leave the people on Lampedusa while they processed their claims to find out who could be at risk of political persecution upon their return. EU law only allows for the repatriation of people if their asylum claims are thoroughly investigated then turned down, but the problem was the time it was taking for the authorities to decide who should stay and who should go. In the meantime, they remained in cramped, filthy holding centres, and the authorities conducted only the most cursory of interviews before loading them back on boats bound for Tunis.

Four years later the European Court of Human Rights would rule that the conditions on Lampedusa diminished the human dignity of the people arriving, and the collective expulsion of the Tunisian people without individual interviews was in breach of

European law. But that would be too late for Majid, who arrived at 2 a.m. on 17 August 2011 and saw Lampedusa at its worst.

His clothes still sopping from the waves and his body still racked with shivers from the motion and dehydration, Majid took his first steps on dry land in a state of disorientated exhaustion. He and the rest of the survivors were thankful to be alive, but desperate for comfort and assistance. That comfort proved elusive. Armed men in uniforms herded the refugees onto buses. Some of the police even snapped photos on their mobile phones, a memento of human misery saved on a SIM card. The only compassion was from a few citizens of Lampedusa who had come down to the port and were pressing bottles of water into the hands of the passengers.

Dazed, Majid followed the orders and clambered on a bus, staring out the window at the dark night. After they had driven through the two gates of the reception centre, the men were told to peel off their filthy clothes. After a strip search, they had to put them back on again. There was no medical attention, and the only place to sleep was the concrete floor of the outdoor courtyard. Not that sleep was on offer: first the new arrivals had to line up and give their name, date of birth and fingerprints. Majid had no idea at the time, but the moment the ink on his fingertip met the Italian stationery, he was trapped. Under EU rules known as the Dublin Regulation adopted in 2003 to determine which country should process an individual's asylum application, a person should request refugee status in the first EU nation they arrive in. Once they have registered their claim – signified by the act of giving a fingerprint, even if the person does now know why they are giving that fingerprint – they must stay there until the authorities of that nation either approve their asylum request or decide to send them home. If at any point before then the person attempts to travel to another EU nation, the authorities can check a central database and send them straight back to the country they arrived in. The rules were drawn up under the assumption that each of the EU's twenty-eight member states was equally well equipped to meet the basic human rights of the refugees – an assumption that would over the coming years prove to be woefully inaccurate.

For Majid at that moment, the fingerprinting was just another impediment to the sleep he craved. Finally he was given two T-shirts and a pair of shorts and trainers and left to find a small space in which to lie down and close his eyes. It would be another three days before he slept on a mattress, but at least for now he felt some peace. It would not last. When he woke up, the hopelessness of his situation dawned on him. He was no longer free but stuck in a country that didn't want him and where he didn't want to be, at the mercy of a bureaucratic nightmare which would last for years and challenge everything he had been taught to believe about freedom, democracy and the superior nature of European values.

2012

Number of refugees and migrants entering the EU: 72,437
Number of deaths: 500

4

Married to the Military

Sina: Asmara, Eritrea

No matter how hard her past had been, Sina Habte's future suddenly looked very bright indeed. It was a predictably balmy evening at the height of Asmara's summer in 2012 and Dani, her former university tutor, had just asked the twenty-four-year-old chemical engineer to be his wife. Astonishment washed over Sina, and she was embarrassed to find herself stammering like a schoolgirl.

'But you're my teacher!' she finally managed to say after the wave of shock had passed.

She tried to hold Dani's gaze, but was too overwhelmed to look into those huge brown eyes.

Dani was unlike anyone she had ever met in Eritrea. Here, people tended to keep their thoughts, feelings, talents and any dissenting opinions to themselves. Spies lurked in every class-room, every workplace, sometimes in your own home. People heard rumours that life was similar in North Korea, but at least the rest of the world knew how awful that country was. In Eritrea you just tried to stay under the radar and out of prison. But Dani was the kind of man who could not contain his intelligence, and Sina was smitten from the moment she joined his drawing class in her second year of a chemical engineering degree.

Now he was asking Sina to spend the rest of her life with him, and suddenly everything made sense. This explained that pang she felt inside whenever Dani laughed and joked with other women in her class. She had also wondered why he stayed in touch after her graduation two years earlier.

'Oh, he's just my instructor,' she would tell her parents when they looked inquiringly at the strapping man showing up on their doorstep bearing books and an eager smile.

All this time, Dani had been harbouring the same feelings of awe and admiration that Sina had for him. First it was intellectual: Sina was so quick to grasp the complicated calculations he gave the class, and while the other students sat quietly and took notes, she was always ready with a stream of questions. It had become a running joke on her course.

'Now Sina,' one teacher made a habit of asking after every lecture, 'do you have any questions?'

Once a classmate passed her a note. 'Please, Sina, we are tired, don't ask anything else!'

Dani, however, had endless patience with her inquisitions, sensing a like-minded soul unable to keep quiet even when that was generally considered the best way to survive in Eritrea.

Then of course there was her luminous face, which had a shifting kind of beauty. She conveyed a casual glamour when she had time to straighten her hair, put some hoops through her ears, and apply lip gloss. When her hair fell in its natural curls around her face, there was an ethereal quality which was harder to define.

For Sina, Dani was still the teacher who everyone at the university wanted to be seen with. *He's like my brother*, she thought as their friendship developed, not daring to imagine that his interest in her went beyond a protective kind of affection. So it was shock that made the words tumble out.

'I am sorry Dani,' she replied that hot July evening. 'I will think about what you have said, but I am not ready for these things. You are my teacher!'

But as the weeks passed, they found themselves making plans, and the truth struck Sina like a bolt of pure joy.

Yes, Dani must be mine, he is a great person, and we will start our life together.

Optimism seized the young woman. This marriage would be a genuine choice in a society where self-determination was rare. In Eritrea, no one got to make their own decisions about their life. You couldn't choose where you lived, where you worked, which God you worshipped, which political group you supported, what you owned, or where you travelled. It was all decided by a dictatorship still using the two painful wars with neighbouring Ethiopia as an excuse to keep the entire population in perpetual servitude. But Sina could only see the good in the world as she imagined her and Dani's future together.

We have so much in common.

As well as sharing a passion for engineering, both were members of the Eritrean Orthodox Church, which was lucky: had they followed anything other than one of the four recognized religions they would have been at risk of arrest and imprisonment. Sina and Dani had also both grown up in Ethiopia, their families forced to flee their Eritrean homeland before they were even born.

In 1962, Ethiopia annexed Eritrea, prompting a struggle for independence that would drag the world powers into a three-decades-long war. This small strip of land on the Horn of Africa – a former Italian colony which looks across the Red Sea to Saudi Arabia – became a key strategic sea location during the Cold War, and Washington and Moscow alternately poured money into Ethiopia to try and cement their influence in sub-Saharan Africa. The result was plenty of guns, tanks and planes to beat back a determined Eritrean guerrilla force. The 1970s were particularly brutal, as a Marxist regime took over in Ethiopia and Russians replaced the United States as its benefactors, pouring billions of dollars in arms into the country.

By 1979 Sina's father realized he could no longer stay in his Eritrean home town without the risk of being pulled into the independence struggle. He wanted to start a family, not head to the mountains for a long stint as a revolutionary fighter. So he fled to Ethiopia, followed in 1982 by his wife. They made their home in a suburb on the outskirts of the Ethiopian capital, Addis Ababa, and in March 1988, Sina was born, followed two years later by her sister, and another girl two years after that.

It was a good childhood. Sina's father was a doctor and her mother a civil engineer, and with two incomes they were able to buy two houses and provide their children with everything they needed. Dinner-time conversations about their careers enthralled young Sina, who was interested in the chemicals her father used to heal his sick patients.

Then Eritrea and Ethiopia went to war again, and that life ended.

In 1998, five years after Eritrea's hard-won independence, border skirmishes descended into a full conflict. The Ethiopian government retaliated to the renewed violence by rounding up all ethnic Eritreans living within its boundaries, imprisoning them, then forcing them over the border, even if some of the 75,000 returnees, including Sina and her sisters, had never even set foot in their supposed homeland before.

Sina's uncle called to warn the family about the forced exodus to Eritrea, and her parents tried to keep as calm as possible, telling the girls that they would be going to see their family. Sina had been seized with a childish excitement.

'Oh, we will see our grandmother, we will go to Eritrea!' the delighted young girl told her sisters.

But her mother and father were quietly making preparations for a much bleaker scenario. Stories were circulating of parents being sent over the border while their Ethiopian-born children were forced to stay. Many families were separated in the chaos as the government rounded up Eritreans and forced them onto buses. Desperate to keep her family safe, Sina's mother wrote the name and address of their grandmother in Eritrea on six pieces of paper, and gave each of her daughters two copies, putting them in different pockets and urging the children not to lose them. They must show that address to as many people as possible if they were separated, she urged her girls, struggling to keep her voice calm and reassuring.

Sina would never forget the sound the policemen made when they banged on the door at midnight, erasing all of her naïve excitement. She was asleep, but the crashing noise echoed through the house and she woke quickly with fear in her veins. The five men went room to room looking for her father, not bothering to holster their guns when they entered the children's bedroom.

'You are Eritreans, we will kill you − shut up or we will kill you!' one policeman shouted to the crying girls.

In the end the soldiers left with Sina's father. For a month the family waited for news, but heard nothing. Then the police returned and took her mother, leaving ten-year-old Sina in charge of her two younger sisters. Their Ethiopian neighbours tried to help and would come round and cook, but they had their own homes to go to in the evenings, and Sina would lie awake wondering if she would ever see her parents again.

Two weeks later, their mother came back. But she was not alone. Accompanied by two police officers, she was forced to bundle up her children and take them to the prison. The jail was dirty, the children were only allowed to use the toilet once a day, and Sina was frightened of the Ethiopian soldiers, who did not seem to view them as human.

'You don't deserve water,' a guard said when she asked for more to drink.

They did not stay for long. One morning a few weeks after their arrest, a big bus pulled up outside, and the family began their journey back to Eritrea, still not knowing what had become of their father. It was a long, hard drive. Their mother was trying to comfort other children who had been separated from their parents. One of Sina's sisters had developed a rash – from stress, the heat or the dirty prison conditions – and had scratched her face raw. They did not know that their father was in another bus, and spent much of the journey crying out for him. Eventually, they were unloaded at the border and told to walk. After they had been marching through the scrub for an hour, Red Cross workers guided Eritrea's new wave of refugees to a camp, before they were handed 4,000 Eritrean nakfa – about eighty dollars at the time – for the journey to the capital, Asmara.

At around the time Sina and her family were uprooted from their home, Dani too had been imprisoned. He was a teenager at the time, and the Ethiopian government was not about to send him over the border so he could take up arms against it. The fifteen-year-old spent three years in jail and had to wait for the implementation of a peace deal in 2001 – after the war had killed 100,000 people and created a million refugees – before he was forced back to Eritrea. He eventually made the border crossing alone, leaving his mother behind and hoping to be reunited with his father in Eritrea.

There, his family and Sina's family had to rebuild their lives from scratch, in a country now defined by a perpetual sense of victimhood, paranoia and misplaced righteousness. Eritrea had been used and then abandoned by the world. Despite this, its dogged guerrilla forces had stood up to a much more powerful enemy – twice. President Isaias Afewerki – a veteran of the independence struggle who took power when Eritrea became a state in 1993 and never gave it up – would draw a number of lessons from the country's experiences and distort them to suit his own ends.

In 1995, he introduced compulsory military service for all men and women, notionally to protect the young state from future threats and promote self-sufficiency. Everyone in the nation of five million people would be drafted, starting with gruelling boot camp in the last year of high school, then returning to the ranks upon graduation from school or university. Not completing your service or deserting was one of the many crimes that could get you locked up in the nation's jail network for an indefinite period of time, or even killed. Never mind that military service could amount to a life sentence of torture, abuse, arbitrary detention and forced labour. If you tried to evade it, the regime's vast security apparatus would find you and force you back into the most severe conscription programme in the world, robbing you of a chance of a normal family life.

Sina's father knew this, and did his best to lie low back in Eritrea. He had a family to provide for. His wife had injured her leg on the journey from Ethiopia and could not work, and he had no idea what she and their three girls would do on the ludicrous military pay if he were posted somewhere far away. But without papers from the government releasing him from his national service, Sina's father could not practise medicine. So during the day he hid inside, only leaving the house at night to drive a taxi. Finally the regime caught up with him and in 2001 he was sent for his military training. After six months they gave him a post as a doctor, but he was still bonded to the military and earning less than ten dollars a month. The expanding family – two boys were born soon after their return to Eritrea – was forced to rely on Sina's grandmother, who had farmland and was able to keep them afloat. The government eventually released Sina's father from military service in 2005 owing to his wife's incapacity to work, and he was able to find paid work in a private hospital.

But just as her father was finally free, it was time for Sina herself to report for duty.

Despite her family's struggles to re-establish themselves in Eritrea, Sina thrived at school, and had won a twenty-one-inch flat-screen TV as a reward for coming top of her year in all subjects. That didn't exempt her from life as a soldier, however, and in her twelfth-grade year – at the age of sixteen – she was torn away from her family and sent to Sawa. The short, melodic name of the military base belied the fear it inspired in Eritrea's youth. Every year, tears would flow freely at bus stops across Asmara as the latest intake for the military academy would cling to the parents they would not see for a year.

Sawa, an outpost in the dusty plains near the Sudanese border, was part school, part military training camp and part detention centre. All children went to the former Italian garrison in their final year of school for political indoctrination and punishing military drills. Every day they were forced to march in the desert heat, heavy boots on growing feet creating small dust storms that would settle in time to be churned up again by the next batch of recruits. Education meant being presented with a warped history of Eritrea's independence, and then coerced into joining the People's Front for Democracy and Justice, the only official political party in the country. Meals were three bread rolls and a bowl of lentils. Students were forbidden from practising their religion, and if you were caught praying or reading the Bible you could be jailed, tortured or killed.

Questioning why you were there or criticising the conditions also merited severe punishment, but Sina could not help the questions swirling around her head.

How will I survive without my family? How can I be a soldier when I don't really know who I am yet? Am I strong enough for this?

Everything was frightening and new, from the runs in the desert heat to the cold metal of a gun in her hand. From the moment they woke her at 5 a.m. for morning drill, each hour was governed by rules. The trainers controlled every aspect of life, stipulating where, how and what time to do each task. It was training not only to fight, but for a lifetime of servitude to the state.

Tears soaked her pillow every night for the first two weeks, but then Sina felt herself hardening. The smart ones usually went one of two ways. Stripped of everything they knew, and abused – mentally, physically, and for some female conscripts, sexually – they either broke down with psychological problems they would bear for years to come, or if they were strong enough they quickly adapted to survive. Sina turned out to be a strong one, and for the rest of the year of study and service, her mindset shifted.

I am not a student, I am a soldier.

In this way she got through it. And after the pain of Sawa, university was a relief.

Chemical engineering was fascinating, friends came easily, her teachers – including Dani – encouraged her, and she got a paid part-time job at a Western pharmaceutical company – albeit in secret as she did not have government permission. Just like in high school, Sina shone at university, receiving her degree with a distinction. After graduation in 2009, the government decided she would be one of the rare few spared from active military duty, and allowed her to practise her profession.

For many people, life as a soldier was indefinite. Sina had friends who trained as teachers, and they became soldiers. She had friends who trained as engineers, and they became soldiers. People trained as hairdressers, only to find themselves in fatigues and boots and instructed to stand at some dusty outpost hundreds of miles from home with no clear task beyond never questioning their barely paid job which had no end in sight.

For Sina, home would now be a dusty town in northern Eritrea where she would work as a chemical engineer for a government firm. But she felt blessed: at least she could put her intellect to use working as a supervisor of a small team. Her job was still considered part of her national service, so for working twelve-hour days with no breaks she got paid 450 nakfa ($30) a month. She was also still bonded to the military, and could be called back to active duty at any time. But the morality of her employment was not something that kept Sina awake at night. So extensive was the government's surveillance of its citizens that many Eritreans tried to censor their own thoughts and dreams. More distressing for Sina was the distance from her friends and family, and the long days and hard physical toil that the job involved.

'You have to be like a man,' she would complain to friends, thinking of the overalls which swamped her short frame, the dirty work boots, the scraped-back hair.

By 2012, however, she was spending more time at the company's offices in Asmara, where the uniform was a white lab coat which they let her spruce up with some jewellery and a sparkling hair band. Evenings could now be spent going for walks or out for meals with Dani.

Her future husband had not been so fortunate in his career. He was a fully qualified civil engineer and a talented teacher, but had been pulled out of the university when Sina was in her third year and told to report to the barracks for his new life as a soldier. Sina was never really sure what his job was. It seemed to be a matter of obeying whatever his military masters demanded. For Dani – also a skilled woodworker – that often meant making furniture for his supervisor's friends. He was not paid of course, beyond the same 450 nakfa a month Sina received – the standard sum which all national service conscripts are expected to live off.

Slave was the only word Sina could think of to describe Dani's position.

But he was based in Asmara, so at least they could be together. And as the year went on, his supervisor became a little more relaxed, and turned a blind eye when Dani started to work part time as a private teacher. The young couple still had to depend on their parents: Sina stayed with her mother and father when she was in Asmara and survived on her grandmother's dwindling fortune. Dani, meanwhile, was reliant on the income from his father's supermarket. But when Dani proposed, Sina could imagine a future.

When we are together, we are happy, Sina thought, and focused on her wedding the following year.

Leaving Eritrea never entered her mind.

Many of her compatriots were not so optimistic. The legend of Eritrea's independence had been passed down from the parents who had fought for it to the children who were expected give up their youth to protect it, and a sense of national pride kept the system going for a while. But gradually it dawned on the nation's youth that their servitude was no longer a temporary measure. At the same time, President Afewerki tightened his grip on every aspect of life: the press, freedom of speech, freedom of movement. The number of people leaving increased every year, and by 2012 around 1,500 Eritreans were fleeing each month. Some of the more creative flights from military service made international headlines. When the Eritrean football squad went to Uganda for a tournament in December, fifteen of them refused to go home and were granted refugee status. Two high-ranking Eritrean Air Force officers flew the country's only luxury plane – the President's private turboprop jet – over the Red Sea to Saudi Arabia, donated the aircraft to the kingdom, and asked for asylum. An Eritrean runner who competed in the 2012 London Olympics decided that he could no longer feign alliance to the flag he carried at the opening ceremony, and applied for asylum.

Some of the tens of thousands of Eritreans fleeing their homeland were starting to find their way to Europe, and the EU's border agency Frontex noticed the trend. In 2011, 1,572 Eritreans had been detected crossing EU borders without the correct paperwork; by the end of the following year, that number stood at 2,604. That was still tiny compared with the 13,000 Afghans and nearly 8,000 Syrians who arrived that year, but when Frontex officials looked at the figure by annual quarter, Eritreans represented the biggest percentage increase on some key migration routes. If that trend continued, it could mean a surge in the coming years.

Europe did not want to hear about potential increases in the future. After the chaos of 2011, the number of people trying to reach the EU seemed to be falling. Tunisia was recovering from its uprising. Colonel Muammar Gaddafi was dead. European leaders congratulated themselves on a military campaign well done in Libya, and patted themselves on the back that they had helped democracy flourish. They preferred to listen to the voices arguing that normality was returning to the Middle East, rather than the warnings that it was on the brink of even greater upheaval. The fact that a fresh exodus was happening from a small country lying on the Horn of Africa also failed to register.

Sina too was keeping herself busy and did not want to dwell upon the political situation in her homeland – her gaze was fixed firmly upon her wedding in a few months' time.

5

Sleeping on the Roofs of Police Stations

Hanan: Damascus, Syria

You can't shield your children from the truth forever. Hanan al-Hasan, a Syrian mother-of-four, had tried so hard, but when her two daughters returned from university one day and retreated to their rooms in silence, she knew she had failed. The news reports she had been watching all day must be true. Students at their university had staged a protest, and President Assad's Shabiha militia had responded in the only way they knew how: with clubs and fists and broken skulls in the campus car park. Rim and Bisan had seen blood spilt and now everything was different.

It was this violence and fear that Hanan had been trying to protect her two sons and two daughters from. Growing up, Hanan's parents had given her and her siblings so much, including a sense of social justice, and she was grateful for that. But that belief in justice had sent two of her brothers into exile and one to jail.

My family has given so much, she thought.

She wanted her own children to have the most beautiful life possible, innocent of the dangers of the regime in Syria, and ignorant of the way their ancestors had suffered. This was very different from the way she had been raised.

Hanan's beloved father had been very open about the sacrifices of their forefathers. Khaled Abd El Haleem Hasan would regale his eight children with tales that made his home village in

Palestine sound like paradise. Throughout their childhood he would tell them all about a farm so fertile that just about anything could grow: olives, grapes, apples, pineapples, lemons and the region's famous oranges. He spoke about how much he loved the land, and how much he missed it. Hanan would listen attentively, always with the same question on her lips.

'Why did you leave? Why didn't you stay?' she asked as she imagined a life growing up in that Eden, rather than the Palestinian refugee quarter in Damascus where she had spent most of her childhood. 'You should have stayed.'

Her mother tried to explain.

'The soldiers came and started shooting tear gas,' she said. 'They arrested and killed people.'

Still, Hanan thought, *it couldn't have been that bad*. If the family really loved it as much as her father said, then her grandmother Watfah would never have bundled up her three sons and three daughters and fled in 1948 when Jewish militias started razing villages as they seized land for the new state of Israel after the British mandate in Palestine ended.

It would be many years before Hanan understood the courage Watfah had shown, and then she came to treasure an old black-and-white photograph of the formidable farmer's wife with her broad jaw and no-nonsense eyes. There was little in the photo to suggest the delicate beauty that her granddaughter Hanan and her great-granddaughters Rim and Bisan would possess, but the face had character. Khaled testified to that: he was just sixteen when he left Palestine – the eldest of Watfah's six children – and remembered his mother's bravery as she strove to keep her children safe, even when her husband decided to stay in Palestine and she had to say goodbye to him forever.

The family first fled over the border into Lebanon, but Watfah didn't like the way the people treated her there, so she travelled on to Syria. The Arab–Israeli war forced 700,000 Palestinians from their homes, a refugee crisis that would last for four generations and eventually encompass more than five million people scattered around the Middle East.

For many Palestinian families, a feeling of displacement, a longing for a land they could never return to, would be passed from parent to child. But Hanan's father made the most of his lot. Arriving in Damascus, the family took shelter in mosques as they waited to find out what the future held. It was there that Khaled met another young refugee from Palestine, fourteen-year-old Khetam. She would later become Khaled's wife, and their home would be Yarmouk, a neighbourhood which the Palestinians built and which was often called a refugee camp, but with its bustle and sprawl it resembled many other satellite suburbs of Damascus.

Watfah's strength and determination was passed down to her children, and Khaled became one of the first Palestinians to study at a Syrian university. With his law degree and a long and respected career, he became the first Palestinian-born judge in Syria. His wife Khetam would give birth to eight children – five girls and three boys – and had boundless love and time for each of them. By the time Hanan was born in 1964, the government had posted Khaled to the northern city of Al-Hasakah, where they would spend six years. Soon after, however, they were back in Yarmouk, which had grown over the years into a thriving neighbourhood.

Of the half a million Palestinian refugees in Syria, around 18,000 of them lived in Yarmouk, and schools and shops and a close-knit community quickly developed, attracting not only Palestinians but also many Syrians who came for the shopping. Low house prices even tempted a few Syrian families to move there. They included Talal Al-Hamzah's parents, who had relocated to the capital from the western Syrian city of Homs.

Talal grew up surrounded by Palestinian friends and attended many youth groups in Yarmouk. He found himself drawn to one young Palestinian in particular, a beautiful and outspoken fifteen-year-old girl who immediately became a close friend. He was only sixteen at the time, but as the years passed Talal and Hanan grew closer, and realized that they were in love.

It was a decade after their first meeting that they were married. First Hanan pursued an education, and when she was twenty-two she gratefully accepted an offer to go and study in communist Hungary on an exchange organized by Fatah, the left-wing Palestinian political organization founded by Yasser Arafat. For a year she threw herself into learning Hungarian, hoping to realize her dream of becoming a translator. When a family matter forced her to return home early, she continued trying to improve her language skills, travelling to Cyprus to learn English.

She never managed to complete her studies – politics and family got in the way – but when she had daughters of her own, Hanan vowed that they would get the university education she never had.

Talal, meanwhile, was working to build a business from scratch. Armed with a degree in economics, he started a small company which offered fixtures for building or home improvements, and he equipped houses throughout Yarmouk and beyond with doors, windows and flooring. Eventually he would employ sixty-two people and start to make good money, but after Hanan and Talal wed in 1989, their first riches came in the form of their four children.

Rim arrived in 1990, followed by Bisan in 1992, then two sons – Ismail and Riad – in 1996 and 2000. Hanan vowed to pass down to her children a pride in their Palestinian heritage without the feeling of displacement which so many Palestinians treasure as the only way of keeping their identity alive. She wanted them to feel safe and wanted and secure, so although she made sure they knew something of their roots, they were to be brought up as Syrians, not as Palestinian refugees.

I am Palestinian, Hanan thought, *but I have never felt the earth there. I don't have anything to remember.*

Her feelings for Syria, however, sometimes overwhelmed her.

She loved the country: she loved it for her education, for her friends, for giving her a husband she adored, for the four children who were growing up to be so handsome and so kind. She loved the way the air felt, and the days she spent tending the flowers on her terrace.

Yes, she thought, *one day I would like to see Palestine, but Syria is my country.*

But while Hanan embraced Syria and its people, the regime was not so tolerant of her family, members of which had a history of opposing the dynasty of oppressors.

Hanan's eldest brother Samir disappeared in 1984. He was twenty-eight years old, and had met with a group of friends who criticized the rule of Bashar's father, Hafez al-Assad. They distributed leaflets calling for greater freedoms, an offence which Hafez would not let go unpunished. Samir's wife was pregnant when he failed to return home one day, and for seven years the family heard nothing. After the long wait, they were informed that he was in one of Syria's notorious political prisons serving a fifteen-year sentence, and short family visits were allowed. But by then his daughter was a stranger to him, and his wife had long given up on their marriage. When Samir was eventually let out, he wouldn't speak about what had happened behind bars, so the family let him keep his traumatic memories to himself and tried to help him rebuild his life and relationship with his child.

Samir's fate had not diminished the courage of the rest of the family, however, and Hanan's youngest brother Riad was just eighteen when he joined a small protest. A few days later, ten police cars surrounded the family home. The officials demanded that the family hand over Riad, so he went into hiding and then fled over the border to Lebanon, the country his grandmother had rejected as unwelcoming a few decades earlier. Riad never set foot in Syria again, and Hanan could only see him if they arranged a meeting in Lebanon or Jordan. As a tribute to him, she named her own youngest son Riad, and was so proud to see him grow up with the same big heart that she loved in her brother. Her third brother Usama also left and travelled to Dubai.

It wasn't just Hanan's brothers who pushed against the oppressive regime of the Assads. One day in 1984 Hanan and her two sisters joined a small group of protesters who rushed into the street and screamed 'Freedom!' at the top of their lungs.

If you live in a country and you can't say anything, what do you do? You keep silent? Hanan thought. No, she was young and fearless and she wanted to try and make life better for people.

The women were promptly arrested and sent to the prison cells. Police went round to their home and took their mother Khetam too, locking her away for the night in the hope that she would give up other potential dissidents in the family. She stayed silent, so Hanan spent a month in a filthy and overcrowded prison, with not enough food to eat and watched over by guards who had no qualms about beating up the women in their care.

When she was let out, she knew she never wanted to be imprisoned again, or for anyone she loved to have that experience, so politics became a taboo subject in the household she made with Talal. Hanan gave up any activism, and threw herself into raising her children and making a home.

As Talal's business grew, so did their ambition, and the couple bought two adjacent apartments in a new build just outside Yarmouk. They knocked the flats together to create a five-bedroom home. Hanan populated the balcony with jasmine, roses and camellias, which filled the air with a beautiful scent. She could afford to go to the salon to have her hair dyed when the grey began to show, and to pay someone for manicures and pedicures. The family even employed an Indonesian maid to clean up after the children. Like most teenage boys, Riad and Ismail had a habit of leaving their clothes on the floor wherever they took them off.

The two boys went to a private school where they learned fluent English, while Hanan's two daughters were working towards the university education Hanan had dreamed of for them. Rim was just about to finish a degree in information systems, while Bisan was in her third year of an architecture degree. Family holidays were to the Meridien hotels in Dubai.

The children were spoilt, but their parents were unapologetic. They could hope for nothing better than to have raised normal self-interested teenagers completely indoctrinated by their Syrian education to speak with love and pride about Bashar al-Assad. They fit in. When the children came home from school praising the president, Hanan and Talal would nod and hold their tongues, happy that their ignorance meant they were safe. Hanan knew if she told them how much she hated Assad, they could let it slip out to friends, and the whole family would be in danger.

The ruse was completely successful, as became evident when Rim was young and they took the angelic five-year-old to see Samir in prison. Hanan and Talal reasoned that she was too young to fully understand why he was there, but the child still seemed to grasp that her uncle was unhappy. So she decided to cheer him up by belting out a song praising Hafez al-Assad, much to the astonishment of the roomful of political prisoners. They saw the funny side, however, especially when the regime guards decided that her act of loyalty meant visiting hours would be extended by one hour.

Overall, it was a good life, and Hanan and Talal were glad their children didn't know how much it was costing. As they were not from Assad's Alawite sect, the expenditures piled up. The children's passports, their education, keeping the business running – Talal had to work every day of the week for fourteen hours a day to pay for everything. Hanan also helped out with the accounts and other aspects of the business. They had hardly any time for themselves, but they didn't mind.

What we have seen, we don't want our children to see, Talal and Hanan told each other. What we missed, we don't want our children to miss. So we must stay quiet – when you stay quiet in Syria, nobody comes for you.

The couple remained happy with their benevolent deception until early 2012, when it was becoming increasingly difficult for them to maintain their vow and leave their politics at the door. The good life was being was chipped away, to be replaced with a growing revulsion at what they saw happening across the country.

Since the first demonstrations in Deraa in early 2011, Assad had offered a few carrots to the protesters – releasing some political prisoners, lifting the forty-eight-year state of emergency – but mostly he had been wielding the stick. He sent tanks into rebellious neighbourhoods, and unlike in Libya, the world was not going to stop him. Any attempt at serious international sanction was vetoed at the United Nations by Russia, which had a naval base in the Syrian port of Tartus and close historical ties with the Assad regime. One by one cities rose up, and the protests were crushed. Opponents of the regime saw no other solution but to take up arms. Nearly a year into the revolution, it became clear it wasn't an uprising confined to the students and middle class of Syria's cities: the country was in the grip of a civil war.

By early 2012, Assad was determined to crush the challenge to his rule, and he was going to start with the central city of Homs, Talal's hometown. Artillery pounded neighbourhoods he considered hostile to the regime, and the bombs ground centuries-old buildings into the dirt with their occupants still inside. At least 700 people were killed in an assault of heavy weapons and machine-gun fire in the city in February, many of them civilians. Assad hoped he could turn the tide by wiping out communities he believed to be strongholds of the opposition. Instead, news of children killed in the bombardment, historical streets reduced to dust, and families trapped without food, water or medical supplies enraged people up and down the country, and dissent grew. Many of Homs' 1.5 million people fled to Damascus, but while they found a degree of safety there, the cost of living was soaring and the capital was struggling to house all the new arrivals.

Talal's extended family turned up on their doorstep first, with a car full of belongings and sadness in their eyes. Many of his cousins and other relatives had gone out on the street in Homs to call for Assad's downfall, and six of them had paid with their lives. The rest fled to Yarmouk, and Hanan immediately made up extra beds in the living room and busied herself with trying to find them an apartment. She soon realized that it wasn't only her husband's family who needed help – hundreds of others did too, so she started opening up her home to strangers as well. More than thirty families passed through, sleeping on air mattresses which now filled every cranny in their dream home. When the guests moved on, Hanan would buy more air mattresses, bedding, pots and pans – whatever the displaced families needed – using her own money and funds sent from her brothers and sisters in exile.

They joined forces with other humanitarians in the city and started renting properties in their name for the displaced people. She could not look at the orphaned children, the sick, the elderly and just turn away. What if it was her own family? She would hope for kindness to be shown to them, so she felt a duty to offer this kindness to others herself.

As the scale of the massacre in Homs became clear, Hanan became more active in the aid networks, sourcing medical supplies, clothes for the children and food. She knew it might draw the attention of the authorities, but she didn't feel like she had a choice.

Then her daughters got involved, and that changed everything.

For most of their life Rim and Bisan had interests typical of young women all over the world: their studies, their clothes, going out with friends. Politics didn't interest them, much to their parents' relief. But when people they knew started to disappear, Rim and Bisan took a look at what was going on around them and it became clear they were their mother's daughters after all. First they tried to attend the Friday demonstrations, but Hanan did everything she could to stop them leaving the house. She could not stop them going to school, however, and had no idea what they were planning when they dressed in black one day and got on the bus.

Students at the Arab International University, where they both studied, had organized a demonstration through Facebook. When Rim and Bisan arrived that morning they found speakers across the campus, and at 11 a.m. those speakers started to play revolutionary songs. The two young women joined the chorus of voices chanting 'Freedom!' and 'We don't want Assad!', relieved to finally be able to speak out against the dictator they had once adored.

When news of the demonstration reached the regime, coach-loads of Shabiha were sent in. The gang of men and women marched through the campus, waving batons which they were not afraid to use, their battle cries of 'We will die for Bashar!' mingling with the students' chant of 'Freedom forever!' The air on campus fizzed with confusion, defiance and adrenalin, as the militia waded in with their clubs.

They stalked through the halls and the canteen, looking for the protest organizers. Rim and Bisan fled to the car park, where they boarded a bus which they hoped would take them away from the university. But the Shabiha got on the bus and pulled people off. Rim watched from the window as they pushed students to the ground, their faces in the concrete and their arms twisted behind their backs. Some of her friends were forced to kiss photos of Bashar al-Assad. Ten regime thugs set upon a young man who Rim thought must be at least six feet tall. But his height and strength didn't matter: the man crumpled under the blows until his blood flowed across the car park.

Rim could not shake the image from her mind. She had seen violence on the television and Internet before, but it was different close up. After that day, Hanan noticed a change in both her girls. They seemed frightened and withdrawn. Then she received a phone call from a friend in Homs. A man suspected of being Shabiha had asked after Hanan by name, and had details of her home. One of the people Hanan had sheltered in her home had been an undercover Shabiha officer who was gathering intelligence on people working against the regime.

'Take care,' were her friend's final ominous words.

Terror gripped Hanan, but she still could not quite believe that her country was tearing itself apart. So the family stayed a little longer, hoping that things would calm down. Then in July, the regime decided that Yarmouk was becoming a haven for opposition fighters, and it went in. Gun battles shattered the peace on the streets around the family home, and the shells started to pound Yarmouk. Hanan was forty-eight years old, and realized it was going to be impossible to keep her children safe any more if they stayed in Syria.

As she pulled down the shutters, watered the plants, and locked the doors of the family home on 18 July 2012, Hanan struggled to process how quickly her carefully constructed life had disintegrated. The business Talal built from scratch had already been abandoned. Two days earlier, the children had moved to a hotel in central Damascus. Hanan and Talal tried to stay and guard the house, but after a night in a neighbour's basement sheltering from the shelling, they gave up all hope. They had to pack their iPads and laptops, along with a handful of old photographs to remind them of their old life, and leave too.

That day, a bomb hit the Damascus headquarters of the National Security Council. The blast killed some of Assad's top security advisers, including his brother-in-law. No corner of the country was safe, not even the heart of Assad's capital. They had to escape, and Hanan began putting their plan in motion. Ismail's passport had expired, so before they could leave one had to be acquired through unofficial channels. Then she needed to arrange safe passage over the border to Lebanon. Both were bought at considerable cost, the first of many outlays which would strip the proud family of all their life savings and leave them reliant on handouts from relatives scattered across the globe.

Then it was just a twenty-mile drive to a new life reliant on the kindness of strangers. Finally Hanan understood why Watfah had left the place she loved all those years ago.

Nart: Damascus, Syria

All across Syria families were facing atrocities they could not have imagined a few months earlier. In August, the first barrel bombs fell on Aleppo, the metal containers stuffed with explosives and shrapnel dropped from the air and indiscriminately tearing through the flesh of anyone who happened to be living where they landed. By December, the regime was using chemical weapons against its own people. After a mysterious gas attack in Homs, people started feeling sick, their vision blurred and their breathing laboured. Seven people died; many more fell ill.

One of the victims found his way to Damascus and to Nart Bajoi, the Syrian lawyer and computer expert whose life was now a constant battle to outwit the regime and help those in need. Nart didn't know what to do with the man whose hair was coming out in clumps and whose body trembled all over. His physical condition made a dash over the border to the hospitals in Lebanon impossible, and there was little expertise in dealing with the aftermath of chemical warfare among the doctors willing to help the opposition. The dying man knew the hopelessness of his predicament, and begged Nart for one kindness: to return him to Homs. So he was smuggled back to die in the ruins of what was once his home.

Such cases were becoming more and more common for Nart.

Tens of thousands of people needed help, but the resources for his aid network were drying up. In the past year, the Syrian diaspora in Saudi Arabia and further afield had donated money, but now the donors' own families were in need of help so their funds went to their relatives instead.

Nart and others in his network had set up an email account. They would leave messages in the trash folder and sign out so that other members could sign in, read the messages and reply while evading the eyes of Syria's intelligence. Each day Nart would sign in to find out about the latest donation of medical supplies, food or money. When two months passed and not one message offering supplies appeared, he knew that he was reaching the point where he could not be of much more help.

By now, his own neighbourhood resembled a full-blown war zone. The regime had set up an artillery rocket just behind his apartment block, so every day he heard the shells fly overhead and would watch from his balcony as they landed on some unknown target, and all he could do was watch and imagine those suffering at the point of impact, knowing that his power to help them was diminishing.

Then members of his network started to disappear.

They were not only co-conspirators, but his friends. Many of them were students, about ten men and four women who were studying subjects like economics and engineering. Others were professionals like himself, using whatever skills and resources they had.

The first to go missing was a religious scholar, Sheikh Moham-med. He had a spare room in his house where clothes and medical supplies were stored before they were ferried across the country. One day the police turned up and headed straight to the spare room. The first Nart heard about it was when Sheikh Mohammed appeared on state television accused of building a bomb in his apartment. It was a setback, but Nart was not surprised. Someone must have reported his friend: the walls certainly had ears, and there were plenty of people willing to whisper to them, often for no other reason than spite. One friend who worked at a mobile phone shop had had nothing to do with the revolution, but he disappeared after a disagreement with his boss, who promptly filled out a report accusing his disgruntled employee of being a terrorist. Nart had even heard of a jilted woman avenging her lover in the same way.

That was what Syria was like now. You couldn't trust anyone any more.

Four more members of the network disappeared when security services searched their car at a roadblock and found supplies in the trunk. Snipers claimed six more colleagues. Tasked with delivering flour to the Ghouta suburb in the eastern part of Damascus, the men had to run a gauntlet of wooded roads to reach the neighbourhood. While the trees afforded them some cover, the security services also used them to surprise opposition activists. The soldiers didn't even search the car and discover the illicit cargo. They just opened fire, killing everyone.

The surviving members of his network were getting agitated.

'We are spending all this money on food and medicine,' one friend said, 'but if we buy weapons instead, we will finish Assad off.'

The friend left to join the Free Syrian Army, and others went with him. Still Nart resisted, thinking of the young boys from his neighbourhood who had been forced into military service. While he respected his friends' decision to fight against the oppressor, his own moral compass could not allow him to take a path which could end with one of those lives lost at his hands, no matter how much he wanted to oust Assad.

Nart had stayed in Damascus as long as he could, but with no resources and no colleagues, there was little more he could do for his countrymen. And there was little more he could do for himself. His money had run out and demand for his services as a systems engineer was dwindling now that there was hardly any electricity in Syria. No one could afford to pay legal fees either, and with rents rising as Damascus remained one of the few reasonably safe places in Syria, Nart could no longer afford an office.

Once again he contacted his friend in intelligence.

'Will I be arrested if I try to leave?' he asked.

This time, his friend refused to help, so Nart – recalling an old Syrian saying that good thieves sleep on the roof of a police station – headed to the regime stronghold of Latakia. Among the Assad supporters and members of the Shabiha, Nart found a taxi to take him to the Turkish border about twenty miles north.

Leaving turned out to be easy. Near every frontier there will be enterprising people looking to make a little extra income by illicitly transporting goods to the other side. On the Turkish border, it used to be cigarettes and coffee. Now, it was people without papers. Many, like Nart, feared that if they handed their documents to a Syrian border guard they would be condemning themselves to torture and death at the hands of the regime they had failed to topple. And so the thirty-two-year-old who just a year ago had been looking forward to starting a career and a family became another of the rapidly rising number of Syrians making a clandestine escape from their own country.

6

Three Friends

Mohammed: Damascus, Syria

Mohammed Kazkji always respected his parents' wishes. That was the kind of son he was, and he made his mother and father proud. But their job was to keep him alive, so when the papers arrived in the post ordering the twenty-year-old trainee electrician to report for military service, they set in motion the chain of events which was meant to keep him safe from harm. He was their priority: for the time being, their Damascus neighbourhood had escaped the worst of the fighting, and Mohammed's two sisters were immune from the draft, which applied only to men. At fifteen, his youngest brother was also safe from military service, while his older brother had been granted permission to carry on his studies of the Koran. It was only Mohammed who was at immediate risk of a brief and bloody military career, so all the family resources went towards getting him out of the country.

Leaving was the last thing Mohammed wanted to do. He could not imagine a life without his family, away from the home he had grown up in, and all the friendships he cherished. He had never travelled outside Syria before, he only spoke Arabic, and he was happy with his small, familiar world. A gloom enveloped Mohammed, but he was not going to disrespect his mother by ignoring her pleas that he leave for safety, so soon after the conscription papers arrived, he and his father presented themselves to the Syrian authorities.

Early in the uprising, the government still had a provision allowing young men to defer their military service until after their studies. So in August 2012, Mohammed and his father crossed town to a drab government office to try and convince whoever was behind the desk to grant him permission to finish his electrical engineering course abroad. The bureaucrat was sceptical, but not fastidious enough to bother probing too far. He asked a few cursory questions before warning Mohammed that he must remain in the Arab world and return within a year, or else they would find him and bring him home by force.

Mohammed managed a mumbled 'OK' before leaving clutching a passport now bearing the permit granting him permission to leave.

Within the month, he was at the boarding gate at Damascus International Airport waving his anxious mother and father goodbye. He tried to shake off the feeling creeping over him that he was leaving his home for ever. When an immigration officer stopped him and asked if he had finished serving in the army, he almost hoped he would turn him straight back round again. But his papers were in order, and all too quickly he was boarding a plane to Cairo.

Mohammed became one of the half a million Syrians who would be scattered throughout Syria's neighbours and other parts of the Middle East and North Africa by the end of 2012. It was an exodus of alarming speed. At the beginning of the year there were 9,500 Syrian refugees in the world. Six months later that number had ballooned to nearly 100,000, and by the end of the year, to 500,000.

Where the Syrians went depended on wealth and family connections. Mohammed's parents made enough money from the cobbling business to buy their son a plane ticket, but poorer families could only manage a taxi journey over a land border. Many Syrians also preferred to stay within a similar culture and closer to home, and both official tented camps and informal dwellings sprang up in Turkey, Lebanon, Jordan and Iraq. A lot of people stayed with friends and family, but for those people with no connections abroad and no money to pay rent, the only option was a camp.

Resigning yourself to a refugee camp meant putting your life on pause, receiving just enough food and water to get through to the next day, but robbed of any chance to provide for a family or plan for a future. Education was basic if it was offered at all, work was non-existent, and it was a daily struggle to keep yourself and your family clean and healthy. Rates of depression, suicide, self-harm, alcohol abuse, drug abuse and domestic violence soar in refugee camps all over the world, a reaction to the frustration arising from the sense of material impotence. In camps, there is nothing to do apart from sit and dwell on the horrors you left and the hopelessness of your future. Children re-live the bombs and the bullets they fled, and find little solace from depressed parents. Doctors working in the camps reported insomnia and bed-wetting among their young patients, with hardly enough funding for food, let alone counselling.

Syrian families with a little money were aiming further afield and trying to get to whichever countries offered the opportunity to continue life with at least a semblance of control over your own destiny. Mohammed certainly didn't have any plans to build a life in a dusty refugee camp. When he landed in Egypt, however, everything felt strange. The language was familiar, but the air and the people seemed so different.

I know I will never see Syria again for thirty or forty years, he thought.

But he had to keep moving forward, not to look back, just like his father had taught him. He boarded a bus which was making the two-day trip over the border to the Libyan port city of Misrata, where his uncle Nidar was waiting for him.

*

Less than a year earlier Misrata had been the focus of Colonel Gaddafi's rage. The city had always had an independent streak, and it was an early and enduring rebel stronghold. Gaddafi had responded with intense shelling, killing civilians and leaving the streets and avenues littered with shells and the rubble of the buildings they had brought down. Nidar had left Syria fifteen years earlier. Like Mohammed, he had fled the draft, and set himself up in Libya with a small car repair business. He had stayed even as the fighting raged around him, and his allegiance to his adopted city appeared to have paid off. Despite the pummelling of the civil war, the residents of Misrata were finding their feet again fast, and there was plenty of business for him and for his newly arrived nephew.

At first, life in Libya wasn't as bad as Mohammed had feared. He could not find a college at which to finish his studies, but his uncle was a gregarious man, and soon he had called in some favours and Mohammed was working as an assistant to an Italian electrician and had started to learn some English. When word got around about the trainee electrician's natural skill, the jobs started piling up and Mohammed was out almost every day putting his knowledge into practice for the first time. He loved learning the intricacies of the trade on the job, and his evenings were spent studying tutorials on the Internet. It was still a lonely life, but at least it was a life away from the bullets and the bombs which were slowly closing in on his family's home back in Damascus.

As the months passed, Mohammed got to know other Syrians living in Libya and struck up a friendship with two young men, Omar and Yahea. Fate had brought them together when Mohammed was sent to Tripoli to do the wiring on an apartment. Omar – a decorator who had also left Syria to flee the draft – was already there working on the drywall. On that same trip Mohammed bumped into another friendly young Syrian on the street and they quickly got chatting. Yahea spoke as passionately about his vocation as Mohammed did: he was an expert in crafting traditional Syrian sweets sticky with pistachio, rosewater and honey, and had dreams of opening up his own shop somewhere in Europe. Yahea and Mohammed were from the same neighbourhood in Damascus, and the men had a laugh about all the friends they had in common. They also shared a sense of displacement from a homeland they were forced to leave, and a feeling that they could be doing more to help their families back home.

When Mohammed returned to Misrata after the job was finished, the three friends promised to stay in touch and share any news they heard about better opportunities.

While Mohammed had a home, a job and some new friends, nothing could replace his mother and father. The phone calls back to his family were becoming increasingly painful. Fighting was closing in on their neighbourhood – Mohammed knew this from reading online news reports – but whenever he was able to get through to his mother to find out how they were, he always received the same reply.

'We are fine,' his mother would reassure him, 'we have food, we have drink, so be good and be strong.'

Mohammed knew she was lying. The phone line was faltering, and often they would be cut off just when he tried to press his mother on the reality of their situation. When four months passed and he was unable to even get through, panic started to take over every waking moment. Mohammed was convinced his family had all been killed as the shelling and gunfire erupted around them. At night, his dreams were haunted by images of his mother coming to harm. Finally, his desperate daily ritual of pressing re-dial over and over again paid off and a faint voice came on the line. It was his mother.

'We are fine,' she told him, 'don't worry, be strong.'

But he could tell by the tone of her voice that she was not fine. Nothing was fine any more. He learned that his grandfather had been killed in a round of shelling on their neighbourhood, and a sniper's bullet had claimed his aunt. The time was approaching when letters might arrive in the post asking his youngest brother to serve in the military. And Mohammed didn't want to let on to his parents, but Libya was no longer that much safer than the bombed-out suburbs of Damascus.

Another war was coming – Mohammed could feel it in his bones.

Libya's uprising had reached a crescendo on 20 October 2011 when rebels dragged Colonel Gaddafi out of a storm drain near his home town of Sirte and killed him, a merciless execution documented on shaky camera phone. The man who had once seemed invincible over nearly half a century of rule cowered in blood and sweat-soaked robes as rebels gathered in an excited crowd, hands flying out to smack his face and pull his hair, feet kicking sand in his face as the metal barrels of guns flashed in the periphery of the shot. The beeping of horns and shouts of 'Allah Akbar' mingled with the gunfire, as Gaddafi was beaten and repeatedly stabbed in the buttocks with a bayonet. It was a prolonged and confused death, the autopsy claiming a stray bullet inflicted the final fatal wound. But with so many injuries it was hard to tell.

That cathartic spasm of extreme violence was followed by a bout of self-congratulation from Western leaders who were well aware that they were lacking glowing success stories from their other recent military interventions in Iraq and Afghanistan. So Libya was hailed a victory for democracy, and the NATO war planes returned to their bases.

For a few weeks, Libya's various factions let the opposition forces who formed the National Transitional Council attempt to establish their authority across the country. With long-standing animosities between tribes, divides between the secularists and Islamists, and rebel groups competing for a slice of what they assumed would be Libya's continued economic prosperity, it was a mess that would take time and investment to fix. The West unfortunately had neither. There were no troops on the ground, and as well as not nearly enough funding there was an insufficient number of expert advisers to help the fractious country in its difficult transition. By late summer of 2012, the National Transitional Council's brief honeymoon period was over. The country was awash with weapons and it was proving impossible to rein in the militias which had formed and united to fight Gaddafi, but which had very different interests in a vast desert nation with a city-state mentality rather than acting as a unified country. The result was a gradual slide into civil war, and Libya was on its own. The leaders who had helped oust Gaddafi had no intention of being dragged into another intractable war.

As if the country needed another blow to its reputation, on 11 September the US consulate in Benghazi came under mortar and rocket fire. A group of heavily armed Islamic militants stormed the building, forcing the US Ambassador to Libya, J. Christopher Stevens, and two other embassy employees into a safe room. The men tried to escape as flames engulfed the building, but the thick black smoke claimed the lives of Stevens and a foreign service staff member. Two more Americans died in a gun battle with militants later in the day. Initial reports that the fire was caused by an anti-US protest which got out of hand were quickly disproved, and the al-Qaeda-linked group Ansar al-Sharia became the prime suspect. Mohammed watched the reports of the consulate attack with horror – this was the kind of violence he had tried to escape, and Libya was becoming a very dangerous place.

For some people, however, chaos proved the perfect cover, and the lawlessness became a draw to a new wave of the displaced. The transitional government in Tripoli was struggling to exert its authority over the city boundaries, let alone the country's vast borders. While there were hardly any border police to stop people entering, there were plenty of armed factions willing to give people a helping hand to enter – for the right price. Just like Gaddafi just a few months earlier, Libya's new power groups saw dollar signs in the desperation, and people smuggling became another vital source of income to fund their armed movements.

While more Syrians than ever were arriving along Libya's vast Mediterranean coastline en route to Europe, they were now joined by many others fleeing conflict from all corners of the globe. In Mali, insurgent Tuareg tribesman had joined forces with the Islamist Ansar Dine group. As the rebels swept over the north of the country bringing their extreme version of Sharia law, families fled over borders. Reports of extreme violence were also seeping out of the Central African Republic, where rebels advanced on the capital. More Eritreans were looking for escape every day. Sectarian violence in Nigeria and long-running conflicts in Sudan and Somalia also sent people on a long odyssey to safety, while Afghans continued to spill out of their homeland. Many Iraqis were on the move again, seeing nearby Syria in flames and sensing troubled times ahead.

These new huddled masses were gathering not only on Libya's unguarded coastline, but also in other countries within reach of the European Union. As the Syrian refugee communities in Turkey, Lebanon and Jordan swelled, those families who didn't want to build a life in a tent or an abandoned building were also looking towards the land and sea borders with Greece and Bulgaria. Very few had attempted the dangerous journey yet. Just under 8,000 Syrians were detected trying to cross an EU sea or land border without a visa in 2012. But as more people left Syria and started moving towards safety, it was inevitable that the number would rise fast.

To many people outside it, the European Union remained the beacon of freedom, democracy and human rights it had aspired to be when it emerged from the wreckage of the Second World War, shamed by its failure to prevent the massacre of millions in the Holocaust. Europe's reluctance to offer sanctuary to Jews fleeing the Nazis in the 1930s had helped embolden Hitler, and when the war finally ended in 1945 an unprecedented number of shell-shocked refugees were displaced from their countries, left to wander ruined cities searching for a home. A Herculean effort saw the 50 million refugees returned or re-settled within a year, and the crisis led to the creation of the United Nations refugee agency, the Office of the UN High Commissioner for Refugees (UNHCR).

The UN's 1951 Refugee Convention was drafted to ensure the rights of those post-war refugees, but it faced another test with the advent of the Cold War. The new wave of refugees fleeing Soviet aggression and proxy wars in all corners of the globe benefited from the unshakable Western narrative of the Cold War as a game of heroes and villains, and they were largely welcomed and absorbed. In 1956, as Soviet tanks rolled into Budapest to crush an uprising, 200,000 Hungarians fled over their borders and into Austria and Yugoslavia. Starting in 1975, the western world managed to find new homes for the 1.3 million Indo-Chinese refugees fleeing repressive Communist regimes in Vietnam, Laos and Cambodia.

When the Cold War ended, however, it left in its wake a minefield of dormant conflicts. In Pakistan and Afghanistan, the flood of weapons and money that had poured in for the mujahideen fighting the Soviets in Afghanistan would help create the Taliban. African nations which had been propped up as client states for one side or another found themselves on their own, and civil wars erupted. Sierra Leona, Liberia, Somalia – the brutal conflicts mounted, scattering terrified victims far and wide. By the 1990s the Iraq war and the break-up of Yugoslavia sent even more people on the road with their families, but the spirit of solidarity that had united Europe after the Second World War had been replaced by individualistic societies driven by the pursuit of economic growth. Europe was no longer the world's main source of refugees but, rather, an increasingly inward-looking place deeply suspicious of asylum seekers, the term itself used as shorthand for the kind of person who should be feared and mistrusted.

The proliferation of conflict in the 1980s coincided with the global economic downturn and with globalization opening up borders for people to move more freely to follow work and money. Increasingly the distinction blurred between those arriving in a European country to seek work and those in need of protection. As Europeans worried about their jobs and pensions, calls to keep economic migrants out grew, and governments tightened visa restrictions. Passport checks multiplied at airports, surveillance increased, and reception conditions for asylum seekers steadily deteriorated to remove the incentive for people to come to Europe. No matter if a person was fleeing the genocide in Rwanda or the retribution of Saddam Hussein rather than poverty and unemployment: everyone was initially treated the same. Then the border fences started going up, and gradually the European Union became a fortress.

The politicians would continue to argue that they were protecting their borders from people illegally entering Europe to work, and many of those wishing to come were indeed economic migrants fleeing poverty rather than persecution. By 2012, however, the mix was tilting towards people who should be granted some form of humanitarian protection if they survived the long journey to the European Union.

But it didn't seem to matter. Anybody trying to reach Europe became an easy scapegoat on a continent at a crossroads. The eurozone crisis was battering economies well beyond the worst-hit countries of Greece, Ireland, Spain and Portugal. Unemployment was soaring and hit a record high across the EU again early in 2012. Governments kept slashing their growth forecasts and many member states saw their credit ratings fall along with quality of life. In hard times, people look anywhere for their saviours, and fringe political parties on both the left and the right were doing well. Playing on racism, xenophobia and old animosities was an easy vote winner, and mainstream politicians didn't try too hard to battle the perception that the desperate people intent on reaching Europe would steal jobs and deplete scarce resources.

So border fences were built even higher, making them even more lethal for those who attempted to scale them, and the EU funnelled money to security forces on the other side to keep people away from Europe no matter what. The leaders could just about convince themselves that it was working – the number of clandestine arrivals was down in 2012. Gaddafi's alarmist rhetoric about unleashing an unmanageable flood of people – a barbarian invasion threatening the very fabric of civilized European – had not materialized, and leaders across Europe relaxed a little. Lampedusa could return to being a holiday island rather than an asylum centre stranded at sea. EU states which had resisted offering assistance to Italy could kick the issue down the road again.

While 141,051 people were detected on Europe's border in 2011, just over 72,000 had tried to enter in 2012. So rather than look around at the neighbourhoods in flames in Syria, the conditions for refugees in neighbouring countries, and the chaotic power vacuum developing in Libya, the European Union took its eye off the Mediterranean and the Middle East and returned to worrying about its own economic troubles instead.

The fact that Europe was in a slump didn't really register with Mohammed, Omar or Yahea. They all remained convinced that it could offer them a better future and an escape from the violence that was once again creeping into their daily lives. Then one day Mohammed heard from a friend of a friend who had crossed the Mediterranean and was safely in Italy.

'Look man, if you want to continue your future, if you want to continue to study, you have to come to Europe,' the friend said.

'OK,' Mohammed replied, 'tell me the way.'

2013

Number of refugees and migrants entering the EU: 107,365
Number of deaths: 700

7

A Family Betrayal

Hanan: Beirut, Lebanon

Fleeing war doesn't always mean a frantic dash through a heavily guarded border with crying children in your arms and belongings spilling out of bundles on your back. Sometimes, it is as simple as going for a short drive, the mundane journey disguising the seismic life change for the people involved. Leaving Syria in two taxis, Hanan al-Hasan and her children could easily have passed for a family heading on holiday. From the outside, no one would have been able to see the tears which streamed down Hanan's face all the way from Damascus to Beirut.

They crossed the border with ease, just as they had many times before when they went to visit family and friends. The frontier between Syria and Lebanon had always been fluid, drawn up by the French after the Second World War and treated as a colonial imposition by many citizens on both sides. Visas were not required – at least not until 2015 – and people and goods flowed freely between two nations which regarded one another like estranged siblings: there had been plenty of political differences over the years, but the bonds of history were strong.

At first it seemed possible to forge a future in Lebanon, and a ray of hope remained in Hanan's heart. By staying so close to the shuttered factory and the family home, it was easier to believe that the war would one day end, Assad would be ousted, and a more promising future would be on the horizon for the children.

In one and a half hours I could be back in my house, Hanan would think to herself when she felt despondent. *I can stand on the hill and almost see my home. I am sure I will go back to Syria.*

The family had connections in Lebanon, and an old friend immediately offered a floor in his home to the displaced family. Hanan, Talal, Rim, Bisan, Ismail and Riad felt safe for the first time in months. But the strain was already showing on Lebanon, a country of 4.5 million people with its own deep sectarian divides. At the start of the conflict in Syria, when only a few thousand people had crossed the border, the overwhelming feeling in Lebanon was one of sympathy for its neighbours, combined with a little gloating. After all, it was Lebanon which had spent much of the last few decades in the grip of a civil war, fuelled in part by Syrian meddling. The government in Damascus had always regarded Lebanon as a client state, sending thousands of troops there in 1976, supposedly for peacekeeping. But even after a peace accord was reached in Lebanon in 1990, the troops remained, allowing Syria to wield considerable influence. The final straw came in 2005 when Prime Minister Rafic Hariri – a proponent of sending the Syrian soldiers home – was killed in a car bombing, and few were in much doubt that the Assad regime was behind Lebanon's worst political assassination in years. A wave of protests eventually ousted the final Syrian troops, but the two countries remained close. Their economies were interdependent and they shared a sense of solidarity in their policy towards Israel. But patience was dwindling as Syria's civil war started seeping over the border, and Lebanese citizens started dying. It wasn't just the errant shells landing on Lebanese territory. While the power-sharing government in Beirut which encompassed all sects tried to remain neutral to avoid exacerbating communal divisions, members of Lebanon's Hezbollah Shia militia headed to Syria to fight for Assad, who came from the Shia-derived Alawite sect.

The delicate sectarian balance that kept Lebanon from tumbling back into civil war was being tested, and the resources were also being stretched to the limit in a small strip of land that already housed a large population of Palestinian refugees.

When Hanan and her family crossed the border, there were 26,000 Syrian refugees in Lebanon. A year later, in July 2013, the number had risen to half a million, eventually reaching nearly 1.2 million – the equivalent of a quarter of the population of Lebanon, with nearly one in five people who were living in the country having fled Syria.

Unlike in Turkey and Jordan, there were no official refugee camps in Lebanon. The government was wary of encouraging a long-term refugee population, so Syrians instead lived in rented accommodation or with relatives or friends. Those who could afford to do neither fashioned their own settlements in abandoned buildings or on disused land – unofficial refugee camps with very little assistance. The refugee population put a huge strain on infrastructure and public services, costing the Lebanese economy up to $2.5 billion. While the schools were struggling, the water supplies dwindling, and the wages falling with an increased labour supply, the influx of mostly Sunni Muslims was also fuelling tensions between the communities.

Hanan didn't care about such matters. Her family were Sunni, but when she had opened up her home to those fleeing suffering in Homs, she did so regardless of their religious background. She expected the same courtesy to be extended to her and her family in Lebanon.

For the first few months there, life seemed bearable once again. The mental tension that had plagued Hanan during her final months in Syria was lifting. Their host owned a home fixtures company just like the one Talal had left behind, and he quickly offered Talal a job. Rim meanwhile had the ideal distraction: her fiancé Izzat was still in Syria and making plans to join them, so expectation and excitement at his arrival helped the days that were bereft of study or work pass more quickly. When Izzat arrived in May 2013, the family threw an engagement party. At twenty-one, Rim had a quiet elegance, and still possessed the charm of the angelic five-year-old who had won over the hearts of the prison guards with the song for her incarcerated uncle. That night, it shone bright. The beautiful life Hanan plotted for her children may have been on hold, but still she could weave a happiness for those she loved the most, and she was overcome with pride. The turmoil of the past year had worn away their carefree exteriors and revealed not four spoilt children, but four resilient and understanding young people who loved and supported one another. And they were so handsome, Rim beaming in a pink satin off-the-shoulder dress emblazoned with jewelled flowers, Bisan a little more offbeat in a black mini-skirt, with a white vest, a long string of beads and a shy grin. Riad and Ismail put on their best shirts, and for that evening all their worries were put to one side.

Hanan wanted them to enjoy themselves. Life was about to get much harder.

In the weeks that followed, Hanan began to notice a change in the demeanour of their hosts. The wife had an uncle in Hezbollah, and as the death toll for the militia fighters in Syria increased, so did her animosity towards her house guests. Snide remarks turned into outright hostility and veiled threats to their safety, and soon Talal was told his services were no longer needed. So in early 2013 Hanan and Talal rented a house of their own, digging further into the family savings. Talal could not find any more work in overcrowded Lebanon, and Riad and Ismail were missing out on their education. Despite trudging from school to school, they kept being turned down. There simply was not enough room in Lebanon's education system for all the Syrian children as well. Apart from Rim's engagement, Hanan's daughters were not faring much better. There were no places at the public university for Rim and Bisan, and the $40,000 it would cost per year to educate them at private universities was too expensive.

'My family have given us a lot, but how long can they go on helping?' Hanan asked Talal. 'We can't just stay here waiting for my sisters and brothers to send money.'

Ismail tried to help, finding a job at a local mall selling gym equipment. He used to go to the gym five times a week back home, so it was at least an area which interested him, but Hanan was not happy with her seventeen-year-old son working eleven hours a day when he should be in school.

In the end, their solution came in an uninvited and unexpected form. Talal had a nephew – Rami – who had left Syria years ago and married a nightclub dancer in Tunisia, a union which had not impressed Hanan. Now the black sheep of the family had separated from his wife and wanted to come to Lebanon, and Talal's sister begged the family to take him in.

'He is changed, he is a good boy, he has work,' she said.

They agreed, and after about six months in which they hardly ever saw their new house guest, Hanan finally found out what line of work Rami was in.

'I am going to Turkey and I will work there,' he told them one day. 'I have a group – we will send people to Europe.'

When Hanan and Talal left Syria, they hadn't considered going to Europe. They wanted to stay close to their country and in a familiar culture. But Hanan's instinct was to offer her children the best future possible. If Talal had no job and the children couldn't even go to school or university, she was failing to provide the very base for them to build their lives on.

A few weeks after he left, Rami called Talal.

'I will send you by aeroplane to Europe, just come here,' he said.

On 1 September 2013, the family packed up what remained of their belongings and moved on again, flying into Istanbul with the money Ismail had saved from his job at the mall.

Rami might have been family, but he wasn't in the business of offering discounts. He met his uncle at the airport and took the family to a rented apartment. Talal and Hanan had let Rami stay with them in Beirut for six months for free, but his first request was for €1,000 in rent. Then he asked for $6,000 to get fake papers for the whole family, which now included Hanan's future son-in-law Izzat. They would need these to board the plane to Europe, he explained.

A few days later he returned with bad news.

'You can't go on the aeroplane, there are too many police,' he said, without explaining the disappearance of the $6,000. 'You will go by ship.'

The family reluctantly agreed, on the condition that it was a large vessel.

'Sure,' Rami replied. The price? '$32,000.'

The figure represented most of their savings, but was worth it for a shot at safety. They agreed to give him $20,000 up front and the other $12,000 when they left.

Hanan wasn't too worried about the crossing. Sure, she'd heard that boats were going down between North Africa and Italy, but her family was paying extra for a good vessel. It was not as if they would be locked in a hold with hundreds of others and launched into the waves with 200 miles of open seas ahead of them. It wasn't exactly first class though – the safest way to apply for refugee status in Europe was to get on a plane with a genuine passport and a valid visa, and then turn yourself in to the authorities when you landed. But which country would now grant a Syrian a visa? She wished there was another option, and despaired of the West's reluctance to punish Assad for his crimes against his own people, and its hypocritical support for the rebels while abandoning the real victims of the war.

I'm sure the Americans, the Europeans and the French could stop this war if they put their mind to it, she thought.

But what could she do? Lebanon was becoming a hateful and dangerous place, and there was no way she would allow her family to end up in a Turkish refugee camp. Hanan could imagine no worse horror than sitting in a tent, helpless and impassive, waiting for someone to come and give you and your family a meal. Her best chance at getting her children to Europe alive was to go by sea to the Greek islands. Many perils remained: as well as the risk of drowning, Greece was doing all it could to prevent people from reaching its shores. Naval vessels were carrying out illegal push-back operations, dumping people who had crossed into EU territory back over the border without processing their claim for asylum, flouting the union's laws stating that a country must examine each individual case.

A few months later, a boat would capsize as it was being towed behind a Greek naval vessel. Eleven Syrians and Afghans, including eight children, drowned, with the survivors insistent that they were being dragged against their will back to Turkey. It was not only Greece: Spain, Italy and Bulgaria also stood accused of breaking EU law by failing to process claims for asylum. Countries would keep doing it though. This was one of the many international laws addressing the rights of refugees which nations broke with impunity. The European Union had a mechanism to punish member states which flouted its laws. It could launch infringement proceedings, which cut off EU funds. But while EU officials in Brussels were quick with words of condemnation about the push-backs, they did not start infringement proceedings against any nation, leaving little in- centive for governments to fall into line.

The push-backs didn't deter people from attempting to cross either, but they did make the smugglers and some refugees take desperate measures to stay in Europe. Smugglers often scuttled the boats on purpose while they were still at sea, fearful that unless the passengers were in the direst of circumstances, the Greek coastguard would tow them back to Turkey. Inflatable boats would be punctured near the coast, people forced to put their lives at risk in a desperate bid to be granted a basic human right.

Hanan's first challenge, however, was to convince the smugglers that they had actually paid for their voyage. After a month of waiting in Istanbul, Rami finally called and instructed the family to go to İzmir on the western Turkish coast. But upon arrival at the bus station, three smugglers – Hilal, Mansour and Shadhi – demanded money.

'No, you didn't pay Rami anything, that's not true,' Hilal said.

Talal and Hanan told them to contact Rami, and after a whispered phone call the smugglers took them to the holding house, a shell of a building close enough to the sea that they could hear the waves and smell the salt in the air. Before their trek to the beach, the family were forced to hand over all their belongings. Shadhi shrugged at their protests – this was their payment, take it or leave it.

'Rami told us that Rim, Bisan, Riad and Ismail will have three laptops and three iPads,' Shadhi explained. 'Rami said, "Take everything they have with them. If they go to police, take one of their children."'

Hanan was stunned. This was Talal's flesh and blood, and he was willing to sell them. How could their life have come to this? Her disillusionment was complete when they walked for two hours to the coast and found themselves on a beach with a handful of other families looking at the two-and-a-half-metre piece of blue rubber which had cost them more than $20,000.

It was dark by the time they arrived. Stars were spreading across a velvet black sky, with the crescent moon of the early October sky struggling to illuminate the few wisps of cloud remaining from the day. But it was just enough light to see that the tiny dinghy rocking on the waves was not what they had been promised. Pure fear gripped Hanan as she looked at the inflatable raft, and she felt the weight of her decision. Endanger the lives of her children on this pathetic vessel, or start the search for safe crossing all over again.

The smugglers were agitated, urging the men, woman and

children gathered on the beach to wade out onto the craft and set off blindly into the sea with no instruments to guide them. Hanan's four children were silent, but she could feel their eyes on her and Talal. Her reserves of strength were ebbing away. She had risked so much already and come so far from that summer morning more than a year ago when she finally locked the door on the family home in Damascus. And Greece couldn't be that far away, could it? But in her heart she knew that drowning was a risk no matter how close European Union soil was, and Hanan had not dragged her family this far only for them to die on the rocks of a foreign shore.

She turned to the smuggler with fire in her eyes.

'If God comes to earth I will not go with this boat!'

'No, you must go, it's very near,' Hilal insisted, waving out to the black sea.

Talal had also recovered from his shock and found his voice.

'No, it is impossible, I will not take my children in this boat,' he said. 'Where will we sit? In the water? We want our money or we will speak to the police.'

The rest of the group had a bargaining chip. While Hanan had paid up front, the other passengers had left their money with a middle man in Istanbul who was under instruction to pay the smuggling gang only upon their safe arrival in Europe. So, faced with this mutiny, the smugglers threw their hands in the air and abandoned their cargo on the beach. A short while later, the police arrived, with Hanan in little doubt that Hilal had tipped them off. Those without passports were rounded up and thrown in the cells for a few days, while Hanan and her family returned to İzmir to begin another wait for their passage to Europe. Once again they called Hilal – they didn't have any other contacts in İzmir and there was nowhere else to go.

A week later Talal returned to their rooms with news: a large ship was leaving the next day. He had been given an address for a taxi, and at 3 p.m. they set off. Hanan had nagging doubts as to whether the boat would be any better than the raft she had already rejected, but she had been holding her family together in limbo long enough: it was time to make the next step. Talal did everything he could to reassure his wife. He had checked the shipping forecasts, and he held his hand steady in front of her.

'The sea will be like my hand – don't worry,' he said.

As the taxi began its journey, however, Hanan's apprehension intensified. The car appeared to be climbing into the mountains rather than skirting the coastal roads. After about half an hour they stopped in the middle of nowhere. 'This is the address,' the driver shrugged before leaving his bewildered fare abandoned in the Turkish countryside. *Have I let myself be cheated once again?* Hanan wondered. Then a small bus appeared round the corner and the family was loaded aboard for another winding journey further into the mountain.

They drove for about three hours and the sun had set when they were finally bundled out and met by a gang of seven large men shouting instructions. Their message was simple: 'Walk, walk, walk.' There was no time to rest after the hours on the road, but there did appear to be time for the men to ransack their belongings, and the family's remaining laptop and iPad – the ones they had managed to hide from Hilal – were quickly appropriated as further payment for the arduous journey.

The stoicism which seemed to run from Hanan through each member of the family was breaking down. Tears streamed down Rim's face. One of the smugglers had taken her aside and waved a knife at her.

'Give me your bag.'

She had handed it over, losing one of her most treasured possessions: a scrapbook which she had filled with photographs and other mementos of her life. She decided not to tell anyone – if Izzat or her father knew she had been threatened, they might challenge the smuggler, and she would not let them risk their lives for her. So she cried, mourning her loss and the trauma of the robbery all alone.

The family had no choice but to march on through the night – *like animals*, Hanan thought as she observed her daughters trudging along. As the hours passed, the bottles of water ran out. At first Riad went ahead, pushing away the bracken and trying to clear a path.

'Come, Mama,' he urged.

The family all had a soft spot for Riad, the baby of the family who loved to sleep by his mother and whisper secrets in her ear. Finally, the thirteen-year-old reached for Hanan's hand, and clutched it for the rest of the journey over mountains and through forest. But while her youngest son was still able to draw comfort and strength from his mother's touch, the older boy was nearing the end of his teenage years and the end of his patience. Ismail's time as a refugee had leached away some of the innocence that can linger from childhood. As his sisters wept and Hanan struggled over the rocky path, she could feel him bristling at the anonymous men who were leading them further into the darkness. Hanan groped in the dark for Ismail's hand. She was proud of his instinct to protect his family, but knew that he was outnumbered.

'They will kill your sister, they will kill me, they will kill your father. They have guns, they have knives, we don't have anything,' she told him. 'Please your mama – don't say anything.'

His answer was quiet but she was reassured: 'OK Mama.'

It took three more hours of hiking before they scrambled down a slope, to find themselves once again with the foreboding sea lapping at their feet.

And there was the boat that Hanan had been thinking about since the idea to go to Europe first lodged in her head. It still wasn't the cruise liner she had initially hoped for, but it was bigger than the flimsy vessel of the previous week. In the darkness, she looked around her and was astonished to see just how many others were on the beach. Once again Hanan had been lied to – she was told there would be seventeen people on the boat, but she counted thirty-two others huddled together, silent with fear. But she was not turning back now, and she melted into the crowd, ready to let fate take over. There was one aspect she could try and influence though, and that was her children's safety. First there was the matter of life jackets. Hanan had been promised jackets for the family when negotiating their passage, but now the men laughed and said none existed.

'Well then, we won't go,' Hanan said. The men carried on laughing, but Hanan rallied the others on the beach.

'With no jackets, none of us are going,' she said, and watched as the men dragged a sack out from behind a rock. The jackets had been there all along: they just wanted to make more money selling them to the next wave of refugees.

The smugglers selected one of the younger men from the crowd and told him he would be piloting the boat. With just five minutes' instruction, the lives of all those people, including those Hanan loved most in the world, were entrusted to a man she did not know.

'If you return,' the smuggler warned the man, 'we will kill you all.'

With these threats, the men, women and children boarded the boat, crouching down with whatever belongings were not stolen bundled in front of them.

Before they cast off, there was one last measure Hanan took to try and protect her children. She had brought them up to have the things she didn't when she was growing up, and that included a knowledge of how to swim. She would not let them sacrifice their lives trying to rescue their drowning mother should the worst happen. If the boat sank, she wanted them to leave her and save themselves. So she took two strong sleeping tablets, reasoning that they would be more likely to respect her wishes if she was already comatose and could not be saved.

'Take care of the two girls and let me go, don't touch me if anything happens,' she told her husband and sons.

'Mama, don't say that, we will save you,' were the words she heard as she drifted off to sleep, and the boat launched off in the direction of Europe.

8

An Indefinable Suffering

Sina: Asmara, Eritrea

After months of excited planning, Sina and Dani's wedding day finally arrived. They had decided on a traditional Eritrean ceremony, and on 17 July 2013, more than 300 friends and family gathered to watch the young couple exchange their vows. Dressed in a luxurious black cloak trimmed with gold and draped over white robes, Sina solemnly vowed to devote her life to Dani, then danced with the exuberance of a woman who knows that there is no one else in the world who will take such good care of her.

'Are people having a good time?' Sina kept asking Dani, anxious that their happiness be shared with their loved ones.

Music filled the hall, and between songs the newly-weds amused themselves by identifying the secret Pentecostals – a banned religion in Eritrea – who were giving themselves away by staying glued to the walls while the other revellers enjoyed themselves on the dance floor.

But when Sina glanced around the room, she couldn't help but notice the absences. Many friends had already fled Eritrea and were living in refugee camps in Sudan and Kenya. Some had travelled further afield to try and escape the long arm of the Eritrean security apparatus. No matter where you went in sub-Saharan Africa, if you had left Eritrea illegally the state could reach well outside national borders and drag you back for a cruel punishment. Security forces in at least four countries had colluded in the forced repatriation of Eritreans, so many people had decided to try and reach Europe, the only place where they would feel safe.

Sina was now used to these strange and sudden disappearances. One day she would be chatting to an old friend, the next day there would be no trace of them. People didn't share their plans. The government had eyes and ears everywhere.

'Ah, he has already left,' Sina would say to herself, feeling happy that the friend was finally free. With around one hundred Eritreans leaving the country every day it was unsurprising that some people on their wedding guest list would be among them. Not that Sina would ever discuss these disappearances. That alone could be enough to be thrown into a cell. And she and Dani were trying so hard to follow all of Eritrea's arbitrary rules. They had applied to their respective military officers and received the government's permission to become man and wife. Dani had even invited his military supervisor to the wedding, although the man never showed up.

Many friends had been refused permission to leave their posts to see Dani and Sina marry. Around seven guests who had their requests turned down decided to travel to the wedding anyway, knowing full well that it would mean a prison sentence when they returned. They just factored that into their decision: that was what life in Eritrea was like. For everything you did, you had to weigh up whether you were willing to stomach the resulting punishment.

The most brutal retribution was reserved for those the government deemed traitors. A simple slip-up like asking the wrong person about a missing friend or discussing general government policy could be enough to warrant the accusation of betraying your country. Other 'crimes' included practising a banned religion, plotting to leave the country, wandering too close to an external border, working for a foreign company, or simply being related to someone suspected of deviant behaviour. As formal charges and trials did not exist, most people never actually found out which totalitarian diktat they had broken when suddenly they were marched off to a cell.

Given the number of people President Afewerki was locking away, there was a need for creativity when it came to the logistics of incarceration. The official prisons were supplemented with secret facilities that included caves, holes, open-air camps and converted old buildings. A particularly horrific innovation was the underground dungeon, a metal shipping container measuring twenty feet by eight feet buried in the desert. No light could seep in, temperatures reached forty-four degrees, and screams would echo around the metal box, the sound unable to penetrate the soil above.

Heat was a problem in Eritrea whether you were under or above the ground. In the open-air prisons, the thorny branches of felled acacia trees counted as walls, and there you stayed as the desert sun baked the land to over fifty degrees. Sometimes your jail was just a hole dug in the earth with a piece of corrugated iron thrown over the opening. Any structure could find a second life as a prison: a water tank, a cattle house or even an unfinished slaughterhouse. Conditions in all facilities were inhuman, with inmates crammed into small spaces with no toilets, forced to sleep in their own waste. Sickness was common, and many people died of illness. Others took their own lives.

With no trials or records, it was impossible to know exactly how many people were buried below Eritrea's earth or suffering in cells. Estimates of 14,000 in military detention facilities alone hinted at the scale of Eritrea's prison population. Imprisonment was an everyday occurrence – everyone knew someone who had disappeared – and that was exactly how the regime wanted it. Fear was its most powerful weapon, and it sowed it with expertise.

Locking people away wasn't enough: torture was also widespread. People who survived told of being trussed up and left in agony for hours or days, limbs contorted and bound behind their backs in a position referred to as 'the helicopter'. Others were told to dig their own grave and lie there as the earth was heaped on top of them, only freed after a gunshot smacked the earth beside them in a mock execution. Sometimes the torture was as simple as a beating with sticks and electrical cable, other times more elaborate. Inmates could be bound by their wrists to a tree or the barrel of a tank, arms spread wide in an excruciating stance known as the 'Jesus Christ'. Interrogators had free rein to inflict whatever horror came into their head. And they always made sure that the screams were heard in the cells next door, so the other prisoners knew what was coming.

For the more minor offence of leaving their post without permission, Sina and Dani's friends expected to serve around two months in a military facility. But they reasoned that it was worth it to be able to share in the couple's happiness. And for that weekend, Sina's happiness outshone all the clouds gathering on the horizon.

Everyone agreed they made a handsome couple, Dani towering a head over Sina, she nuzzling perfectly into his frame, a broad smile across her face whenever those long arms enveloped her and tucked her head protectively under his chin. Their children would be beautiful, and Dani's father was already dropping hints that a grandchild would be very welcome. But it was hard for Sina to imagine bringing in a baby into their life. The couple refused to discuss such matters on their wedding day, but a few months earlier bad news had reached them. Dani's supervisor, who had once seemed friendly and had turned a blind eye to Dani's work as a part-time teacher, had become hostile. It wasn't clear what had upset him, but Dani could sometimes rub people up the wrong way. He was educated, and had opinions he was not afraid to express. The problem was that his military superiors – often less educated than Dani and envious of his easy manner

– took such behaviour as insubordination, and had plenty of scope to punish him. The supervisor demanded money, but it was unclear where this was meant to come from when Dani was only earning $30 a month. The demands became more insistent in the run-up to Dani's wedding. The implication was clear: pay up or split up.

And while Sina had been enjoying her time in Asmara preparing papers and organizing conferences, her employers were demanding that their chemical engineer return to work in the field. Sina could just about stand getting back in her overalls and work boots, but the thought of a life without Dani was unbearable.

The couple had discussed their options, and decided to ask the military to transfer Dani to a post near Sina's office in the north of the country. Asmara would have made a better first home for the newly-weds. Their families were in the capital, which was the closest thing Eritrea had to a tourist attraction, with its Art Deco buildings, its streets filled with jacaranda blooms, and only pleasant mementos of its colonial occupation by Italy – pizza parlours serving fresh pies under sunny pavement awnings, and old coffee machines filling the air with the smell of roasting beans. Nothing like that existed in the northern badlands where Sina was headed, but they would be together, and this was all Sina wanted.

The request was turned down. Dani's supervisor had another plan for him. He was to be sent 500 kilometres south of Asmara to take up his new post as a guard on the border with the neighbouring nation of Djibouti.

This is the worst thing that could happen in our lives, Sina thought.

How could they ever build a life and a family if they could not see each other, or even talk? Deprived of national ID papers which give you freedom to travel, every potential trip to see one another would mean a protracted application to military supervisors, who had a habit of turning down requests just to keep recruits in line. Sina and Dani would not even be able to speak on the phone. Mobiles were banned during national service, and possession of an unauthorised phone was one of the many crimes that could land you in prison. If their service had an end it would not be so bad, but no one ever seemed to leave the military until they were well past the age where they could bear a child and enjoy their vitality.

You can't find any kind of definition for this kind of life, Sina thought, perplexed about what they were being punished for.

The couple had completed their military training, followed a state-sanctioned religion, worked hard even when their jobs didn't pay, and never discussed taboo subject like politics, freedom or democracy. Eritrea was home and they wanted to stay, but the government was thwarting their every attempt at happiness.

They spent just two and a half precious months together as man and wife before Dani boarded a bus down to the southern city of Assab. There he would spend his days standing in the desert heat on the sun-baked southern plains of Eritrea, notionally keeping watch to prevent some of the tens of thousands of border jumpers escaping to Djibouti and other neighbouring countries.

For Eritreans who decided that their future lay outside their country's borders, the danger began the moment they left their designated post. Giving military superiors the slip was no easy feat. If they did make it to the border, they had to dodge the bullets of soldiers. For years the government had a publicised shoot-to-kill policy for anyone caught trying to escape. Unless you had the money to bribe someone for safe passage, you had to run over the rocks and scrub and hope the darkness afforded you the cover needed to make it into Ethiopia, Sudan or Djibouti.

For those who managed to make it to a refugee camp or a city, the next step was finding a smuggler to get you as far away from the grasp of the Eritrean authorities as possible. But desperation is easily exploited by the ruthless, and wherever the refugees went, opportunists followed.

The difficulty was knowing who to trust, and Eritreans who had only ever known their tightly controlled life became easy targets. The lucky ones ended up being overcharged for a voyage which was gruelling and dangerous, but got them to a Mediterranean shore alive and unharmed. The unlucky unknowingly put their trust not in a smuggler but in a trafficker, whose aim was not to facilitate a voluntary voyage, but to profit from a roaring trade in torture and extortion. Lurking around the Eritrean border were such men, apparently eager to help the recent escapees.

'OK, we'll get you a car that will take you to a UNHCR refugee camp,' they would promise.

But when the unfortunate traveller climbed in the car, the chains went round their wrists.

These men and women found themselves sold like livestock to Bedouin tribesmen: some were transported to the Sinai Peninsula, others kept in Sudan in a kidnapping racket which has killed as many as 10,000 people. Held in deplorable conditions, the captive would be tortured while the kidnappers called their family, demanding money. Sometimes the family was forced to listen on the phone to their anguished son, husband, mother or father being raped, beaten, or having molten plastic poured on their skin or electrodes applied to their body. Some of Dani's fellow Eritrean security officials were complicit in this trade, taking a cut for tip-offs about people coming over the border.

Even the UNHCR refugee camps were not safe havens, with the kidnappers preying on the tens of thousands of bodies squeezed together in desperation with little protection. Up to 30,000 people – ninety per cent of them Eritreans – were victims of this trade.

Others perished on the route north. The trip over the Niger desert which Majid had survived a few years earlier claimed more lives as the smuggling routes grew busier. Around forty people could be packed onto a pick-up truck designed for four or five, and these vehicles would often give in under the punishment of the weight, the bumpy desert tracks, and the unrelenting heat. In October, the bodies of ninety-three women and children were found strewn around a truck in Niger's Sahara desert. The placement of the corpses at different distances from the broken-down vehicle suggested they had been running, walking, crawling to find water, each dying at a different point in their struggle for survival.

While UN agencies roughly tracked the deaths in the Mediterranean and on the EU's land borders, no one knew how many people were dying before they got anywhere near Europe. Not that Europe's leaders paid much attention. When they filled Colonel Gaddafi's coffers on his promise of keeping the tide of humanity on his shores, many people were just dumped in the desert to die. The Moroccan police were also on the EU payroll, getting €20 million in funds and under pressure to stop people attempting to jump the fences barricading two Spanish outposts on the northern Moroccan coast.

Ceuta and Melilla represented the only land borders between the EU and Africa, and had long been a magnet for those fleeing poverty, war and repression. The borders became an early symbol of Fortress Europe, as people camped out on the mountain slopes within sight of Europe's lights, most bearing scars from their attempts to cross the formidable barrier. Between them and their dreams of a better future stood three fences tipped with razor wire, the trenches between each fence packed with more coils of razor wire and steel cable. Motion sensors and thermal cameras monitored every sign of life, ready to trigger the floodlights and pepper-spray dispensers rigged up along the barrier. Moroccan police stood on one side of the fence, and on the other were the Spanish Guardia Civil armed with batons and rubber bullets. Every few weeks hundreds of people charged the fence. A few made it over and claimed asylum, but most ended up in the hands of Moroccan police after gouging themselves on the razor wire, breaking a limb in a fall, or being overwhelmed by the pepper spray. The Moroccan police would then bus the men to the border with Algeria and leave them there. But there was nowhere else for them to go, so they would trek the 150 kilometres back to the lights of Europe. While in the past most of the people huddling on the wrong side of the fence near Ceuta and Melilla were young men from sub-Saharan Africa fleeing poverty rather than persecution, by 2013 Syrian and Malian families joined them on the inhospitable slopes.

Whatever their backgrounds, they all faced the same nightmarish limbo, constantly under threat of death, injury and exile. Moroccan police – under pressure from the EU – had burnt down their camps and started sweeping the mountainside in the day, arresting anyone they found. Human rights groups documented cases of assault, rape and unlawful killing by the security forces, but the EU funding continued. So the men and women spent their daylight hours hiding in small groups among the cacti, waiting for night to fall. Some had spent years trying to get to Europe and most of the people on the mountain had injuries from the fence. Dozens died, though these deaths hardly ever made the news, so it was easy to pretend they weren't happening.

Then one day, the bodies started washing up on Europe's beaches.

Eritrea's coastline is the eighth longest in Africa, measuring 2,234 kilometres from north to south. But very few of its citizens know how to swim. With most hours of the day spent in national service, there was no time for leisurely pursuits like sunbathing and paddling on the Red Sea coast. Only a few people tried to flee Eritrea by boat, given that the nearest country by sea – Yemen – had a habit of locking Eritreans up.

But for Eritreans who hoped to get to Europe, it was almost impossible to avoid the water for ever. Whatever circuitous route they took through sub-Saharan Africa, tens of thousands would eventually end up looking out at the Mediterranean, fearing the waves but imagining no other route to safety. By the end of 2013, at least 11,300 more Eritreans would have made it to Europe, up from 2,604 the previous year, and they just kept coming.

In theory that should have kept Dani busy at his post near the border with Djibouti, but just like in Asmara, most of his days were spent standing around a neglected military post. He was idle most of the time, left to dwell on his separation from Sina and struggling to come up with ways to be close to her again. His thoughts were not yet focused on compatriots who were heading to Europe, but at around the same time that Dani arrived in Assab with a heavy heart, several hundred Eritreans found themselves on the Libyan coast, about to embark upon what they hoped would be the last leg of their journey to Europe.

On 1 October 2013, more than five hundred people – most of them from Eritrea – gingerly stepped aboard a retired fishing vessel. The deck was scratched and worn, and a cheap red curtain hung by a string over a window in an empty cabin, the only sign that other people had once considered the 66-foot vessel seaworthy. Even when it did trawl the Mediterranean for fish, its capacity was only thirty-five. Now nearly fifteen times that number were struggling to find a tiny bit of space to call their own.

Each of them had faced the threat of bullets, kidnapping gangs, prison, torture and death to get this far, so getting onto a decrepit boat was a calculated risk.

For much of their journey at sea, their gamble appeared to have paid off. It took thirty-six hours for the overladen vessel to force its way through the resilient waves, but as dawn was about to break, the Italian coastline came into sight. With half a mile to go, the passengers started to relax and celebrate their imminent arrival in Europe. But when the crew switched off the engines, water started pouring in. In desperation, the captain lit a rag to try and attract the attention of the coastguard. But it fell to the deck and the old wood caught fire. It didn't take long for the flames and panic to spread. As people flung themselves into the sea, the boat tilted and slowly disappeared beneath the dark waters. Most of the passengers were unable to swim. Just a few miles from Europe, they thrashed about in the sea, trying to stay afloat or to locate husbands or wives and children. Gradually the passengers started washing up on the white sand beaches of Lampedusa, a few lucky ones alive, staggering ashore amid some of the 368 corpses.

The tragedy wasn't the first smuggling-boat disaster in the Mediterranean, but its proximity to Europe's coast made it harder for the world to ignore. European Union leaders got on planes and stood, stony faced, by the chequerboard of coffins. In front of the rows of dark wood boxes adorned with a single red rose were a handful of smaller white coffins. Inside them the drowned children were laid to rest, each coffin decorated with a pink flower and a tiny, smiling teddy bear with a bright red heart in the centre of its chest. More telling were the digits scrawled in marker pen across the front. '19', '15', '14', '92': the children didn't have names, only numbers. Most of the victims would never be identified.

In the days after the sinking, Europe's leaders made their solemn promises to the dead and to the hundreds of thousands still living in Eritrea, Syria, Libya, Turkey and Lebanon, some waiting to board a boat within days, others still holding on to hope that they could make life work closer to home. The European Commissioner for Home Affairs, Cecilia Malmström, proposed a search-and-rescue operation 'covering the Mediterranean from Cyprus to Spain'. The President of the European Commission, José Manuel Barroso, vowed that 'the kind of tragedy we have witnessed here so close to the coast should never happen again'. The Italian Prime Minister promised a state funeral for the victims.

One by one, all those promises were broken. The state funeral was quickly forgotten, and instead many bodies would remain at sea, others unidentified and buried in unmarked graves. No EU leaders wanted to back a search-and-rescue operation. Covering the costs was not a priority as the economic crisis continued to bruise government coffers. And it took less than a fortnight for Barroso's words of 'never again' to prove the shortest lived.

9

Never Again

Mohammed: Zuwarah, Libya

Three days before Barroso and Malmström made their promises in front of the tiny coffins on Lampedusa, Mohammed Kazkji had arrived in the Libyan coastal town of Zuwarah. There he had moved into a crowded, partially built apartment block, awaiting news of his own voyage to Italy. He was not alone. With him were his uncle Nidar's wife and her mother, and Nidar's three children: a three-month-old baby, also called Mohammed, and two girls – five-year-old Siham and six-year-old Maram.

When rumours started to circulate that a boat full of Africans had just sunk attempting the same trip, Mohammed chose disbelief: if you accepted that such a thing could happen you couldn't logically undertake the journey, and he was determined to get to Europe. His thoughts were shared by many of the hundreds of Syrians who sprawled on the floor around him trying to fashion something resembling privacy among the huddle of listless bodies. What choice did they have? Their homes were destroyed, their lives in danger every day, and desperation had driven them to this crumbling halfway house where they were simply waiting for the smugglers to decide when they had assembled enough human cargo to make the voyage to Italy worth their while.

But as more people started piling into the apartment, Mohammed's faith in the smugglers' promises dwindled. It wasn't just his life at stake any more. Baby Mohammed rested in his arms, and he was already troubled with the uneasy feeling that the tiny life was too precious to risk on the 200-mile stretch of water separating them from Europe.

Mohammed's uncle Nidar had started planning an escape for his family a few months earlier as it became clear that Libya was on the verge of a full civil war. He was determined to remain in the country himself though: his car repair business continued to do well despite the unrest, and Nidar had started using some of his profits to buy medical supplies to send to the Syrian refugees living in Turkey. Even though he had not set foot in Syria in years, they were his people and he could not watch impassively as the violence forced millions from their homes.

By then at least 125,000 people had died in Syria's war, and it wasn't just Assad's wrath sending Mohammed and Nidar's compatriots into exodus. There was no unified Syrian opposition: dozens of armed factions were fighting for their own varied goals, often battling each other as well as Assad's still-formidable army. Shaky video footage had emerged on YouTube and Islamic extremist websites showing atrocities that included beheadings, mutilations and the desecration of corpses. Syria's civil war was heading into even darker territory, and the world seem paralyzed by indecision. A full military intervention was ruled out. No one wanted a repeat of Libya. With a delicate sectarian balance in Lebanon, Iran and Iraq which could be easily upset by events in Syria, it would not be as simple as bombing a coastline and then leaving the nation to its own devices. The United States, Britain and France took a few steps, providing some military assistance to whoever they decided was 'moderate', despite the difficulty in actually tracking where their aid ended up. Saudi Arabia had its own interests, and channelled money and weapons to several rebel groups, including ones with Islamist leanings. On the other side, Shia fighters from Lebanon and Iran continued to enter Syria to prop up Assad, and horror piled upon horror for the Syrian people.

Among the various rebel factions were the al-Qaeda-linked al-Nusra Front and the Islamic State in Iraq, which in April combined to form the Islamic State in Iraq and the Levant – ISIS – a group with an uncompromising view of how Islamic law should be applied in territory which was swiftly falling to its fighters. Slowly the fight for freedom and democracy in Syria had for some people become a battle for an Islamic caliphate.

Watching news reports, Mohammed had wondered if he would ever be able to return home. At first Nidar thought that he and Mohammed should travel to Turkey and start a new life there, but suddenly that didn't seem safe either, with fighting occasionally spilling over the border. So when Nidar heard about a cruise ship heading to Italy in the coming weeks with spots available for a few clandestine refugees, he decided to pay $1,200 per person for a berth for his family. He sent Mohammed along with them as their guardian. Nidar knew some people in Italy who could then take the family to Sweden, the one EU nation which had promised residency to any Syrian.

But to claim asylum in Sweden, they first had to get there. Despite his bravado when discussing the journey to Europe with friends, Mohammed had been hesitant about making the voyage. Ever since he was a child the sea had filled him with a sense of foreboding. If you were killed by a bullet, at least it was quick. Drowning seemed like such a slow and awful way to die, and he avoided watching films about the sea or shipwrecks.

One day, I will be swallowed by the sea, he used to think as he looked out at the waves.

There was a voice somewhere in his head telling him that no matter how calm the waters looked on the surface, the sea had depths and should be approached with mistrust. He only learned to swim out of embarrassment. When he was ten years old he went to a pool with two friends, and could not bear the humiliation of stories spreading around school of Mohammed and his fear of water. So he forced himself to jump in and stayed in the water until his survival instinct took over and his uncontrolled flailing morphed into a haphazard stroke which kept him afloat.

Still, the prospect of hours at sea brought back that dread of his childhood, and it was with reluctance that he accepted Nidar's proposal and found himself waiting to set sail from Zuwarah, just a few miles west from the spot where Majid had launched to sea just over two years before.

Conditions for the sea crossing had deteriorated significantly in the years since Majid's forced crossing. In the past, the smugglers operated semi-officially with links to the Libyan coastguard and navy, and therefore with some knowledge of the sea. In the new, anarchic Libya, the business was open to anyone with enough firepower to out-muscle the other militia getting in on the lucrative trade. While a few years ago it had been in Gaddafi's interest for the boats to reach Europe as it gave weight to his threats of flooding the continent with migrants, now the money was being paid up front. As long as the smugglers could launch the boats past Libya's paltry coastguard operation, it didn't really matter what happened next.

Some smugglers only provided the boats with enough fuel to reach a major shipping channel, reasoning that the ancient rules of the sea requiring any boat to come to the aid of a stricken vessel meant that someone somewhere would pick them up. Other boats were scuttled on purpose so that they could not return to the Libyan coast. The safety of the refugees was not the priority, and stories circulated about smugglers killing and throwing overboard anyone who questioned their actions. All the while the criminal networks kept growing across continents to meet the surging demand from those wanting to make the journey. These networks ranged from small operations – the taxi drivers along borders and low-level criminals producing fake documents – to existing crime syndicates like the Italian Mafia, which quickly got involved in the lucrative trade. Within a few years, the business of smuggling people into the European Union would be worth nearly as much as the illicit drugs industry. Billions of dollars would change hands each year, with tens of thousands of criminals profiting from people's desire to reach safety. As long as there remained no legal routes for people to ask a European country to grant them refuge from war and persecution, they had no choice but to pay criminals: the EU's policy was actually creating the smuggling networks it kept vowing to dismantle.

Zuwarah was a perfect location for this thriving new trade. The former coastal resort had long stretches of deserted beach, and there were plenty of unfinished apartment blocks which the developers had started building for holidaymakers before the war came. These abandoned blocks made ideal holding houses for the growing numbers of people making their way from the world's war zones to the Libyan coast. The sparse rooms filled with concrete dust may not have been pleasant, but the lack of furniture and fixtures meant more human beings could be crammed into all the available space.

At first Mohammed didn't consider his handlers too inept. When he arrived at the apartment block along with Nidar's family, there were only a few dozen people there, and the three smugglers running the operation seemed knowledgeable enough about the sea to advise against getting into the boat in the current choppy conditions.

'There will be a sturdy boat with a Tunisian captain. You will be two hundred people on the boat, you will have food,' the handler told Mohammed. 'You will go today, tonight or tomorrow.'

While this wasn't exactly the cruise ship his uncle had been expecting, it didn't sound too bad, so Mohammed settled baby Mohammed, Siham, Maram and their mother and grandmother in a corner of the dusty apartment and set about making life as pleasant as possible while they waited. The women were apprehensive, but Mohammed kept everyone's spirits up and took charge of his tiny namesake, rocking the baby to sleep and walking him up and down the street when it got too hot inside.

But as the hours passed into days, the smugglers' promises that they would leave soon seemed less and less credible. Instead, more people started arriving. They packed into all corners of an apartment designed to house one family, and soon the handlers had taken over another floor and siphoned off the single men into a different building.

What is all this? Mohammed asked himself, questioning whether there really was a problem with the sea or whether they just wanted to wedge more people onto the boat.

Already he counted two hundred people in the apartment where he was sleeping, and adding the single men housed elsewhere, he estimated there were at least 400 people waiting for the calmer conditions which never seemed to arrive. And people were getting impatient, each day demanding answers from the smugglers, the adults' voices getting more tense with agitation and apprehension.

Most of the people in the apartment were Syrian – the smugglers tended to keep nationalities together. Even in the desperation of an illicit journey at sea, there was social stratification. The Syrians were assumed to have the most money of all the people trying to reach Europe, and tended to be charged more. It meant that on the crowded vessels, it was usually the sub-Saharan Africans who had paid less for the journey who had to endure the terrifying claustrophobia in the hold, often with the doors locked so they couldn't escape to the deck during the journey, even if the diesel fumes were overpowering them and threatening death by suffocation. So the passengers remained separated by nationality as they waited for their voyage, as it was not in the smugglers' interest to have them all living side by side for days discussing what they had paid.

The smugglers did provide food, water and cigarettes, but it did not stop an aura of fear and desperation settling over the crowd. Some had endured President Assad's barrel bombs and chemical weapons attacks, others the terror of Islamist militia, and they had fought their way to the Libyan coast at terrible cost to their families. Now they were suddenly idle and helpless, their fate in someone else's hands, and this was the most unbearable part. This fear started to affect Siham and Maram, who would spend much of the day crying and struggled to sleep on the hard floor. Mohammed would stay up for most of the night, holding the baby in his arms and trying to comfort the other children.

For three days the people just kept coming, and Mohammed's mind kept returning to the rumours about the fishing boat that had sunk off Lampedusa. He made a decision then which would help alleviate some of his terrible guilt in the years to come: he called his uncle and told him to come and pick up his family. He could not promise to keep them safe any more.

At first Nidar was angry.

'This is happening for all the Syrians – it is what we have to do: be strong.'

But Mohammed had made up his mind.

'I am strong,' he told his uncle, 'but the women and children are not. You must come.'

The next twelve hours felt like they lasted a year. Mohammed feared that the smuggler would suddenly order them all down to the water and his efforts to keep his extended family safe would be undone. Eventually his uncle arrived, but the smuggler resisted letting anyone out of the cramped apartment. It was impossible, he told Mohammed. If a few were allowed to leave it could create a mutiny, he reasoned, and suddenly everyone would be demanding their money back.

But the young man squared his shoulders and remembered his father's mantra.

'Nothing is impossible,' he said. 'If you don't let them go, I will make a scene.'

The smuggler backed down, and Mohammed rushed the family to his uncle's car, only to have another round of abuse hurled at him when he told Nidar that he was planning on staying and taking the boat to Europe alone. He had made up his mind: he wanted to find a way to make a decent life so he could help bring his family out of Syria. Eventually Nidar threw his hands in the air, telling Mohammed he would pray for him.

There was just one more call to make to the person Mohammed had always trusted to know what to do.

'What do you think, Mamie – should I go to Europe and continue my job and my studies?' he asked. If his mother told him to stay in Libya, he would have to obey. But she knew her son and wanted him to follow his heart.

'If you see a good opportunity,' she said, 'God will keep you safe.'

So with her words of approval, Mohammed watched his uncle's family disappear into the distance. He celebrated his small victory with a coffee and a cigarette, before slowly making his way back to the apartment block which he had come to regard as the only gateway left to a better future.

Yahea and Omar could hardly believe their eyes when Mohammed walked through the door. Despite their promise to keep in touch with their new friend, the pair had been caught up in the preparations for their sea voyage to Europe and forgotten that he too had been keen to hear of opportunities to escape Libya.

It was an overheard conversation which had led the two of them to Zuwarah. News of a sturdy vessel heading to Europe had spread through the Syrian community in Tripoli, and there were plenty of people who were just waiting for the best opportunity to get out while they still could, willing to believe the assurance of safe passage. Omar heard two Syrian women talking about it on a job one day, and convinced them to give him the phone number of the smuggler. A few weeks later, he and Yahea turned up at the given address and a taxi took them to outskirts of Zuwarah. There had been the small matter of Omar being about $600 short of their fee, but the smugglers let him stay anyway.

They could find another full fee-payer and they might as well take his money and stuff the boat a little more.

When fate brought the three friends together again, there was some gentle ribbing from Mohammed about Yahea and Omar's broken promise, but they soon settled back into easy conversation about the journey ahead of them. It was Yahea who brought up the issue of investing in some life jackets, just in case. Mohammed teased his friend.

'Look man,' he told him, 'if we're going to sink in the middle of the sea, what good is that going to do?'

That was easy for Mohammed to say: his uncle had bought one for him, and despite his nonchalance he was guarding it closely. Yahea asked around, but the response from everyone in the apartment was the same: boats that go from Libya to Italy don't sink – everyone arrives safely, so there is no need to worry about taking precautions. Denial was the best way to keep any dark thoughts at bay. No one was talking about the tragedy that had occurred in sight of Italy a few days earlier – no one wanted to believe it. Better to keep busy. So Yahea stopped asking about life jackets and made himself useful cooking and cleaning for the families. Finally, after fifteen days of waiting, the smuggler returned with news: they would leave the day after tomorrow at 6 p.m.

Mohammed finally left the airless apartment on Thursday, 10 October and piled into a large truck with a hundred other young men. Zuwarah was a Berber town which had a few years ago been making its way onto travel blogs for its unspoilt beaches. But there was little sign of life now in a place which had become the epicentre of the new smuggling trade. Mohammed only spent about fifteen minutes in the back of the truck at dusk, but it was enough time to register the town's sinister silence. Nobody seemed to live there: either the civilian population had fled, or they knew better than to be seen on the streets during the day. There was no sign of the armed militia, but he knew they were there somewhere in the dark corners of the town, the same young men in flip-flops and cheap sunglasses who had once torn though the desert determined to unseat a tyrant.

Mohammed didn't even see the gunman who opened fire on their truck. The first sign of trouble was the driver yelling.

'Everyone down and start running!' he shouted. 'You have to move.'

Mohammed didn't think too hard about his options, but followed the driver's lead and ran, barely looking back to see the confused stragglers melting into streets which would take them away from the coast. Mohammed's long legs just kept on moving, propelling him forward with an instinct which cast the whole evening in a haze. It was as if he were watching someone else.

He ran with the dwindling group until the sun went down, running out of the town and into the darkness. There was nothing there, no houses or street lamps to light their way. He just kept in time with the beat of the footsteps around him. After about an hour, he was able to stop running. He could feel the sand beneath his trainers and hear the lapping of the waves. They were at the coast, joining the hundreds of men, women and children who had already arrived.

Mohammed didn't take the drama of their arrival as a good sign. *If we start like this, how will it end?*

And he couldn't find Omar and Yahea. They had been on a different truck, and in the pitch black of the unlit coast there was no way of picking them out from the crowd. He could barely see a few metres in front of him over the dirty sand and black rock, covered in a litter of belongings cast off by other transients hoping a lighter load would lessen their chances of being swallowed up by the waves.

Mohammed pushed his way down to the water's edge to examine the vessel that would take them across the Mediterranean, but all he could see were two small motor boats.

'Where is the big boat?' Mohammed asked.

'Don't worry,' the smuggler told him, gesturing out into the darkness. The small boats would ferry them out to a larger vessel at sea, he said, and Mohammed strained his eyes toward the horizon. He couldn't make out any boat in the darkness, but he had no choice but to trust these people who were moving quickly to get all 400 people onto the water before the light came up.

The small boats could only ferry forty people out at a time, but it didn't seem to take very long to clear the beach. When Mohammed finally arrived at the larger fishing vessel, all remnants of trust evaporated. Disembarking from his bumpy ride, he found himself clambering aboard a boat which he estimated to be decades old and little better than scrap. It was around thirty metres long and painted the same bright blue as every fishing vessel he had ever seen. Such boats may have had some charm lined up on a busy marina as fishermen milled around with their catches, but as their means of crossing the Mediterranean, it filled Mohammed with more dread.

A long wooden deck tangled with fishing nets led to a structure near the prow which had once been the captain's room, and which was soon filled with people. Beneath that in the hold was another room where more people squeezed into the black crannies. The roof of the structure was commandeered as another level on which to pack even more people, creating the appearance of a floating human pyramid.

Any protestations about overcrowding were met blankly by the captain, a young Tunisian who told everyone to find themselves some room, sit down, and shut up. Mohammed had little choice but to obey, and elbowed a small gap on the open deck towards the back of the boat. It wasn't just people competing for space. Many passengers had bags of luggage and crates of water weighing heavily on the creaking vessel. Mohammed was travelling light, and had just two bags packed with his essentials. He sat on his life jacket, reasoning that it would be safest there.

As the smuggler cast a torch around the vessel to seek out any remaining room, Mohammed caught sight of Omar on the roof.

'Where is Yahea?' he shouted to his friend, who gestured beneath him to the two cabins. Mohammed nodded, then tried to settle down for the journey. There was too much humanity in one small space to worry about staying together now. More important were the women scrambling to keep hold of their children in the dark amid the confusion and restless bodies.

If I had a family, Mohammed thought, *I would not risk their lives like this.*

But he was not going to judge those who did. On the beach a man he had recognised from the apartment in Zuwarah asked after the three children. When Mohammed explained that he had sent them back, the man quietly congratulated him, before gesturing towards his own family.

'Maybe you can do that, but I can't, my wife and kids…' he said, his voice trailing off with sorrow at the circumstance which had forced him to subject them to this ordeal.

Mohammed nodded and mumbled something about how he hoped for a safe journey, before slipping back into the dark crowd. Now, squeezed between bodies whose faces were obscured by the darkness, Mohammed felt an immense relief that he was on his own with responsibility for just one life. Soon after midnight on Friday 11 October, the motor finally spluttered into life and the Tunisian captain started off under cloudless skies.

For a while the travellers abided by the smugglers' instructions to avoid any torches, lighters or cigarettes until they were well out to sea to avoid detection from any security forces or rival militia. It made no difference whether Mohammed opened his eyes or closed them – the darkness was the same – so he rested his head on his hands and tried to think about the life that awaited him in Italy. He passed the hours with quiet thought about the different electrical systems in Europe that he would soon be able to study, reasoning that with experience on three continents, perhaps he truly could become the world's best electrician.

After about three hours of sailing, someone on the boat lit a cigarette and it barely registered with him: Mohammed just took it as a sign that the journey was progressing and Europe was within reach. But when, a little while later, he was suddenly blinded by a search light, he was lucid enough to know that that was not part of the plan. He was momentarily confused: were they being rescued already? Or had the Libyan police caught up with their vessel, and were they sending them back? But when Mohammed peered over the side of the boat and to the source of the light, he saw neither the Italian coastguard nor Libyan police. Looking straight at him from a dinghy were the cold eyes of a man with a Kalashnikov rifle slung over his shoulder.

It was the first time Mohammed had seen a gun. Had he stayed in Syria and survived his military service, by this point he would be carrying a gun himself, perhaps hardened to the weapons. But he had taken a different path, one that was meant to take him away from the instruments of war, yet here he was in the middle of the Mediterranean Sea being terrorized by six heavily armed men in an inflatable dinghy, who had spotted the lit cigarette and aimed their vessel towards the rich pickings. The families on board the fishing vessel had taken everything they could with them to try and start a new life in Europe, and the pirates knew that pockets, wallets, bags and bundles would be bulging with cash. For each family their savings may only be enough to survive for a few weeks when they reached Europe, but for the robbers a few hundred from each of the 400 passengers would make a fine bounty.

'These are militiamen,' the Tunisian captain shouted above the drone of the waves and the dinghy motor. 'They want money and mean to kill people, so we have to go on.'

When a few men on the boat protested and said they should turn back, the captain refused.

'They will kill your wife and take everything – we have to keep going.'

And so began a night of cat-and-mouse over the bumpy black sea. For a while it would appear that the trawler had outrun the gunmen, only for the screams on the boat to rise up again as the pirates returned with fresh threats to sink the boat unless everyone on board handed over their money and valuables. Still the captain ignored them and kept going – a panicked call back to the traffickers in Zuwarah was met only with the instructions to carry on towards Europe no matter what. Each time Mohammed thought they were finally rid of the gunmen, they would return fifteen minutes later, determined to stop the vessel. Utterly helpless, Mohammed followed his instinct and buried his head deeper in his arms, trying to ignore the edge of fear in the captain's voice as he urged his cargo to keep still.

Then the gunfire started.

From his position on deck, Mohammed couldn't tell whether the pirates were firing directly at the boat, into the water, or over their heads. He figured they were trying to scare everyone on board, and it was working. Terrified passengers tried to scramble away from the sides of the boat, but there was nowhere else to go and it just caused the boat to rock more fiercely in the rising waves. A woman hoisted her two-year-old son above her head, pleading with the attackers to stop shooting and spare his life.

'Please,' she screamed, 'I have a baby.'

The mother's appeals went unheard, and Mohammed winced at the *phhut* of a bullet striking wood. Still the captain sailed on, even as the militia crossed back and forth in front of the boat, firing into the air and at the boat from all sides, then ramming the vessel and sending it careering back and forth in the water. More gunfire rattled the vessel, the sound of old wood giving in to its force mingling with the cries of a handful of people hit by the flying bullets. His head down in prayer, Mohammed heard a bullet strike the engine, and he was sure of his fate now: he was going to die in the cold sea far away from his mother and separated even from his friends. With each burst of gunfire, he braced himself for the bullet which would end his life.

Then the moon disappeared and as the rising sun slowly brought an end to their hellish night, Mohammed raised his head from his hands. The dinghy had gone, the militia retreated back to the Libyan coast to find other human cargo to scare into submission. No one on board was dead. The woman who had tried to protect her child sat now in a huddle, enveloping him with her body, having done her duty and kept him safe from harm.

For a brief time, Mohammed was happy. He had survived another ordeal and was still moving forward. Then he looked over the side of the boat. It was undeniable: the trawler was sitting lower in the water than when they had left six hours earlier. The water was not the gentle lapping which had lulled Mohammed into a sense of security as they set off, but a fierce swell that took their boat lower in the water with each buffeting wave.

It didn't take long for others on board to notice their fresh predicament, and now in the dawn light he could see panic on people's faces. One man who remained calm was Mohanad Jammo, a doctor from Aleppo. When it became clear that the pirates' bullets had caused irreparable damage, the captain asked for anyone who could speak English to make a call for help on the satellite phone. The doctor had come prepared: he had a screenshot on his phone of numbers to call in case of emergency – he had found it on one of the many Facebook pages devoted to the Mediterranean crossing.

At 11 a.m., he called the Rome Rescue Coordination Centre and gave them their position, reporting that there were 400 people on board including 100 children, and they were sinking fast. The line was cut off. They got through again just after midday, only to be told by an officer in Rome that their coordinates placed them in the Maltese search-and-rescue area so they should call them instead. Eventually the Italians also contacted the Maltese, and a rescue operation was launched at around 1 p.m. The Italian coastguard had informed the Maltese that two commercial vessels were sailing through the area, while an Italian patrol boat was also within a few hours' sailing of the stricken vessel.

But no boats came.

Having spent the last few hours preparing for death, Mohammed was at first optimistic with each communication that they would be saved. Mohanad Jammo's increasingly urgent calls to the Maltese armed forces at around 3 p.m. had elicited a promise that help would arrive in forty-five minutes. But the sun was sinking lower in the sky, and the rescue boats had still not arrived. Panic was spreading. Some men had gone below deck with empty water bottles and were attempting to bail out the water. Voices shouting conflicting orders rose from the crowd. Some chose defeat, wailing that the boat was going down and they would all drown. A few men screamed that they were going to throw themselves overboard, but Mohammed didn't see anyone make good on that threat. Many people tried to save themselves with a misguided surge toward the side of the boat which was higher in the water, causing the vessel to list more sharply. Older passengers with more experience of the sea shouted that everybody must stay still.

A voice in the crowd urged people to cast their belongings overboard to lighten the load. Mohammed opened his bag and looked at the contents, symbolizing his life up until that moment: the engineering manuals that represented his studies, and some of baby Mohammed's clothes that reminded him of his year in Libya. He didn't dwell on the symbolism for too long before throwing it over the side, hopeful that his act was one of many which would keep them afloat for that little bit longer while the European navies raced towards them.

They were still waiting for the rescue boats at 5 p.m., when the trawler gave one last lurch in the swell and disappeared beneath the waves.

10

Fortress Europe

Nart: Antakya, Turkey

Just go and you will find your destination, Nart Bajoi told himself as he walked for an hour across the Syrian border to meet the taxi which would take him deeper into Turkey. It was 1 May, he had left his home and the war behind, and he had to trust that life would steer him in the right direction.

The journey from the Assad stronghold of Latakia had cost him €200, leaving him with €800 left in his pocket. The rest of the money saved from his two jobs had long ago been spent on medical supplies, food, fuel and other necessities for the opposition network. But Nart had a bullish faith that his abilities would see him through.

After a long drive from the Turkish border town of Antakya to Istanbul, he headed to an Arab quarter and quickly found his people. A few friendly exchanges later and Nart was deep in conversation with a man from the same neighbourhood in Damascus, who advised him on where to find a hotel and set him up with a job at a computer and mobile phone repair shop.

The hours were long, but the promise of $700 a month was good enough for him to bear up through the eighteen-hour shifts. The Turkish owners even promised meals and a place to sleep, and Nart thought he would soon earn the money he needed to apply for papers to officially work in Turkey and hopefully find something more stable.

Since Syria's chaotic civil war had erupted on its doorstep, Turkey had managed to be simultaneously welcoming and inhospitable to the people pouring over the border as bombs destroyed their neighbourhoods and the conflict starved them out of their homes. Syria and Turkey were never real friends. Territorial disputes and Hafez al-Assad's decision to support the Kurdistan Workers' Party at a time when the Turkish state was at war with Kurdish rebels soured relations well into the 1990s. A delicate rapprochement after the death of Hafez al-Assad in 2000 proved illusory. The Turkish government still viewed his son Bashar with suspicion, and a few months after the first bullets hit civilian targets, President Recep Erdoğan began to back the movement to topple him.

This backing went beyond words: the political opposition in the Syrian National Council set up a government in exile in Istanbul. As the opposition swiftly took up arms, various rebel factions were allowed to cross the border and operate from bases on Turkish soil. The government in Ankara took the gamble that one of the many factions would topple Bashar, and it would be in their interests to have helped them do it. With the fighters came first a trickle and then a tide of refugees, moving largely unhindered across the 900-kilometre border. A few years later, as the fighting spilled over onto Turkish soil, the government would question its open-door policy. But in early 2013 the majority of refugees were allowed through.

When Nart arrived in May, there were 320,000 Syrian refugees in Turkey. That number would swell to half a million by the end of the year, eventually reaching more than 2 million. Those families who registered at a refugee camp found their basic needs met, and had access to healthcare, food and schooling provided by the Turkish authorities despite little funding from the rest of the world. Turkey had spent more than $4 billion on the refugees, but it had received just a fraction of the €497 million promised from the UN, which was struggling to convince other governments to contribute to its fund to aid the displaced Syrians.

The twenty-two official Turkish camps only had a combined capacity of 220,000 though, and they filled up fast. The hundreds of thousands of people unable to secure a spot in a camp or unwilling to subject themselves to a life of perpetual handouts had to fend for themselves, struggling to find accommodation, work, school or medical care. They had no access to World Food Programme assistance, and many people found themselves sleeping rough. Syrian families lined the sides of motorways under a few sheets and tree branches near the camps in the hope that a space might open up, or took shelter in abandoned buildings with no running water or working toilets. They slept on building sites, in tents, on the floor of overcrowded apartments, trying to get to the end of each day with enough food. Access to education was limited, with only about a quarter of Syrian children living in Turkey attending school.

Syrian refugees were not permitted to work, and although those with passports could apply for a work permit like any other foreigner living in Turkey, these were extremely difficult to acquire. For unscrupulous employers, that meant a large workforce of people who could be exploited for minimal pay, creating tensions with members of the Turkish community who found themselves competing with this barely paid workforce of the dispossessed.

Nart had imagined himself above the daily struggle for survival of many of his compatriots. He was thirty-one, a multi-lingual lawyer and a computing specialist, and with his skills and talents he was convinced that a reasonable life could be his in Turkey. So for two months, he worked night and day fixing laptops and mobile phones, grabbing some sleep in a chilly apartment where his bed was a sofa with a thin blanket. He had been told that he would be staying with the shop owners, but they only turned up to play poker in the flat, before returning to their more comfortable homes. The promised meals only amounted to a few tomatoes and a hard-boiled egg each day, and no one seemed forthcoming with his wages. Finally, after a month, he challenged the shop owner.

'We don't have money,' the shop owner replied. 'Maybe next month there will be money. If you want you can wait, if you don't want to wait, you can leave.'

Nart was stunned, but without official papers, there was nothing he could do. He walked straight out of the shop and boarded a bus. He didn't know where it was heading. He just wanted to escape, calm down, and think about his options.

Just go and you will find your destination.

He almost didn't recognize his former boss when he got off the bus at a random stop. It had been ten years since Ali had hired Nart to work as a systems engineer at an IT firm in Damascus. At first Nart didn't want to burden his old friend with his woes, but it all soon came pouring out.

'I am going to Sweden with my family – come with me,' Ali replied.

Nart wasn't sure about Sweden – he hadn't thought about heading to Europe before. Turkey was a Muslim country close to home, so his heart told him to stay. He did, however, immediately accept his friend's invitation to spend the night in his home, and listened attentively as the older man laid out his plans. Ali had paid €56,000 and had been promised passage all the way to Sweden for seven members of his family.

The next day, Nart called the smuggler.

In Syria, he had been somebody. He had felt important, first through his work and then as an activist in the underground opposition. Now he was just another Syrian refugee, robbed of his money, his dignity, his sense of self. He understood now that he was not special after all.

You cannot find a job and the Turkish hate us, he reasoned as the smuggler answered the phone. Nart quickly explained that Ali had put him in touch.

'I don't have this kind of money, but I have €700,' Nart told him.

The smuggler had a ready solution: 'OK, give me €200 and I will send you to Bulgaria.'

To enter the European Union by land, there was really only one route left, and that was over the hills from Turkey to Bulgaria. Before the Arab Spring opened up the smuggling bonanza on the North African coast, the Greek land border with Turkey had been the most popular crossing for migrants and refugees trying to reach Europe safely, with 49,513 making it over in 2010. Back then, it was mostly Afghans, Palestinians, Iraqis and Somalis fleeing conflict and trying to float across the Evros River – which delineates most of the 203-kilometre border with Turkey – or hurry past Greek border guards on the twelve kilometres of dry land. It was still a tense journey, but at least they were not out on the open water of the Mediterranean, at the mercy of the weather and the waves.

Most of the new arrivals were not interested in staying in Greece: it was a stepping stone to other countries where they could find work and assistance. But in 2011, Greece was in the grip of an economic crisis, and support for anti-immigrant parties was rising. Foreign citizens were accused of taking jobs, homes and other precious state resources, and policies stigmatizing them proved popular. That year, Greece began work on a fence along its land border with Turkey, and by the time it was completed in 2013 the number of people crossing by land had been slashed to 12,968. Trying to penetrate the frontier meant braving concrete pillars, barbed wire, thermal cameras and Greek border guards operating under the harsh rules of Operation Xenios Zeus, a crackdown on undocumented migrants that was named after the god who prized hospitality to travellers.

Greece had pulled up the drawbridge and sealed off the safest route to the EU just as Syria plunged into its long and bloody civil war and millions fled the country.

For the tens of thousands of Syrians who found life in Turkey unbearable, Bulgaria was now the obvious choice. The crossing was more mountainous than the Greek frontier, but at least it was dry land, and safer for the women, children and elderly people who were now joining the mostly young men who had made up the first wave of Syrian refugees trying to reach Europe.

By the autumn of 2013, more than 8,000 people had arrived in Bulgaria, up from 2,000 the previous year. The government was quickly overwhelmed. While Greece was suffering from an economic crisis, Bulgaria was still the poorest country in the European Union. It had joined the union in 2007 with dreams of future prosperity, but EU membership had so far failed to haul living standards in line with the rest of the continent.

But Nart didn't know that as he embarked on his journey over the border.

Two hundred euros hadn't bought him much. His guide drove him the 150 kilometres from Istanbul to the border, dropped him off by a forest and pointed into the woods.

'That is Bulgaria,' he said to Nart and a teenage Syrian boy who was also making the journey. 'On the other side of a small mountain in that direction you will find a village.'

The pair set off eagerly into the thicket – the route sounded easy. Just follow the side of the big mountain, then over the small mountain. As they pushed on, however, the small mountain did not seem to get any closer, and the vegetation grew thicker. Nart didn't know what kind of trees they were hiking through, but the branches had thorns and he and the boy had to get on their hands and knees at times. The forest was dark and quiet. Nart was not scared by such things after everything he had seen in Syria, but his young companion was frightened, and cried quietly for most of the walk. At least the weather was on their side though. It was 16 June, and it was dry. Some Syrians who had attempted the journey earlier in the year had frozen to death, lost and alone in the snow-covered forests, unaware which country they were in or why they hadn't been saved.

If it had been winter, Nart would have been in trouble – after about six hours moving in what he thought was the right direction, he realized they were lost. His suspicions were confirmed when they came across a military base with watchtowers and searchlights. They could go on no further, and tried to retrace their footsteps until they reached a village.

'Maybe it's Turkey, maybe it's Bulgaria,' Nart said to his companion, and they walked up to three men sitting outside and asked. Nart was not that surprised to hear that they were still in Turkey. But they were clearly not the first Syrians to have passed through.

'You want to go to Bulgaria?' one of the men asked. Nart nodded. 'OK, it's a hundred dollars.'

Nart offered him 100 Turkish lira instead – about $35 – and the man made a call. When a car pulled up it looked familiar, and sure enough, the man who got out was the same smuggler who had dropped them off about twelve hours earlier.

'What happened?' he asked.

When Nart explained, the smuggler took them to his home, where his wife cooked the two Syrians dinner, made them sandwiches and mended Nart's shirt, which had been ripped by the trees. With a new set of instructions, the pair set off again. This time, Nart was more confident, and led the boy under the thorn trees and round the military base. After about ten hours of walking, they finally reached the Bulgarian village, and found the police station. The officers were sleeping.

'Syrians! Syrians!' Nart shouted. When the police awoke, they bundled him and the teenager in a car and drove them for about two hours, before dropping them off at a larger police station. When Nart tried to explain his plight, he was immediately thrown in one of the cells.

There is no such thing as an illegal asylum seeker. The UN convention on refugees allows a person fleeing conflict to enter a country without the required paperwork, and prohibits any penalty on those who do so. Nart's incarceration would only have been legal if he had had his refugee application turned down – highly unlikely given that most Syrians were deemed to be genuinely fleeing persecution – or if he as an individual posed a specific threat to security. But none of that mattered to the Bulgarian security services, and Nart spent sixty-four nights in detention: one night in the first jail cell, four nights in another cell, fifteen nights in a refugee camp on the border with a locked door and guards on the gate, and then forty-five nights at a closed camp in Sofia.

Bulgaria was breaking international law, but the detention of asylum seekers had a long tradition in Europe – Italy, Malta, Hungary and Greece had all locked up people seeking refugee status over the years – and no country had ever been penalized for it. UNHCR officials could express moral outrage and demand the cessation of the practice, but there was no mechanism for enforcing the refugee convention, and no country was interested in championing one.

So the government in Sofia packed the increasing numbers of men, women and children into refugee camps, then jails, then disused buildings, and then simply erected tents and surrounded camp sites with corrugated iron.

Plenty of people never even made it much further than the Bulgarian flags fluttering on border posts. In an effort to deter more people coming, border guards threatened, beat and set guard dogs on some new arrivals. Many were forced back to Turkey, even though denying admission to a person seeking asylum was illegal. Those who made it in and were allowed to submit their claim for asylum found themselves trapped in a web of bureaucracy, with very few people to help them navigate the maze of paperwork beyond the opportunists who always prey on the helpless.

An Arabic translator at the second police station told Nart he needed to pay for a lawyer unless he wanted to stay in the cell for ever, so he parted with €130. The lawyer came and left again quickly. Nart was not sure what he paid her for, because soon after she left he was escorted to a room to have his fingerprints and a mugshot taken – he was being charged with illegal entry. After four days in the cell, he was taken to court and found guilty. He got a six-month suspended sentence and an order that he would be jailed for two years if he crossed a Bulgarian border illegally again, and was told to pay a €100 fine. He was still not free to go, however. Now he had to file his refugee application, and that meant another fifteen days in detention on the border before a transfer to Sofia.

In the Bulgarian capital, Nart found himself in yet another jail for forty-five nights, and he did not understand why. When someone asked him for another €150 to guarantee his release, he paid up. He just wanted to be free. Conditions in the prison were terrible, and when he and some other refugees staged a small protest in the yard to demand their release, the guards threw cold water at them and prodded them with electric batons. When Nart was finally allowed out, he slept on the streets for a few days, before finding a cheap hotel room. By then, he had gone through most of his money, given his fingerprints and condemned himself to stay in Bulgaria until his application was complete, although it wasn't clear when that would be. The authorities still had his documents, so he couldn't get a job. Instead, he began helping a local non-governmental organization (NGO), trying to make himself useful as he had done back in Syria.

One day in late October, Nart visited the Voenna Rampa wood-work school, where Syrians were staying and needed help with translation. The autumnal sun was shining on the playground, but it didn't bring much joy beyond catching the light in the broken glass where the children played. At least the carpet of sparkling shards helped parents see where a window had shattered, enabling them to steer their children to a safer place. That was why his compatriots were in Europe after all, Nart thought, trying to make the most of their tiny square of allocated space in the disused Communist-era academy on the outskirts of Sofia. The Syrian families tried to turn the classrooms into habitable dormitories, fashioning tents from sheets and tree branches to grant their families some semblance of privacy. The Bulgarians had long stopped using Voenna Rampa for their own people. The building was a relic of a different time, a boxy three floors in concrete, with the red paint that was meant to create the illusion of cheeriness having weathered away and the bars over the windows caked with rust. The interior was equally decrepit. On the third floor, a boy of around seven stood on tiptoes as he peered through the window at the sunny yard. He couldn't go outside. He didn't have any shoes or trousers, just a pair of thick woollen tights pulled up over a polo neck jumper. It was an outfit which would have attracted ridicule from peers at home. But here in Sofia – so much colder than Syria – this donated item of girl's clothing was so treasured that panic spread across the child's face when a stream of water trickled down the corridor, and he desperately hopped from foot to foot to try and keep his tights dry.

The team of volunteers was scrubbing the floors again. The young Syrians who tried to keep their temporary home clean would scrub these floors over and over again, especially when the toilets overflowed, but no matter how hard they tried they couldn't rid the corridors of the smell of urine and souring food. This place was designed for young people to come in the morning, learn some carpentry skills, then go home. It was not built to house eight hundred men, women and children. At least the hot water was working now. When the five thousand beds for refugees in official reception centres across Bulgaria filled up earlier in the year, the authorities didn't have time to get all the facilities at Voenna Rampa working before moving Syrian families in, and the shocked new arrivals found themselves bathing in cold water in the sinks.

Could this really be the Europe they had been so desperate to reach?

Nart watched with sadness at the pitiful state his fellow Syrians found themselves in, although he thought they were lucky not to have been jailed like him. Nevertheless, each of the people he spoke to said the same thing.

'No one will stay here,' an English language student told him. 'You see the situation here. It is too bad. If we get our travel documents, we will leave this country.'

Another young man, Ahmad Maruan Sahed, twenty-three, had been shot by a sniper near his home in Damascus. The bullet shattered his hip, and his mother sent him to Europe with medical records and a doctor's recommendation that he undergo surgery to correct his heavy limp. But there was no one in Bulgaria to look at those papers. He borrowed money to buy the medication he needed for the pain and his high blood pressure, but that was running out.

'Take me to another country to get medical attention,' he pleaded. 'Have some humanity.'

Nart was starting to realize that humanity in Europe was in short supply.

Bulgaria could not afford to provide clothing, medicine, food or even enough beds for the refugees, and relied on donations from charities and ordinary Bulgarians, who turned up at the gates with bundles of clothes. Like Italy in 2011, the Bulgarian government turned to colleagues in the European Union, but found little sign of the post-war dream of a shared humanitarian spirit. Despite pleas for assistance, Bulgaria received very little money from other EU nations.

Towards the end of the year, the European Union agreed to make €5.6 million available in emergency funding, and Slovakia, Hungary, Slovenia and Austria donated 2,000 folding beds, 4,200 blankets and some cutlery. The mattresses, blankets and kitchen sets arrived, but so did more refugees. In December 2013, while conditions at the camps in the capital slightly improved, the situation at the border was worsening as winter set in. More than 11,000 had now crossed over. In Harmanli refugee camp, heavy rains bogged the soil and children had to wade through the freezing sludge in sandals. No amount of tarpaulin could keep the damp from infiltrating the tents where many of the refugees slept. Children's eyes streamed, irritated by the smoke from the fires their parents burned to try and keep them warm.

Bulgaria didn't just want a few charity-shop handouts and a one-off payment. It wanted other EU nations to resettle some of the refugees and forge a long-term solution to a crisis which was getting worse by the month. There was only one country – Turkey – between the EU and a war which was killing hundreds of thousands of people. Charity workers and government officials in Bulgaria tried to sound the alarm, making statements to the press warning that more people would try and leave Syria and come to Europe. But the rest of the EU didn't want to hear it.

As the winter months set in, fewer people would arrive as the seas and mountains which marked EU borders became impassable. Talks on setting up an official resettlement programme and on ensuring a fair distribution of Syrian refugees across Europe failed to make headway, and were postponed until a meeting of EU leaders in June 2014.

So Bulgaria followed the lead of its neighbour Greece, and announced that it too would start building an impenetrable fence. With Ceuta, Melilla, Greece and Bulgaria now behind steel and razor wire and Russia providing a buffer on its eastern flank, Fortress Europe was in full lockdown.

Nart had at least managed to make it in before the drawbridge was raised. But although he managed to secure his liberty from the detention centres, far-right hooligans had started turning on the Syrian refugees and demanding their removal from Bulgaria, and Nart began to fear for his safety.

11

Our Sea

Mohammed: The Mediterranean

There were at least three doctors on board the fishing trawler when Mohammed Kazkji and the 400 other passengers were pitched into the waves, but they were as powerless as everyone else to stop the dying. Hasan Yousef Wahid, a physician who had been practising at a hospital in Libya, could not save his own four daughters, Randa, aged ten, Sherihan, eight, Nurhan, six, and Kristina, two. A childhood illness had left him with a limp, and the smugglers had forced him to sit at the back of the boat with the elderly and infirm while his wife went with the children towards the prow. So he didn't even have a chance of rescuing his little girls when the boat tipped its cargo into the sea.

Mohanad Jammo, the intensive care doctor from Aleppo, had tried to save lives by making emergency calls to the Italian and Maltese authorities, but he was unable to get them to respond in time. A female doctor spent the last few hours of the voyage delivering a baby boy in the darkness of the hull, her attempts to bring life into the world undone by the sea moments later.

The cry of that newborn baby was the last thing Mohammed heard before the boat finally gave in to the growing swell. He sensed it was coming, but while fear had seized every muscle during the pirate attack, that terror had given way to a calm resignation. Mohammed knew they were going to sink, and his mind was processing that information logically.

If the boat tips this way, I will jump the other way, he thought. *Then I will swim and try and find my friends.*

It all played through his mind like scenes in a film, and his body braced for a cold swim.

At the last moment Mohammed peeled off his shirt, and he had just slipped the life jacket over one shoulder when the trawler toppled with such speed it was like being sucked into a whirlpool. A large wave had tossed the boat onto its port side, sending everyone who could move surging starboard to level it, only for the shifting weight to give the crippled vessel the final nudge it needed to turn over completely. And Mohammed was on the wrong side of the boat. While passengers on the roof or on the port side were able to use the brief moment of imbalance to jump off the teetering ship, it was the starboard side which disappeared beneath the waves first, dragging the men, women and children down with it.

The cold sea which was meant to carry Mohammed to safety was instead pulling him into its dark depths, the light of the surface quickly receding. Still there was no panic – it was as though it was all part of the same dream he had been stuck in since the previous night, and now his legs were kicking with the same ferocity he had experienced when running from gunmen through the streets of Zuwarah. But this time, nothing happened. The expected release and ascent to fresh air didn't come. One of his feet was tangled in a fishing net. His kicks became stronger, but they just seemed to drag him further away from life and towards the sea bed. No amount of struggling seemed to free his body, and the effort to stay alive suddenly seemed futile. All around him people were dying: what was one more life lost when there was so much suffering?

Then Mohammed's mother appeared to him in the water. Peace enveloped him as he looked into her eyes. Almost a year had passed since he had seen his mother's face, and here she was to comfort her son in his most urgent moment. He noticed the tears in her eyes, and Mohammed knew he would do anything to stop her crying. The vision in the black sea lasted until the young Syrian felt a force pushing against his leg, and finally he was swimming upwards. He hadn't been aware of the other bodies around him engaged in the same struggle against death, but someone must have shoved his foot out of the netting. Or perhaps the desire to make his mother happy gave him the surge of strength needed to free himself of the ropes. With his lungs stinging, Mohammed kicked up towards the light, the life jacket which he still grasped with one hand helping to pull him to safety. He kicked off his jeans to lighten to load, and the sodden denim sank to the bottom of the sea along with the €400 in cash he had stuffed in his pockets to pay for his life in Europe.

As he surfaced, Mohammed was only able to take one breath before another force dragged him back towards the darkness. Arms wrapped around him, as a survivor who could not swim grabbed on to the nearest floating object, which happened to be Mohammed, to try and stay alive. The survival instinct of the drowning man threatened to take both lives, and Mohammed now found himself kicking and struggling to free himself from the tangle of desperate limbs. His youthful strength prevailed, and the other man disappeared.

Mohammed would save many lives that day, but this man was not one of them.

When they had boarded the boat, chance had placed Mohammed on the edge of its deck, slightly increasing his odds of escaping as it was sucked underwater. His age, his ability to swim and the fact that his brain was wired for survival also played in his favour. Unencumbered by family members, he was able to devote all his strength to keeping himself alive, helped by the life jacket his uncle had bought him.

Those who had spent the journey below deck had been dealt the worst hand.

Even before the boat capsized, the cramped wooden hull was

a scene of suffering, with the two men injured by the pirates' bullets slowly dying of blood loss as they waited for the rescue boats. When the trawler sank below the waves, they were too weak to swim. Even if they had the power to fight the force of the water gushing in, there were few escape routes. The handful of people who had brought life jackets were not safe down below either: as the water rose in the hull they were pushed up to the celling, trapped by the devices they had believed would offer some insurance against a voyage gone wrong.

They would never surface, and when Mohammed reached the open air again he could only see a small number of the 400 people who had started the journey with him. The high swell didn't help, with the waves at first hiding all other signs of human life from sight. For a moment, he thought he might be the only survivor. Then heard the cries of mothers searching for their children, husbands searching for their wives. All across the sea, turned an inky blue by the approaching twilight, huddles of survivors clung to debris. Heads and shoulders of those who had wrestled free from the trawler bobbed in the water, moving in unison with the swell. Flashes of bright red and dull yellow marked the lucky few who had life jackets, while the flailing limbs singled out those who could not swim and would likely not be alive for much longer.

For those clinging to life, there was little time for the realization that they were stranded in the open water a very long way from land. Everybody was busy searching for somebody, fighting against the waves and the currents and the mouthfuls of nauseating salt water to find their loved ones.

My friends, was Mohammed's first coherent thought.

He pulled himself through the water with his clumsy stroke, searching for Omar and Yahea. He didn't find, just more bodies that he knew were beyond help, as well as a few survivors he could try to assist. One group bobbing in the water seemed to consist of four people who could not swim, yet were managing to stay afloat by grabbing each other in turn, the heads disappearing underwater before grasping another body to push themselves back to the salty air. Mohammed flung an empty fuel tank towards them. But he didn't know what to do with the tiny body floating a little further away in the water. He swam towards the baby and recognized the tiny boy from the smuggler's house in Zuwarah.

I know he is dead and I can't do anything.

For a moment he considered scooping up the lifeless child and dragging him along in the water with him – at least his mother would be able to say goodbye to her son. Then he saw the baby's father swimming around searching for his family. At that moment the father still had hope that his child was alive, and Mohammed could not bear to be there when he discovered the truth. So he left the body of the drowned baby and swam away.

All across that area of sea similar tragedies were occurring. Hasan Yousef Wahid was searching for his four daughters, but no matter how hard he tried to battle the waves and swim back to the wreckage after being flung out to sea, he just seemed to drift further away. Another father swam in circles with his young daughter under one arm, trying to find her twin sister and his wife, who was heavily pregnant with another set of twins.

'Where is your mother? Where is your mother?' he kept asking the mute little girl.

A man watched his young son drown in front of him: if he had let his arms loosen their grip on his nine-month-old daughter, she would have perished too.

And still the rescue boats did not arrive.

Frantic voices mingled with the sound of the waves buffeting bodies and the debris, and then Mohammed spotted Omar battling the swell.

'Where is Yahea? Where is Yahea?' he shouted to his friend.

But Omar hadn't seen him either. Omar had been perched on the roof for the night's ordeal, but had surprised himself by falling fast asleep during the long chase with the pirate vessel. When he awoke at sunrise and found that they were safe, he attributed his hours-long blackout to shock and fear: his body couldn't cope with the constant idea of death so had shut it out the only way it knew how. He had more control when the ship tumbled, though. With his bird's-eye view, he could see the mass of people below shifting from one side to the other like the surge of a crowd at a rock concert. When the boat finally went over, Omar was able to jump and throw himself clear of the vessel. When he looked behind him, the boat had gone, leaving a scattering of bodies in its wake.

Since plunging into the water he, like Mohammed, had been battling against the swell to try to save lives and find friends. The pair quickly told each other who they had seen and who was still unaccounted for, before their voices were drowned out by the thudding of the rotor blades.

Finally, as the light of the day faded, the first help had arrived for the 400 Syrians. But this wasn't a rescue mission: a Maltese coastguard helicopter had merely swooped by, scattering a rain of life jackets and two inflatable boats from the sky. The survivors raced towards the boats, those who could swim trying to help others to safety.

Omar started swimming towards the smaller lifeboat, an octagonal raft which could barely hold ten, let alone the scores of people who had survived the sinking and were now exhausted and freezing and fighting to stay alive for that little bit longer until proper help arrived. Mohammed wanted to continue his search for Yahea, and tried to keep his spirits up even though his limbs were getting colder and heavier as the hours passed.

Finally he stopped searching

If Yahea was in the hold, now he is three kilometres under the sea, he thought.

Instead he devoted his dwindling reserves of energy to reaching the larger rescue boat which had fallen from the skies and raised false hopes that a full rescue effort would soon be under way. He hoisted himself on board before realizing that it could not bear the weight of everyone who had clambered on. There were already forty people on a boat designed to carry half that number, so Mohammed gave up his place for those more in need – children, the elderly, women and men who could not swim – and once again he plunged into the cold water. He clung to the black rubber of the boat, kicking his legs to stay afloat, trying to reach out his long, cold arms and hoist other less able bodies onto the raft. Fresh cries of fear now mingled with the shouts of the survivors, still searching for loved ones hours after the boat went down.

'We will sink again!' a man on the raft cried as it dipped lower in the water.

A lethargy was starting to envelop Mohammed. He was so cold, the light was fading, and hope was ebbing away, along with all his strength. How much longer could he cling to the rubber dinghy, before he slipped away beneath the waves, more bones to settle on the seabed and never be recovered?

When help finally arrived – six hours after Mohanad Jammo had first called the Italian coastguard – Mohammed felt a sense of detachment and disbelief at the sight of the huge naval vessels looming over the specks of human life in the water. Then suddenly the waves were alive with smaller zodiac vessels manned by Europeans in smart uniforms, and the collective moan of hopeless suffering from the life raft changed, the tone shifting to sharper, higher cries of 'Help!'

By this time, so many lives had already been lost. But Mohammed was just overwhelmed with relief that he was not going to drown.

After hours of batting the distress call between them, the Maltese and the Italians had both sent vessels in response to the call, and they were now racing through the water to save who they could. Some survivors ended up in Italian coastguard vessels, others in Maltese, with families separated and bewildered children trying to find comfort in the arms of strangers. Silently the survivors huddled in the life rafts and rescue dinghies, many just in their underwear after the force of the sinking ripped their clothes away. Parents cradled the children they were able to save, frantically searching for any injury on small bodies motionless with shock and cold. Young men helped the elderly clamber up the rope ladders onto the decks of naval vessels, where the shocked and bedraggled would reanimate as they once again continued their search for people lost at sea.

But still Mohammed waited, treading water steadily trying to keep his sluggish arms and legs moving. A vessel had zipped up to them and a rescuer shouted that there was another group more in need so they had to wait. Mohammed and the dozens of others in and around the life raft stayed where they were. But thirty minutes passed and still nobody had come back for them. The sun was setting, the sea suddenly seemed empty, and Mohammed felt the panic rising again. Perhaps they couldn't see them or had forgotten about them? His limbs could not hold out much longer, and he could hear some people crying on the boat.

'They are going to forget us, they are going to forget us for sure,' one woman said.

Mohammed tried to reassure those around him, but he was filled with doubt himself and once again prepared himself for death, hardly able to believe that he could have got this far only to die when so many others were rescued. He started screaming for help, but the light of the boat only seemed to recede further into the distance. Finally one of the people on board the dinghy found a flare and fired it into the sky, now almost as black as it had been for their departure. A boat turned around, threw them a rope, and at last they were being towed towards one of the naval frigates.

When Mohammed finally realized that he was going to survive he was filled with joy. He wanted to collapse with laughter, but knew he could not when so many of the people alongside him had lost so much. So he laughed inside, and thought back to when he was a child and troubled by premonitions of drowning and terror of the sea. Now he had survived what he had always worried was his fate.

What's next? the young man thought. Finally he had a future.

I did not choose to be alive or dead, but now I choose how I want to go on with my days. The new Mohammed will live a normal life — I have finished my nightmare.

Within the space of two weeks in October, as the Mediterranean holiday season was wrapping up and the beaches of Europe became a little quieter, more than 550 people died at sea. Bodies washed up on stretches of sand normally used for sunbathing, where in the summer months Europeans lay under their umbrellas and gaze out to a sea which to them symbolized only recreation and relaxation.

In the presence of such a jarring contrast, Europe's leaders felt compelled to offer heartfelt words. As Malta's armed forces were engaged in a chaotic and mismanaged rescue of Mohammed and the other shipwrecked Syrians, Maltese Prime Minister Joseph Muscat uttered a phrase which would become shorthand for the tragedies at the heart of Europe.

'We are building a cemetery within our Mediterranean Sea,' he said, and called for compassion and a respect for human lives. 'I don't know how many more people need to die at sea before something gets done.'

At around the same time, Mohammed, Omar and some of the other 212 survivors were on their way to a Maltese detention centre. There they would be locked up and treated like criminals, continuing a long tradition in Malta of detaining men, women and children who arrived on their shores.

Malmström, the European Commissioner for Home Affairs, meanwhile praised the Italian and Maltese authorities, 'whose courage and quick reaction have contributed to reducing the death toll'. Again she called on the EU's governments to come forward with funds for saving lives at sea.

'We heard solidarity expressions from all EU countries, but these will remain only empty words if they are not followed by concrete actions,' she said.

But her promise a few weeks earlier of a Mediterranean-wide search-and-rescue operation would never progress further than a few hurried words uttered on a beach. Most European countries were not interested in investing time, money and political will on a problem which they thought could be safely contained in the south. The Italian government, however, had finally had enough of their shores becoming saturated with so much suffering. On 15 October, they announced a new naval search-and-rescue operation called Mare Nostrum – 'Our Sea'. Six ships staffed with between 80 and 250 crew members and equipped with helicopters and drones would trawl the Mediterranean right up to Libyan territorial waters for the fishing vessels, dinghies and other flimsy craft which were ferrying their cargo into deep and dangerous waters. The life-saving operation would cost the Italian government at least €8 million each month. The Italians hoped that once Mare Nostrum was up and running and thousands of people were being saved, their partners in the European Union could be convinced to help fund the operation.

For the moment, though, the nations on the peripheries of the European Union watched as the brief burst of united compassion faded away, and Greece, Bulgaria, Italy and Malta were left to their own devices.

'We feel abandoned by Europe,' said Prime Minister Muscat.

So did most of the refugees.

12

Europe Turns Ugly

Hanan: The Aegean Sea

The sleeping pills had done their job. Five hours at sea passed and only once did Hanan al-Hasan stir, turning drowsily to her husband.

'Talal, why haven't we arrived yet? They told us the journey was just eighteen minutes.'

The pounding of the boat soon sent her back into her chemical sleep, and Hanan's family let her be as they watched the dim lights of the Turkish coastline fade away. As Talal had predicted, the waters were as calm as a steady hand, the sky was clear, and the hum of the outboard motor accompanied by the rhythmic thump of the boat on the shallow waves had a hypnotic quality which seemed to calm the thirty-nine passengers on the inflatable dinghy.

Talal and the children settled into stillness, which was disturbed only once in the night when a sharp cry rang out from another passenger.

'Sharks!'

Hearing the unexpected shout, Ismail leaned over the side of the boat, and sure enough, huge forms were leaping all around them, creating shimmering arcs as they danced in the water. Ismail smiled: *dolphins*. He nudged Riad, and the two boys watched the creatures glide alongside their boat, playful guardians vaulting the hull and clearing a path through the dark water.

Finally, a dull light somewhere on the horizon indicated a sun preparing to rise, and the mass of Greece crept closer. The inexperienced captain had somehow steered his craft safely to shore, only veering off course once to evade a coastguard vessel which they feared would tow them back to Turkey.

When Hanan woke at 5 a.m. they were washing up on the rocky shores of Samos island and a voice was yelling at her to get up and run. Members of the Greek coastguard were on the beach, so they needed to stay out of sight. People quickly scrambled over the crags and up the cliff. Hanan's sluggish legs were unable to respond, and she was only able to get moving with her sons pulling her by each hand and her husband pushing her up the steep incline from behind. Boulders tumbled around them from the other passengers' struggles and in the hazy dawn light Hanan worried about losing sight of her family. They had made land a few kilometres north of the main town, on a rocky outcrop where the cliff faces and sharp stone beaches kept the tourists away.

Elsewhere, however, Samos was stirring.

It was early October, and although the high season had ended, there were still a few holidaymakers on the island, escapees from northern European climes trying to make the most of the last vestiges of sunshine before another grim winter. For them, the rising sun promised another beautiful day of coastal walks and cocktails. For Hanan and her family, it meant an increased risk of detection and detention as they trekked for a few hours to Samos town.

Soaked through with crusting salt water and with sand and fragments of rock rubbing at their skin, all Hanan wanted to do was to get her children clean and dry before they presented themselves to the police. As soon as the shops opened, she hurried her family inside a small department store, but they had been spotted. While many Greeks on the islands where refugees washed ashore were sympathetic to the people fleeing war, others were more concerned about the impression their bedraggled appearance could give the tourists.

Hanan was distraught. If only the people of Samos could have seen her children a few months earlier, in their beautiful outfits at Rim's engagement party in Beirut. But her beautiful, healthy family were now reduced to this, begging to be allowed to change into fresh clothes.

'We are Syrian, we will go to the police, but please let us buy clothes,' Hanan pleaded in broken English. 'Look at us – we are in a bad condition, we are wet and sandy.'

Her appeals were ignored. Two police officers had arrived. A young female officer was shouting at Hanan and Talal, ordering them to leave the shop and get in the police car. The blood rushed to Ismail's head and he leapt in to protect his parents. This wasn't like him: in Damascus he had never been quick to anger, any adolescent aggression channelled into his bodybuilding exercises. But the war that had forced him from his home, the year of rejection in Lebanon, the betrayal by Rami: it had changed him, as it had changed them all.

'You can treat us better, you can speak to us better, be cool with my mother and my father,' he told the unsmiling female police officer. But she had little interest in trying to understand what the seventeen-year-old had just been through.

'Be cool?' she asked. 'OK, I will show you cool.'

She beckoned the burly male officer over, and Hanan thought he would strike her son. She didn't think before placing her body in front of her boy, even though he towered over her now.

'Don't touch him,' she warned. 'You can make us go back to Syria, but don't you touch him. I will not allow you to hit him.'

The policeman backed down, but mumbled a quiet threat: 'You will see, I will make you go back to Syria.'

When they arrived at the police station – still in their damp, sandblasted clothes – the family gave their names and had a number scribbled on their wrists with a marker pen. Hanan was now known as '3', Talal as '1'. The family put their wrists together in a circle as another refugee snapped a photo: this was what Europe thought of them.

Their new home was an old building on the outskirts of Samos which Hanan thought might be an abandoned farmhouse. The police called it a camp, but Hanan didn't think it was even up to keeping animals in. The room was four metres by five metres in size, there was one small window with bars, and a broken toilet with no running water. In this room were fourteen other Syrians, including an elderly woman and a seven-month-old baby, with only the hard floor for a bed.

Police stood guard at the door, and pleas for soap so they could at least wash their hands were ignored. After a few days a Greek lawyer turned up. He didn't have many answers to Hanan's questions, so in the end she just begged the man to please bring them some soap. When the lawyer returned five days later with no soap, she was furious.

'Don't come back here – you are a liar,' Hanan shouted, the fierceness which had propelled her onto the streets to protest against Hafez al-Assed in the 1980s now re-emerging in the face of these indignities. 'You just want to pretend you are working but you are not working. You can bring with you soap. You can pay for one soap.'

The lawyer never returned, and for seven days the family waited for the paperwork which would allow them to travel to Athens. No one was allowed to leave, but the men and boys trapped in the building kept their spirits up by singing Arabic songs.

'Shut up!' the policeman guarding the door would bellow, but the boys would just sing louder, a little bit of resistance to a life slipping out of their control.

Hanan and her family had given their fingerprints and officially registered as refugees, but in Greece that didn't mean much any more. Crippled by the debt crisis, the country had long realized that it could not offer the refugees a life and gave them little incentive to stay. Like Bulgaria, Malta and Italy, Greece had for years systematically detained migrants and refugees arriving on its shores. Conditions in the centres, however, were some of the worst in Europe. Illness was common in the damp, badly heated camps. With men and women crammed into the over-crowded centres, sanitary conditions were appalling, and respira-tory, gastrointestinal and dermatological diseases were common. Finding themselves living behind bars again when many had escaped arbitrary detention, torture and abuse back home also took a mental toll, and doctors at the camps despaired at the cases of self-harm, attempted suicide and hunger strikes.

Because conditions in the Greek detention centres were so appalling, most other European nations had stopped returning people to Greece under the Dublin Regulation, which states that a person seeking asylum must stay in the country where they first lodged their application. The European Court of Human Rights in 2011 ruled that the return of an Afghan refugee from Belgium to Greece breached the prohibition on ill treatment. But just because the rest of Europe agreed that Greece's treatment of refugees was so inhumane that they would not send people back, it didn't mean there was any legal way for the refugees to leave Greece and apply for asylum elsewhere. The European Commis-sion instead handed Greece more than €227 million between 2011 and 2013 for border security measures to keep the refugees out, while allocating just €19 million to helping it improve conditions in the holding centres.

Hanan never had any intention of keeping her family in a country where more than half of the population's young people were unemployed and the chances of Talal finding a job were negligible. Greece was only ever going to be a staging post on their way to northern Europe. A week later, when the police finally returned to their cell with their paperwork, they im-mediately boarded a ferry to Athens to join tens of thousands of other people plotting their onward journey.

*

Greece in 2013 was the poor man of Europe. The debt crisis which brought the country to the brink of bankruptcy had inflicted a massive blow on people's quality of life. The other nations in the euro currency, along with the European Commission and the International Monetary Fund, had foisted upon Greece a punishing austerity regime in exchange for the billions in bailout funds the country needed to stay afloat. Men and women in tattered clothing queued at food banks, the sick could no longer afford their medicine, malaria reappeared on the islands, and an army of homeless grew on the streets. People were living in poverty in one of the richest regions in the world, and there was dwindling sympathy among them for the refugees who continued to arrive from the world's war zones: when you have your own mouths to feed, you don't hand your food to strangers.

These extremes of suffering in Europe led to the emergence of extreme political views. The far-right Golden Dawn political party – whose leaders gave Nazi salutes and whose supporters prowled the streets assaulting foreign workers – took nearly seven per cent of the Greek vote in elections in 2012, and support for the party was growing.

Rather than challenging the openly hateful rhetoric of Golden Dawn, the governing coalition launched Operation Xenios Zeus, the crackdown aimed at curbing illegal immigration which ended up targeting people who had fled state brutality elsewhere in the world and had not been expecting similar treatment in Europe. Around 85,000 people would be stopped on the streets and taken to a police station, simply for looking foreign. All but 4,811 had the legal right to be in Greece, but still they were locked away for hours, sometimes after suffering physical violence and threats. It didn't take long for Hanan's children to see this dark side of their new home in Athens. Riad was out one day with some other Syrian youngsters when the police turned up and pushed some of them into a van and drove off. After that, Riad and Ismail decided to stay inside.

The family had sensed the hostility the moment they arrived in Athens at 8 a.m. on 17 October and spent the day roaming from street to street searching for a place to stay. Hanan carried in her hand a crumpled piece of paper. A woman she met on the street had taken pity on the family and scrawled some Greek script on the scrap for her to show to prospective landlords.

'We are Syrian and we are looking for a place to rent.'

Hanan hoped it would afford the family some sympathy, but each person she showed it to in the squares and side streets shook their heads and turned away. At 1 a.m. the family finally went to a hotel, only for the person behind the reception desk to tell them that their papers were not in order. That didn't mean they could not stay, of course. It just meant they had to pay more. It was a predicament Hanan was getting used to, and so their savings quickly dried up, followed by the savings of all their extended family. A few days later, they moved into a small flat with another Syrian family. Twelve people shared three bedrooms. Ismail slept on the floor, and Riad had the sofa.

Their next stop was Agios Nikolaos, a square with a Byzantine church at its centre that was at the heart of the Athens smugglers' network. Talal and Hanan took the metro, and found themselves somewhere that seemed to be a cross between a market and an open-air travel agency, the brokers and smugglers openly lording over the masses heading their way, crocodiles waiting for their prey to walk right into their mouths.

Like kings, Hanan thought, a bitter taste in her mouth at the thought of Arabs exploiting their fellow men.

As they began to ask around, they found it was a sellers' market. One broker was rumoured to have the images of 500 stolen and forged passports on his SIM card, from every country in the world. As a family would sidle up to his table and sit down, he would slowly scroll through his phone, glancing every now and then at the hopeful faces in front of him, then back at his phone. Eventually he would speak.

'Yes,' he would say, 'I have a passport for you.' Then he would demand €7,000.

Hanan had her heart set on a new life in Norway, where a relative of Rim's fiancé Izzat lived. They just wanted to find a place where someone could help them settle. A smuggler gave them his price: for €6,000 per person, he could send them by plane with fake documents to whichever country they wanted. Hanan, Rim and Bisan would be easy – they had fairer skin and could pass for European. Talal, however, looked too Syrian, while Riad and Ismail were under age and any attempt to send them alone on a plane would arouse suspicion. The broker had other suggestions: for €3,000 per person, Hanan's sons could be hidden in a van that was travelling on the car ferry to Italy. There would be other people in the back of the vegetable truck and they would have to stay crouched in silence for a couple of days, and run from police when the truck stopped. There was no way Hanan was sending her sons on such an arduous journey, and the prices were too expensive, so, as though she were piecing together a package tour for her family from different Internet sites, Hanan set out to buy the fake IDs and tickets individually.

She knew the risks, but wanted some control over her family's fate. Hanan's cousin Iyad had been on the boat with Mohammed Kazkji which had sunk off Libya a few days earlier. Iyad had managed to save his wife and two sons, but only just. Another couple Hanan had met in Athens drowned with their two young daughters and two young sons. They were locked in the hold of a fishing boat bound for Italy. It had not even left port, but the smuggler fled when the vessel started to list, and there was no one to open the door.

Flying was best, Hanan decided. So first the family tried to get Ismail and Rim to Norway. Fake Italian ID cards cost around €150, and Talal then accompanied the pair to Crete, where they thought the airport would have less security than Athens. It was a disaster: crippled by nerves, Ismail got lost and confused and walked up to a police officer. He wanted to ask directions to the departure gate for the flight, but the wrong words tumbled out.

'Where is Oslo?' he asked.

The policemen raised their eyebrows and beckoned him to follow them.

'Come, here is Oslo,' one officer said and took him straight to a room for interrogation. Two more officers went to the gate and picked dark-haired Rim out from the queue of fair Scandinavians.

'Leave and don't come back,' the police told the pair, so Talal returned to Athens with his dejected son and daughter.

Next time, Talal and Hanan spent a little more money and bought Bulgarian ID cards for Rim and her fiancé Izzat. At first it looked like luck was not on their side again. Hanan had bought the tickets on a day when there was a general strike in Athens, a common occurrence as the population protested against the austerity measures. There were hardly any buses and trains, and Rim arrived at the airport after check-in had closed.

Tears welled in her eyes.

'Please,' she begged the woman on the check-in desk, 'my family have a problem, I must leave today.'

Whether the woman at check-in realized the true nature of this distressed young woman's predicament was not clear, but she decided to help. Rushing her through check-in, the airline employee then escorted Rim all the way to the gate, past the police who would probably have pulled her aside and quizzed her, and onto the plane.

Hanan waited in the airport lounge, eyes glued on the departure board, expecting her daughter to return at any moment in the company of police. When she saw that check-in had closed and still Rim was nowhere to be seen, she allowed herself just a little bit of hope. When she saw the plane had taken off she let herself believe that perhaps Rim was in the air. But it was not until her eldest child sent a text message that tears of relief overwhelmed her.

'Mama I left.'

It had only taken fifteen days since arriving in Athens for Hanan to get one child out, and Izzat was close behind her on a flight to Germany. He would get the train through Denmark and Sweden and join Rim in Norway.

But Hanan could not rest: she had three more children to get to safety.

Nart: Sofia, Bulgaria

At around the same time Riad and Ismail were passing their days behind drawn curtains in Athens, a fellow Syrian, Nart Bajoi, was also scared to leave his hotel room. Like Hanan's family, Nart wasn't just afraid of being randomly stopped by the authorities, he was also fearful of being abused by ordinary citizens. A wave of economic hardship and political turmoil was finding an outlet in hatred in another poor European Union nation, and on 3 November, skinheads took to the streets of Sofia with a threat for the new arrivals: unless the Bulgarian government expelled the refugees, they would do it themselves.

Nart had seen the signs. On the drive from central Sofia to the outskirts of the capital where the Voenna Rampa academy housed the refugees, the high-rises got a little shabbier, the streets more unkempt. Swastikas were daubed on the walls of the housing estates. He understood that life for young people in Bulgaria was tough, and they were looking for answers.

Nearly a quarter of Bulgaria's youth was not in education, work or vocational training, the highest rate in the EU. Membership of the union was meant to bring wealth and opportunity, but Bulgaria remained its poorest member. Most of the qualified young people just left – the country's population was expected to decline to 5 million in 2060, half of what it had been in 1989. This was not what its citizens had expected in the mid-2000s, when the EU expanded to envelop Bulgaria and other former Communist nations. Estonia, Latvia, Lithuania, Poland, the Czech Republic, Slovakia, Hungary and Slovenia joined the EU in 2004, followed three years later by Bulgaria and Romania. For the idealists, Europe was finally becoming the prosperous political union they dreamed of when it rose from the ashes of the Second World War. That dream had been interrupted by the Cold War, when the east of the continent was cleaved from the west by ideology. When the Berlin Wall came down in 1989 and successive Central and Eastern European nations shed their dictatorships, the European Union welcomed them in. Expansion was meant to spread EU values of human rights, the rule of law and dignity for all: becoming part of the richer bloc was intended to be an incentive for countries still struggling to emerge from the shadow of repression to be better, to be kinder, to be more humane.

Europe's borders were meant to melt away, and people, goods and capital would flow freely between the EU members, the single currency a cement binding inter-dependent economies. That was the dream, although the reality turned out to be more complex. Europe's diverse economies struggled to fit the single mould of the euro, and soon after the watershed expansion, the eurozone crisis infected all corners of the bloc. Very quickly, the new members found themselves part of an alliance that was facing not just a financial crisis but an existential one too.

A cultural gulf also existed between the more established member states and many of the new ones, which were more conservative and less ethnically diverse since there had been little to attract economic migrants to the Communist nations during the advent of globalization. Then there was the feeling that they were treated as second-tier members, prevented from immediately joining the Schengen Area, a zone of twenty-six European nations which had abolished internal border controls. People could cross freely between the countries by road or rail without having to show their passports, an agreement which took effect in 1995 and was considered one of the key symbols of European integration.

Citizens from new member states also found themselves vilified by the press and political parties in the northern countries, accused of stealing jobs and threatening the cultural fabric of their supposed EU equals. And while the wave of migrants from east to west was adding to the social tensions in the richer countries, those who remained behind were also looking for someone to blame for their economic hardship. The Syrian refugees proved an easy target. As Bulgaria became overwhelmed by the arrivals, first the skinheads marched, then the violence started. A seventeen-year-old Syrian refugee was stabbed. Other ethnic minorities were also attacked, with a group of Algerian boys set upon by the far-right thugs.

The government had plenty of problems of its own with a spluttering economy and a student occupation of Sofia University which had broadened into a wider protest against corruption and state nepotism. Once again, foreigners were an easy target and government-run media featured stories labelling Syrians terrorists, accompanied by inaccurate information about how much was being spent to house the refugees. A far-right party, Attack, had secured seven per cent of the vote in parliamentary elections in May 2013, and became a key power broker in coalition negotiations.

Nart heard about the attacks on Syrians, and started to feel even less welcome. The gregarious lawyer who had offered his translation services for free to charities and the Bulgarian authorities was now being urged to stay inside, keep hidden, and not try to integrate into the country that was his new home.

'Don't go to the centre, don't even try to speak Arabic,' the Syrian owner of a local café told him. The warning spread around the Syrian diaspora: if you're in the camps, stay there. If you live outside, don't leave your accommodation after nightfall. The police won't protect you.

So from 5 p.m. Nart locked himself in his room, wondering why on earth he had come to this godforsaken continent. He pondered his options.

Should I return to Turkey? he wondered.

But how could he? The Bulgarian authorities still had his passport and all his papers as his asylum application wound its way laboriously through Bulgarian bureaucracy. Like 11,000 others, he was trapped in a country that didn't want him and could not protect him, so he hunkered down and hoped the hatred would pass.

It wasn't only in the front-line nations like Greece and Bulgaria that refugees were finding themselves vilified. Across Europe, far-right and populist parties ranging from the violent and openly neo-Nazi movements of Greece and Bulgaria to the less extreme and more outwardly mainstream anti-immigration parties of Britain, France and the Netherlands soared in the polls. But whether the parties were openly giving fascist salutes or more subtly peddling factually incorrect narratives, the overall effect was the same. Despite the bodies washing up on EU shores and the brief outburst of compassion on the beaches on Lampedusa, there was no new money for search and rescue or to help nations on the front line of the migration crisis; no offers of homes and sanctuary to the millions fleeing President Assad's chemical weapons or Eritrea's modern-day slavery; no debate about overhauling a broken asylum policy that trapped the world's most needy in countries unwilling to welcome them and incapable of looking after them.

European Parliament elections were due in a few months, a bellwether for other national polls which were on the horizon, and politicians were determined to claw back ground lost to fringe parties. If that meant ignoring the masses hoping for sanctuary – or even vilifying them for political gain – well, so be it.

13

Escaping 13V105

Mohammed: Valletta, Malta

The year-round temperate weather and crystalline seas attract more than 1.5 million tourists to Malta each year. Every summer the holidaymakers arrive and outnumber the 500,000 residents, who are happy to host the foreigners given that tourism accounts for a quarter of the gross domestic product (GDP) on the small island. Hoping to boost the state coffers during the economic downturn, the Maltese Prime Minister Joseph Muscat launched a scheme to offer citizenship to some of its visitors. But only certain types of foreigners got the golden passport treatment. Those who could invest €1.15 million and live a life of leisure on the island for a year were welcomed; those arriving with their clothes ripped from their bodies and all their life savings lost at sea were not.

Mohammed Kazkji's first taste of Maltese hospitality was a night spent on the deck of a naval frigate as it churned through the Mediterranean on its way to Malta. An autumnal cold had set in now that the sun had gone down, and Mohammed was sopping wet and shivering in his T-shirt and underwear. The young Syrian looked around and all he could see were stunned families clinging to their surviving children, silent with the shock and cold. Some people had fallen into a deep sleep, as if they were under the influence of powerful sedatives. They didn't even stir when a helicopter came and winched away a small, limp boy, leaving behind a mother who screamed for her son without pause until the helicopter returned and took her up into the sky too.

An elderly man was also airlifted away, but most of the survivors had to endure their injuries for a few more hours. Mohammed felt a hot, stinging sensation on his shoulder and reached back to find his hand bright with blood, but the wound did not appear too bad so he made himself useful, helping the Maltese hand out the silver foil hypothermia blankets. When he handed out the last one he found there were not enough for him to cover his exposed limbs too, so he huddled down next to another young Syrian and held out a packet of cigarettes he had found. A Maltese official gave them a light, and the two men sat silently sharing the smoke, a quiet celebration at another chance at life.

Mohammed did not know at that point that Malta was not an Italian island, but one of the European Union's smallest members with a habit of automatically locking up anyone who arrived without the right papers.

As the sun rose on 12 October, the naval frigate docked at the Maltese port of Msida, but Mohammed scarcely had time to get used to dry land before an identity bracelet bearing the number 13V105 was thrust on his wrist and he was herded onto a bus.

Exhausted and hungry, Mohammed went along with the group, barely registering what was happening when a man at the back of the bus asked why a gate was being locked behind them. When the bus stopped, they were taken into a government building and left to wait in a windowless corridor. There was no one to answer their frantic questions or tell them what was going to happen to them. Mohammed was grateful for the kindness of a female police officer who noticed that he was standing in his boxer shorts and ran home to get a pair of her son's board shorts for him. But otherwise the officials seemed unaware or unconcerned that their new charges had fled some of the world's worst human rights atrocities in their home country before spending a night terrorized by pirates and then being flung into the ocean where they clung to life for hours watching their compatriots drown.

Police stood guard at the door, as if the refugees might have the energy to try and bolt out into the streets, while security officials pushed them forward and demanded documents which the survivors couldn't possibly have saved from the sea.

Confusion was soon spreading among the Syrians: no one knew who was dead and who was alive. Everyone was asking the same question.

'Where is the other ship?'

Mohammed and the other 157 survivors who were taken to Malta were finally coming to understand that they were not in Italy, and that they were not about to be reunited with family and friends who they hoped were on the other rescue vessel they had seen plucking bodies, both alive and dead, from the sea six hours earlier.

When they heard that the Italian coastguard had taken the other survivors to Sicily, desperate hope started to spread through the jail. Everyone who had lost a child, a wife, a brother or a friend during the shipwreck was suddenly sure that their loved ones were alive and well in Italy. All around him Mohammed heard voices pleading with officials.

'Where is my baby? Where is my husband?'

The hope infected him too. Maybe Yahea was among the fifty-four survivors in Italy.

The pleas got angrier and more emotional, until a Syrian doctor who lived on the island arrived on the scene. He had been recruited to translate, and told the waiting refugees that they just had to give their fingerprints and have a photo taken, and then they would be taken to Italy to be reunited with their loved ones. At first Mohammed was sceptical: other Syrians living in Libya had warned him against giving his fingerprints to the police, but he didn't really understand the reason. And why would this doctor lie to him? All he wanted at that moment was to be out of the bureaucratic nightmare, have a shower and some food, and call his family and let them know he was safe. So he gave his fingerprints, and at about 4 p.m. they were finally able to leave.

Mohammed was so exhausted that he barely noticed when the police took the single male survivors to jail. He only realized what was happening when he was handed a nylon bag stamped with his name and his number – 13V105 – and told to empty all his personal belongings into it. The only clothing offered to Mohammed and the other men consisted of prison uniforms.

'What are we going to do here?' he asked one of the guards. 'I am a refugee, I am not a bad man, I am not a killer.'

But he was told there was nowhere else for the survivors to go, so they filed into the cells at the Safi Barracks, a detention centre with razor wire around its perimeter and two sets of bars on the windows. Just before the men were herded into the cells on the second floor, they heard the voice of another prisoner, a sub-Saharan African migrant, who leaned on the bars to offer them a warning. 'You'll be here for six months.'

In all the stories Mohammed had heard in Libya about life in Europe, he had never heard of anyone being thrown in jail, and soon he was engaged in furtive conversation with the other detainees about how best to escape their incarceration. One man suggested a hunger strike. Mohammed was not so sure: they had not eaten properly for more than thirty-two hours and he was worried that some of the men might have medical problems. But he held his tongue, and when the guards arrived the next day with breakfast, the men turned it down and demanded to see the warden. It was only then that they were finally allowed their belongings back, and the men ransacked the bags for mobile phones, desperately pushing the buttons trying to will the waterlogged phones back to life so they could call family to let them know they were safe, or find news of the missing.

Mohammed's phone had been lost at sea, but he applied his

technical know-how and managed to get another man's old Nokia working by patiently taking it apart, scrubbing all the salt water from the phone in the sink, and then letting it dry for a day before reassembling it. When he put the SIM card back in, the phone turned on and he found €20 worth of credit. The only number his exhausted mind could dredge up was that of another electrician he had worked with in Libya, so he called him and passed on an urgent message.

'Tell my uncle Nidar that I am safe, and he must tell my mother that I am alive.'

Now that he had done everything he could to let his family know he was safe, he finally allowed himself to shut his eyes. The other men were downstairs praying for the start of the Muslim holiday of Eid al-Adha, but Mohammed didn't want to be near anyone else. He lay down and allowed his body to drift into a deep sleep for the first time since he had left the smuggler's house in Zuwarah four days earlier.

It took eight more days before Mohammed, Omar and the other men were finally released from the Safi Barracks into an open camp. The rooms there were shipping containers stacked two high, behind a wire fence topped with barbed wire. The conditions there were better than the barracks – they could come and go and did not feel like prisoners – but no one seemed to know what to do with them. Tempers frayed as the survivors waited for news of their loved ones in Italy. All people could do was register their details with the Maltese Red Cross. Hasan Yousef Wahid, one of the doctors who had been aboard Mohammad's boat, had arrived alone in Malta but was convinced that his wife and four daughters were in Italy. About 200 kilometres to the north in Sicily his wife Manal Hashash was also alone, telling herself that her children were in Malta with their father. It took twenty days for the husband and wife to be reunited and discover that neither of them had their girls.

After a few days, photos started to circulate in the Maltese camp of the people who had been on the other boat, both the survivors now in Italy and the few corpses recovered from the sea. Determined to find out the fate of his friend, Mohammed pored over the photos, forcing himself to look into the bloated blue faces of the drowned. Yahea was not there.

Each morning the Red Cross came back with the photos. One man went every day to look for his wife, keeping hope alive that another picture would turn up with her beautiful face smiling for the photographer in Italy. It was only on the third day that he realized that he had been looking at his wife every day, but had not recognized her features distorted by the salt and the sea.

Despair infected everyone. One day on the outskirts of the camp Mohammed caught sight of a man he recognized from the safe house in Zuwarah. He walked over to say hello, and it was only when he was close that he saw the tears falling from his face.

'I just saw my wife and two babies in my dream,' he told Mohammed. 'They said "you killed us, you killed us".'

One day a call arrived for Mohammed on the camp telephone. An official came to get him, and Mohammed picked up the receiver and said hello. There was a painful pause.

'You are not Yahea,' a soft female voice said, before the sound of sobs came down the line.

Yahea's relatives were searching for him, and had heard that there was a young man from the same Damascus neighbourhood in the camp. Mohammed didn't know what to say.

'I'm sorry,' he told them, 'but I never found him.'

Relations between the survivors became tense. Any camaraderie from the early days of their incarceration had given way to a quiet mistrust, both of each other and of the authorities. It was clear now that the promise of transport to Italy was a lie. Instead they remained in the camp, with no word on their futures. At the end of each day when Mohammed returned to his shipping container, each bit of hope – hope of finding his friend, hope that the distraught families would be reunited, hope that he would leave the refugee camp, hope that he would become the world's best electrician – slowly evaporated.

Very few economic migrants or refugees wanted to make land in tiny Malta, but boats casting off from the North African coast with no navigation equipment often sailed unwittingly into Maltese waters and the travellers had little choice but to disembark there.

Like nearby Lampedusa, Malta's position between Africa and Europe has defined its problems both past and present. Christianity came to the islands during Roman times, followed by two centuries of Arab rule beginning in AD 870 which left a lasting mark on the Maltese language. The island then found itself conquered by the Normans, Aragonese and Italians before being bequeathed in 1530 to the Knights of the Order of St John, a Roman Catholic monastic order founded in Jerusalem and tasked with protecting Christianity during the Crusades. When the knights were forced out of Jerusalem they went into exile on Malta, fighting off the Ottomans during the Great Siege of 1565 and constructing the fortresses and ramparts of Valletta. It became a city designed to keep foreign invaders out, which worked until 1798, when first Napoleon and then the British forces took over the island.

Malta finally became an independent state in 1974 and joined the EU in 2004, but a barricade mentality remained – perhaps not towards millionaire investors, but certainly towards refugees and migrant workers from outside Europe. Like many other European nations, Malta chose hostility as a deterrent, and men, women and children who arrived in search of asylum could spend up to eighteen months behind bars in detention centres like the Safi Barracks.

Even as war zones around the world scattered their victims and the number of people attempting the dangerous sea voyage to Europe soared, Malta held firm. In July 2013 more than 400 people arrived on the island in a week, most fleeing fighting in Somalia and the Eritrean dictatorship. They had set sail from the Libyan coast, so Prime Minister Muscat tried to put them on planes and send them back to the chaos and strife in Tripoli. He only backed down after the European Court of Human Rights intervened. A month later he refused permission for a tanker which had rescued 102 people from a sinking dinghy to dock. Four pregnant women and a five-month-old baby were on board, but the Maltese authorities insisted that M/V *Salamis* did not have permission to enter their waters. Muscat had already warned the European Union's leaders that his country would not quietly shoulder the burden of a brewing refugee crisis.

'Call us heartless, but we are not pushovers,' he told the European Council President, Herman Van Rompuy.

Muscat used the 102 people on board the M/V *Salamis* to make his point, and it sailed on to Italy, where the pregnant women and the baby were finally able to see a doctor on dry land.

Italy came to Malta's rescue again when it launched Mare Nostrum, relieving Malta of its duty to disembark the world's weary as record numbers were attempting the journey. There was, however, still the matter of the refugees who had already arrived, and to Mohammed and Omar it seemed like no one knew what to do with them.

For a month, the young men waited at the camp for someone to explain what life had in store for them in Malta. But no one came. There were only a few bored security officials to quiz, and one uninterested guard told Mohammed that they could do whatever they pleased. No one explained how the Dublin Regulation worked, but they had a vague idea that they were not meant to leave – another person from their ship had been detained when he tried to get a ferry to Italy. Mohammed desperately wanted to escape – he was plagued by flashbacks, and could not escape the sea on an island just twenty-seven kilometres long and fourteen kilometres wide. Everywhere he went he had the unnerving feeling that he was still rolling in the swell, a seasickness at the very centre of his being. He couldn't escape the sea at night either. The Mediterranean haunted his dreams, and he was lucky if he managed more than a few hours' sleep. It was always the same – he was standing on the beach and a wall of waves barrelled towards him like a tsunami.

'I have to go,' he would say to no one in particular, before waking, terrified.

Omar and Mohammed decided to seize control of their destinies, and found someone in the camp who would make them fake Bulgarian ID cards. There was nothing for them in Malta, but they had heard that the Netherlands was a welcoming place, and they had friends there who could help them find accommodation and jobs.

As soon as the documents were ready, Omar wanted to leave.

'Let's go tonight,' he said.

'Are you crazy?' Mohammed replied. 'Let's wait.'

Given the recent thwarted escape attempt, Mohammed thought the authorities might be on alert for more absconders. But Omar was determined, so Mohammed decided to accompany him to the port to see how the security officials checked the ID cards. They left at 3 a.m. and walked the three miles from the camp to the port. Omar turned to bid his friend farewell at the ticket desk.

'If the police catch me, they catch me, but I want to try,' he said.

Mohammed looked at Omar, thought about his life in Malta, and made up his mind. He turned to the man behind the desk.

'Two tickets to Sicily, please.'

When the ferry finally set sail on 28 December, relief washed over Mohammed. He was once again afloat on the sea which terrified him, but this time he was sure it was carrying him to a better place.

This is the last time I will see Malta, he thought. *The nightmare is over.*

2014

Number of refugees and migrants entering the EU: 283,532
Number of deaths: 3,500

14

Hunted

Sina: Asmara, Eritrea

Now that Dani's superiors had put 800 kilometres between him and his new bride, maintaining any kind of relationship required ingenuity and deception. If Dani heard of anyone travelling to the capital from his remote outpost near the border with Djibouti, he would give them a letter to deliver to Sina, hoping that his trust was well placed and that the note wouldn't fall into the wrong hands. Even more dangerous was the mobile phone hidden in his room. While military conscripts were not allowed mobiles, those who had been released from national service were free to use them. Many parents gave their phones to their children, and Dani's father had handed down his when his son was posted south. At a designated hour of a designated evening, Sina would borrow a mobile from a friend and sneak away. Dani was risking jail with the secret late-night calls, but it was a risk he was willing to take to speak to his wife.

Despite his exile near the border, Dani was unable to contain his individualistic streak. And just as it had done in Asmara, it eventually landed him in trouble again at this remote outpost.

One night, Sina went to her room with her friend's phone, in her usual state of excitement and anticipation at speaking to her husband. But when she dialled his father's number, it did not connect. The phone was switched off. Panic pricked across her skin. She knew Dani had been having problems. He had quickly tired of the pointless tasks and wasted days in the dust and dirt of southern Eritrea, and in an effort to make his unit more productive, he had made some suggestions to his superiors. They had not been well received, and Sina steeled herself for the worst. *If someone hates you, he will find reasons to send you to prison*, she thought. *That is the behaviour of these men with power.*

Sina waited for word from Dani, but it never came. No more letters arrived by clandestine courier. His mobile phone never connected again. Friends were sympathetic, but evaded Sina's increasingly frantic calls. Maybe they knew what had happened to him, but if they told Sina and the government found out, they would be punished too. People were meant to disappear without trace in Eritrea – that was how the government kept the population fearful and compliant.

For the first three months of 2014, Sina heard nothing. She desperately wanted to go to Assab, the town near the border where Dani was stationed, but without an ID card or the government's permission to travel, she would be thrown in jail too, and that would not help Dani. Then in March, rumours reached Sina of a crackdown on Pentecostal Christians in the south. Then she knew for sure. Dani had been locked up and she might never see him again. A crackdown on a banned religion would have been the perfect excuse for Dani's superiors to get their revenge.

The filth and misery contained within Eritrea's jails was legendary, and the one Dani found himself in was no exception. But at least the squalor brought Dani his freedom. Even a young, fit man is at risk of disease in the cells, and a few months after arriving he contracted an intestinal disorder. The prison doctors ordered him to be transported to a hospital in Asmara, but not before the authorities demanded insurance against his escape. He was forced to hand over the deeds to the house of his friend Joseph as a bond for his return. If Dani absconded, his friend's house would be seized.

In Asmara, Dani was finally able to see Sina and explain what had happened. It was exactly as she had feared. Although Dani was an Orthodox Christian, some of his friends were Pentecostal, and one evening they were holding a prayer meeting in a room in the building where Dani lived. If you were Orthodox, Roman Catholic, Lutheran or a Sunni Muslim in Eritrea, you were free to worship your God. But practising any other religion meant clandestine gatherings after dark, hidden religious texts, and hushed prayers behind closed curtains. Sina never asked if Dani was actually in the room during the prayer meeting – it didn't make any difference. The end result was the same. Someone tipped off the military police, and every person living in the building was arrested and thrown in jail, no matter what religion they practised.

Dani's superiors had got rid of him at last. And he had no intention of going back.

When Dani's treatment at the Asmara hospital ended in early summer 2014, he walked out the door and home to his wife. With limited resources and plenty of deserters to worry about, it would take a few months for the authorities in the south to realize that Dani was missing. Sina was determined to enjoy that time together, and for a while they were able to live under the illusion that they were just like any other young couple in the world.

They could enjoy long walks together again, meals in Asmara's restaurants, time spent with their brothers, sisters, cousins and parents. Dani's father even started to drop hints about a baby. He was getting older, Dani was his only son, and he was ready to become a grandfather. Sina was not so sure it was the best time to be trying for a child: they did not have their own home, Dani was expected to go back to prison, and she was only earning $30 a month. But soon the hints turned into explicit demands, and Sina understood that she had to respect his wishes, especially as she and Dani were so reliant on his kindness and generosity. Her father-in-law was so desperate for a baby – perhaps aware that Dani could be sent back to jail any day and that the window for a grandchild could close for ever – that he would accompany her to a private clinic every few weeks.

'Please, check whether she is pregnant or not, check properly,' he would urge the doctor.

One day in August, Dani and Sina went to the clinic together. The doctor smiled. They were expecting a baby. It was a bitter-sweet moment. Happiness at the growing life was tempered by all the problems they would have to overcome to be able to give their baby a safe and secure home.

First there was the matter of Joseph's house. If Dani did not return to prison in Assab, his friend would be homeless. Dani's father proposed selling his own house. Then they could give the proceeds to Joseph to compensate for the house he had lost. But Joseph had his own solution. He had had enough of life in Eritrea and was already making preparations to leave. His house meant so little to him compared with the baby his friends had been blessed with.

'Dani, you should not have to return to prison, it's better to stay with your family,' Joseph said. 'Your child needs to have a father. Your father will be a grandfather.'

It was the summer of 2014. Their baby was due on 15 April the following year. They had nine months to try and make a future worthy of the tiny life they had created.

Gradually, the prospect of being a mother was becoming a little less alien to Sina. When their baby was a concept discussed at length by her parents and father-in-law, she listened passively to all their chat about what clothes their grandchild would wear, what they would call him. Now she found herself getting possessive.

'I am the mother – I will give my baby a name,' she told Dani.

In the autumn, they found out the baby was a boy, and Dani and Sina settled on the name Delina.

But every moment of joy was overshadowed by fear. The military police had finally started to look for Dani. If he returned to prison, he would never be released, and Sina would have to bring up their child alone. Her work in Asmara was also coming to an end and soon she would have to return to the harsh lunar landscape of the north, where there would be nothing to do but watch her belly swell and wonder whether the father of her child was dead or alive.

Life without Dani was unbearable – she knew that now. If Dani had to go on the run, she would go with him. They would never be apart again. So one unbearably hot summer's day, when Sina awoke beside her husband, she stayed there, two deserters side by side wondering what the future might hold. Deserting together carried huge risks. The government had no qualms about locking away expectant mothers, and the conditions for pregnant women were just the same as for the rest of the prison population. If a woman carried her child to term, her baby would probably be born behind bars. But often the beatings and the torture brought on miscarriages and premature labour, and the child never made it into the world alive.

I would die, thought Sina.

Going on the run was their only choice. The couple moved across the country, staying a few days with different relatives, trying to keep one step ahead of their pursuers. Whenever they could, Sina would stop by a private hospital for scans to check on her baby. He was doing fine, but they could not run for ever. They had to reach safety soon, and finally Sina and Dani realized they could not bring their child into the world in Eritrea. They had to leave to keep Delina safe.

By 2014, around 5,000 people were leaving Eritrea every month, and the country was on track to lose nearly ten per cent of its population. Most of them were young people, and increasingly children were among the runaways, their parents preferring to send them on the dangerous journey over Eritrea's borders rather than watch them disappear into military service.

The fleeing Eritreans joined the Syrians, the Iraqis, the Nigerians, the Malians, the South Sudanese, the Afghans, the Palestinians; with fifteen conflicts erupting in five years, the United Nation's High Commissioner for Refugees, António Guterres, warned of an unprecedented crisis.

'The world is at war,' he said.

Finally the global toll of the displaced had exceeded the aftermath of the Second World War. More than 60 million people had been forced on the run, wandering the earth looking for safety. Most of them did not find it in Europe. Eighty-seven per cent of those refugees were being looked after in the developing world. Since the beginning of the Arab Spring, officials with the UNHCR had pleaded with the rich world to meet its moral responsibilities and offer homes to tens of thousands of refugees who were living in the camps in Syria's neighbouring countries. But the response was lacklustre. The UNHCR held another pledging conference in Geneva in June 2014, but Belgium, Ireland, Switzerland and Uruguay were the only countries to step forward. Between them, they could take 565 more Syrians. This pledge came as 42,500 people all over the world were being driven from their homes every single day. Of the twenty-eight EU nations, only fourteen had offered to resettle Syrian refugees. By the end of the year, when Syrian refugees numbered 3.2 million, fewer than 45,000 places had been found in Europe, more than half of them in Germany. Excuses put forward by governments ranged from financial hardship to pressure from the rising support for far-right and anti-immigrant political parties.

These arguments had echoes of the 1938 conference held in the French spa town of Evian, where governments debated whether to offer sanctuary to the growing number of Jewish refugees fleeing Nazi atrocities. One by one, the leaders stood up and offered their deepest sympathies to the refugees, but lamented that the state of their economies meant they couldn't possibly offer any of them a new home. Europe's Jews were left to their fate, and as a result of the continent's self-interest in the early twentieth century, human rights were placed at the heart of the new union that emerged after the Second World War.

Those values continued to attract the ever-increasing numbers of people fleeing war in 2014, despite the vilification of refugees by populist parties and the implementation of government policies designed to keep them out. From January to April, 42,000 people were detected at the European Union's borders without papers, most coming over the Mediterranean in decrepit fishing vessels like the one that had tossed Mohammed Kazkji into the waves a few months earlier. That figure was up from 12,400 in the same period in 2013. The Italian government had heard reports that half a million people may be waiting in Libya to make the journey when the calmer summer seas arrived. There was no functioning government in Tripoli to confirm the reports, but a crisis was clearly on the horizon.

Migration experts were clear about what would save lives: more funding from member states for search and rescue at sea; more refugees resettled from nations neighbouring Syria; and the introduction of more legal ways for people who had fled their homes to get to Europe without risking their lives. Instead the European Union's border protection agency Frontex noticed its budget falling slightly from 2013. The EU's broken asylum system was scheduled to be discussed at a meeting of EU leaders in June 2014, but it fell off the agenda entirely as the leaders busied themselves with a messy scrap over who should become the new president of the European Commission. A few days later, 100 more people were lost at sea in two separate incidents off the Italian coast.

Politicians noted the tragedies but were more worried about problems back home after the bruising European Parliament elections in May, when fringe political parties, many openly espousing policies to curb the number of refugees, saw a fifty-per-cent leap in representation. In Britain, the anti-immigration UK Independence Party won more votes than the sitting Conservative government. France's populist leader Marine Le Pen – who would face trial for inciting racial hatred for comparing Muslims praying on the street to Nazi occupiers – also celebrated as her *Front National* eclipsed the country's two main parties. In Greece, Golden Dawn came third, while in Hungary a party with anti-Semitic links – Jobbik – came second. The views of the extreme right concerning migration and refugees went largely unchallenged during campaigning. Tapping into centuries-old xenophobia was an easy vote winner, and slowly the refugee policies of some mainstream political parties hardened.

Dani and Sina had started their journey just as governments in Europe looked at their asylum statistics and saw a dramatic rise in the numbers of Eritreans asking for refuge. The solution of some was not to look at ways to help the new wave of the displaced, but to try and deny their suffering.

In Denmark, the anti-immigrant Danish People's Party won the largest share of the vote in the European Parliament elections. General elections were due the following year. The government noted the rise in Eritreans arriving in 2014, and commissioned a fact-finding mission to Eritrea to gather more evidence for assessing the claims. The authors came back with conclusions that surprised many people working in human rights and among Eritrea's diaspora. The report claimed that the shoot-to-kill border policy was no longer in operation, there was little evidence of a vast network of political prisoners, and reports of ill treatment during military service were exaggerated. On the subject of the length of national service, one unnamed Western embassy source was quoted as saying the service 'is not really indefinite, but when it ends is arbitrary'. The implication was clear: people were leaving for economic reasons and it was safe to send them back to a country ranked the tenth most corrupt and the most censored in the world, and to a government which the UN would soon accuse of committing crimes against humanity.

The sources for the Danes' surprising findings included an unnamed 'well known Eritrean intellectual' and 'a representative from the Eritrean government', unspecified Western embassies and NGOs, as well as observations of the Danish team on the ground. The report drew its conclusions about the freedoms enjoyed by Eritrean citizens from anecdotal details such as the ability of the delegation to watch CNN and the BBC in their hotel, and the fact that the delegation 'observed many people using smart phones'.

The report named just two sources – two academics based outside Eritrea – and they both swiftly denounced the findings. But the damage was done. The Danish government changed its policy and stopped automatically granting asylum to Eritreans. The British government, also seeing a huge rise in the numbers of Eritreans asking for refuge, took note and issued amended guidelines for assessing Eritrean claims for asylum, heavily quoting the anonymously sourced and largely discredited Danish report.

Should Dani and Sina reach Europe and join the many others weaving their way through an unwelcoming continent, there was now a possibility they could be refused sanctuary. But at the end of 2014, the couple hadn't even considered their final destination.

We need to stay alive. In Sina's head, it was simple as that.

Dani got in touch with his friend Joseph. Having given up his house for them, he had now made it to Sudan.

'Please send someone to help us leave Eritrea,' Dani pleaded.

A smuggler contacted them. He asked for $12,000, and their escape was planned for January 2015, just a few months before the baby was due to arrive.

15

All Alone

Mohammed: Milan, Italy

Milan's Central Station is a shrine to excess, its gilded halls of Art Nouveau and Art Deco flourishes serving as an easy metaphor for the gulf between the riches which built modern Europe and the stricken people it is now turning away. During the Second World War, Jews were secretly loaded onto trains on an underground platform and sent to the death camps. Today, underneath Mussolini's gauche creation fashioned from 11,000 cubic metres of marble, refugees gather with their sparse bundles and gaze up at the departure board. Milan is connected by rail to cities throughout Europe, and for the tens of thousands of refugees passing though the capacious halls, it is a place for a respite from a gruelling journey, a pause in their game of cat-and-mouse with Europe's police forces. Mothers nurse babies on the marble staircases. Men gather for furtive cigarettes to share stories of how to best dodge the police, border guards and immigration officials. Women sit in filthy clothes underneath Dolce & Gabbana billboards emblazoned with skinny models draped in gold and silk.

When Omar passed through, he was wearing four t-shirts and the same shoes and jeans he had on when the ship from Libya went down.

Mohammed and Omar had left Malta a few days earlier, ill equipped for the cold and the snow which greeted them as they travelled by boat and train from Sicily to the Alpine north. It had rained in Malta, but the temperature could still reach eighteen degrees in winter, and they had no money to buy supplies for their first trip to a place where they would truly experience the European chill. Layering every item he owned seemed like the best option to Omar. But soon after their train had left Central Station and crossed into France, his strangely unseasonal attire caught the attention of a couple of police officers who boarded the train.

'Don't you feel cold?' the female officer said, laughing.

Omar and Mohammed struggled to see the funny side when they were asked for their IDs.

'Where are you from?' the male officer asked.

'Bulgaria,' Omar replied.

'No, you are not,' the officer said, pulling Omar's Syrian passport from his bag.

'It's normal,' Omar protested. 'My mother is Bulgarian and my father is Syrian.'

The officer rolled his eyes and escorted the pair off the train at the small French town it had stopped at and took them to a police station. Mohammed was separated from Omar and was asked for his fingerprints. But they had both prepared for such a scenario. They would not give any details about themselves until they reached the Netherlands. They still did not fully understand how Europe's complicated asylum system worked, but they were determined to avoid being jailed again. Playing dumb seemed the best option.

'I need a translator, I don't understand anything,' Mohammed told his interrogators.

'It's eleven o'clock at night,' the officer replied.

But Mohammed stood his ground.

'I am not going to give my fingerprints – I want to go to Holland.'

He imagined Omar's interrogation in another room. Were

they telling him that Mohammed had given his fingerprints in a ruse to get him to comply? Mohammed had seen enough police television dramas to know all the tricks. But after two hours, the police gave up and told Omar and Mohammed that they had twenty-seven hours to leave France. They even offered the young men a lift to a hotel, but it was two in the morning and they didn't have any money so they decided to opt for a night in the cells.

The next morning, an officer dropped by.

'Go, you are free.'

With increasing numbers of refugees traversing Europe, countries were struggling to implement the Dublin rules requiring them to process the asylum claims of each person crossing their borders. Arrival and transit countries like Greece, Italy and Bulgaria had neither the resources nor the willpower to register everyone who arrived. And with their pleas for more financial and practical assistance from other EU members largely ignored, the governments had an incentive to let some people slip though and lessen the burden on their overcrowded refugee facilities. Only around a quarter of requests to return a refugee under the Dublin Regulation to the place they arrived actually resulted in a transfer. With the rules haphazardly applied, refugees never knew what to expect. Families could end up in different countries. One Chechen man was sent back to Poland while his wife and newborn son were allowed to stay in Austria, carving up the family just when they most needed to be together.

For Mohammed and Omar, European discord played in their favour. They got back on the train to Paris, then caught one to Brussels and another to Amsterdam, taking care to stay hidden. They developed a plan for each time the train stopped. One of them would go to the toilet and the other would step onto the platform for a cigarette, thus evading any police walking through the train. At one stop, Mohammed was puffing away when a tall police officer started walking towards him. His heart leapt into his mouth as he looked up at the unsmiling face.

'You can't smoke here.'

Mohammed stifled a laugh and put the cigarette out.

He boarded again, hopeful that they would soon be on Dutch soil. But as the flat grey fields of northern Europe whipped past their windows, Mohammed wondered how they would know when they had crossed the border.

'Look out for cows – there are lots of cows in Holland,' Omar advised.

When they pulled into Amsterdam, they went straight to a police station. Mohammed had never broken the law back home, and he didn't have any intention of doing so in Europe.

'Hello, I just arrived and have escaped the war in Syria,' he said.

The woman smiled.

'And what can I do for you?'

For a few days, Mohammed felt as though his luck had finally changed. Everyone they met in Amsterdam went out of their way to help, giving them bus tickets, pocket money, advice. They were sent to a camp where they had a clean bed to sleep in, and they were no longer treated like prisoners. When Mohammed told a psychologist there that he wouldn't let himself sleep because his dreams were haunted by visions of the waves and his mother in peril, he was given a prescription for free sleeping pills, which helped give his mind some rest from the turmoil of the past few months. It was January 2014, and the year seemed full of promise. But those carefree days were not to last. A month later the authorities ran Mohammed and Omar's fingerprints, and they showed up in the Dublin database. By EU law they had requested that Malta grant them asylum. It didn't matter that they had been shot at by pirates, watched dozens of people drown, and spent hours at sea battling death just prior to the time they were supposed to have made that request. They had to go back to Malta.

'I couldn't even remember my name at the time, let alone re-member that they took my fingerprints,' Mohammed protested, but it did no good. They were escorted from the first place they had felt safe in months and taken to an asylum detention centre. They were prisoners again.

Omar was put on a plane first. A few days later, Mohammed's lawyer came to see him with a copy of a Maltese newspaper report: Omar had been arrested when he landed and sent straight to jail. After a short trial he was sentenced to six months in prison for leaving the country illegally with false identification documents. When Mohammed arrived in Malta a week later, he was prepared for the same fate. Bundled into a police car at the airport, he spent three nights at the station as the officers questioned him about why he left. He tried to explain that he had a phobia of the sea, which earned him a little sympathy. The police demanded that he say sorry for leaving the country illegally, and after the humiliating apology, he was told to leave.

Mohammed asked if he should return to the refugee camp.

'No – because you left Malta, you can't go back to the refugee camp,' the immigration official replied. 'You have to take care of yourself.'

Mohammed didn't know where to go, but the official offered no further help. So the young Syrian electrician walked out into the early spring light with just a mobile phone, a small school satchel, and €30 to his name. He wandered to a public garden in Valletta, and sat on a bench. Mohammed stayed on that bench for two days, sleeping under the stars and trying to think of anyone he could call for help. There was no one. He decided to go back to the refugee camp anyway – he needed a shower and a charger for his phone so he could keep in touch with his parents in Syria.

If they catch me in the camp and take me to the jail, I will be glad, he thought. *Jail for six months would be better for me than this.*

It wasn't just his own fate worrying Mohammed. His two

brothers had now also been called up for the draft, and had fled to Turkey. Syria's exodus was gaining pace, and it would accelerate throughout 2014 as ISIS fighters seized more territory in Iraq and Syria and declared an Islamic caliphate. Families were forced to live under strict Islamic law, and reports of the horrors of that life were seeping out. In August tens of thousands of members of Iraq's Yazidi sect would flee after ISIS fighters seized their homeland in northern Iraq. The extremists separated hundreds of men and boys from their families and executed them in the ditches of the Nineveh plains. Woman and girls were raped and boys as young as eight were forced to fight. Watching a beheading was a crucial part of their bloody induction. Christians, Kurds and Shia also feared slaughter and ran from their homes.

In northern Syria people fled from the threat of execution, public flogging and detention. Alcohol consumption, sex out of wedlock and homosexuality were all considered crimes warranting violent punishment. The dashes into Turkey became more frantic, but the 900-kilometre border was no longer an easy escape route. The government in Ankara watched with increasing concern as a rebellion to topple Assad morphed into an Islamist uprising which threatened Turkey's own security. Deep trenches and coils of razor wire began to appear along the border, and armed guards would refuse entry at the official crossing points to anyone without a passport. But many Syrians who wanted to flee had no passports, so they were forced to try and sneak over the border, only to be abused by guards and forcibly returned to Syria.

Syria's neighbours were near breaking point, but no one was helping. The World Food Programme pleaded for more funds from governments to feed six million Syrians displaced within their own nation or living in neighbouring countries. The money never came, and from October 2014 the amount of food they were able to give to refugees in Syria, Jordan, Turkey, Lebanon, Iraq and Egypt decreased. By December, food vouchers stopped entirely for 1.7 million people outside Syria, just as the winter months set in and their lives became even more bleak.

While in the first few years of the Syrian conflict it was mainly the middle class fleeing with a reasonable amount of money, now the horrors of ISIS compounded the brutality of the Assad regime and sent families from all walks of life over the border with only the few belongings they could carry. They clambered through razor wire into countries where they were not allowed to work and where they could no longer get assistance from international donors. They had little choice but to keep on the move.

Mohammed wanted his brothers to be safe and understood the dangers they would have faced fighting with Assad's dejected and poorly funded army against the dogmatic religious convictions of ISIS. But he was doing everything he could to keep them away from the sea. He knew that such a journey could be just as deadly. However, there was little he could do while he was sleeping rough with no way to charge his mobile phone or pay for credit.

For two nights he slept in the refugee camp's prayer room, until finally he found a friend on Facebook who was still in Malta and could offer him a bed. Now that he had somewhere to stay, he went back to the immigration centre to continue his asylum application, but their advice didn't make sense to him: he had to stay in Malta, but he wasn't allowed to work and he wasn't allowed to study.

How was he meant to rebuild his life under such conditions? At least work might have taken his mind off the wreck, scenes of which still looped around in his mind and stopped him from sleeping. When he asked Maltese officials for some of the sleeping pills which had helped cloak the nightmares in the Netherlands, they just told him to go to the pharmacy and buy some. But how could he pay for them? As the first few months of 2014 passed, Mohammed felt utterly alone: Omar was in prison, Yahea was dead, he could hardly get through to his family on the phone, and no one in Malta seemed to care whether he lived, died, or hovered somewhere in between.

Nart: Sofia, Bulgaria

Loneliness and alienation also consumed Nart Bajoi as he hid away in his hotel room in the Bulgarian capital, fearful that far-right thugs might hear him speaking Arabic and target him. There was nothing for him in Bulgaria. He tried to make himself useful, writing emails to prospective employers and meanwhile offering his services as a translator to the Red Cross, the Bulgarian authorities and local charities. He wasn't even asking for money in return – he would have been happy to volunteer, anything to make the days pass in this strange city where he knew no one and his education and talents counted for nothing. But although he had had a few weeks of translation work the previous autumn, now no one replied to his emails. The only employers who responded were interested not in his two degrees and his linguistic skills, but in the desperation which made him an easy target for exploitation. Nart worked for a few days in a café and a few days at a factory before realizing that no one was going to pay him. It was just like it had been in Turkey – he had stopped being seen as a human being the moment he took the taxi over the border from Syria. He even considered returning home. His life may have been in danger in Syria, but at least he had a purpose there.

Money was also a problem. Towards the end of the previous year Nart had found himself down to his last two euros, and it was only after a long-standing member of Bulgaria's Syrian community lent him €150 that he was able to pay for the hotel room he shared with two others.

No, Bulgaria was not for him. As soon as the authorities

approved his request for asylum and gave him his refugee passport, he went straight to the bus station. It was 17 January 2014, and Nart was surprised by how busy it was. All around him excited young Bulgarians with backpacks milled around with tickets in their pockets and hope on their faces.

He asked them where they were going.

'Britanie! Britanie!'

On 1 January, restrictions on Bulgarians and Romanians working in some of the European Union's twenty-eight nations had expired. When the two countries joined the EU in 2007, some richer countries, including Britain, had worried that their labour markets would be threatened by migrant workers from the poorer new member states. But the free movement of people for work and travel was one of the pillars of the EU, and they had to open up their borders eventually, even if many people remained deeply suspicious of foreign workers.

Since the end of the Second World War, European nations had had a delicate relationship with people coming from outside their borders to work. For most of its history Europe had been an exporter of migrants, with around two million Europeans leaving poverty behind at the turn of the twentieth century to find a new life in the Americas. Roughly one million European refugees were also resettled outside the continent after the Second World War. Outward migration continued well into the 1960s and 1970s, but the rapid post-war reconstruction meant the countries also had to find workers to rebuild the devastated continent, and European nations began to sign pacts with other countries based on their geography and history.

Many countries welcomed people from their former colonies, so Algerians found themselves working on farms in France and South Asians and Afro-Caribbeans came to the UK. West Germany signed a deal with Turkey in 1961 to bring one million workers into the country. The new arrivals were largely welcomed into European societies until the oil crisis of 1973 brought hard times back to the continent, and then the men and women were expected to leave again.

This pattern was repeated with each wave of prosperity: people from far afield were invited in to do the jobs locals didn't want when times were good, only for populations and politicians to turn on them in hard times. Many EU nations shipped in builders, farmhands, cleaners and nannies from Africa, Asia and the Middle East as the introduction of the euro brought a temporary bubble and a building boom. But it wasn't long before they found themselves unwelcome on a continent in the grip of an austerity drive.

The free movement of people who came from within the European Union was also troubling to some populist parties like the UK Independence Party, which campaigned for restrictions on foreign workers both from outside the bloc and from other EU nations.

In Britain, 2014 began with panic and alarmist rhetoric that the country was on the brink of an invasion of workers from Bulgaria and Romania threatening not only Britons' jobs but the very fabric of society. The political debate was driven by fear rather than by facts and figures, and even though the predicted surge of economic migrants never transpired, a toxic tone was set. When refugees started arriving on Europe's shores fleeing terrible conflict rather than unemployment, the language that greeted them in Britain was hostile and defensive: they were not people, but 'swarms' and 'marauders'.

But Nart was not going to Britain. He had another country in his sights: Germany, which, by 2014, was the powerhouse of Europe, its economy booming while others slumped. Its leader, Chancellor Angela Merkel, had been dubbed the Queen of Europe. During the eurozone crisis and as the bloc grappled with the Greek bailouts, she had emerged as the leader with the power to make or break the deals. In Greece, protesters shocked at the severity of the austerity programmes she was championing did not shy away from reviving the ghosts of the Second World War, daubing Hitler moustaches on posters of Merkel and waving them in greeting to any visiting German officials.

But the shadow of that war would also be there for Merkel when she formulated Germany's response to the refugee crisis. She was determined to show leadership as the numbers of those seeking sanctuary crept up, and this time it was going to be a moral leadership.

On 20 January Nart walked into a police station in Munich.

'I am from Syria,' he said, hopeful that those words would finally mean something.

16

A Very Long Transit

Hanan: Athens, Greece

There was not much festive cheer in Greece as the country rang in another year of austerity and political turmoil, but Hanan al-Hasan refused to give in to the gloom: there was no point dwelling on all the setbacks when there was so much more work to do. Three months after arriving, Rim and Izzat remained the only ones who had managed to escape the confines of their tiny apartment and travel to Norway, and the rest of the family were getting desperate. In Greece, there was no work for Talal, no assistance from the government, and Ismail and Riad had the threat of arrest hanging over them. In Norway there would be accommodation and a cash allowance for necessities while their asylum applications were processed, and funding and housing for up to five years once they were recognized as refugees. Most importantly, there were jobs, schools and universities.

It had been one setback after another, however. Bisan tried to fly to Oslo to join her sister, but she dropped her fake ID card in front of a security official, who noticed that it made the wrong sound when it hit the floor. He summoned security to escort the young woman out of Athens airport. Ismail and Riad hadn't even tried flying out of Greece, but Ismail was always on the lookout for creative ways for him and his brother to get into the Schengen Area, the zone of twenty-six European countries which abolished internal border controls. That was the main challenge for people who chose the safer sea route to Greece over the gruelling voyage from Libya to Italy. There were pros and cons to both journeys. To arrive in Greece meant horrendous living conditions, a state with no resources to process refugee claims, and a buffer of non-EU Balkan countries which refugees had to cross to reach the passport-free Schengen zone and find a genuinely safe haven.

On the other hand, if you launched off the Libyan coastline and hit Italy, you could avoid giving your fingerprints and jump on a train to the richer northern European nations. But first you had to make it over the sea alive, and in 2014 one in every sixty people who attempted the journey would die. Nevertheless, the Libya crossing would remain the favoured route in 2014, with 170,664 arriving in Italy or Malta, nearly four times as many as the previous year. Just over 44,000 would arrive by sea in Greece. That was still a massive increase – up from 11,831 in 2013 – and the Greek authorities were under pressure from other EU states to stop refugees leaving and making their way north.

Ismail spotted his first opportunity to try and do just that when he was at Athens' Piraeus port with a friend one day. Two large car ferries bound for Italy were loading, and on an impulse the teenagers ran up the ramp. Greek police spotted them, but in the confusion started searching for the stowaways on the wrong ship. The two teenagers hid under a lorry, and shortly after, Talal and Hanan received an unexpected phone call.

'Mama, Papa, I am in a ship!' Ismail told them.

Using a GPS tracking application on their phone, the couple were able to follow his progress, and once the ferry had set sail and Ismail was far out to sea, they called him back and told him it was safe to come out.

Another child to safety, Hanan thought.

As the ferry steamed ahead to the Italian port of Bari, a British woman approached the two teenagers. They looked out of place, and she asked if she could help. Ismail explained that they were

Syrian refugees, and she told them they should stay hidden – they were not in Italy yet.

'You look suspicious,' the woman warned Ismail. She pressed €50 into his hand. 'You will need this.'

Ismail tried to decline her offer. His family's aim was to get across Europe to find somewhere they could provide for themselves, and he shared his mother's sense of wounded pride at accepting handouts. But the woman was insistent.

'You must take it – God bless you.'

When the ferry finally docked in Bari, Ismail realized that they needed more than money: they needed a miracle. Italian police stood by the ferry doors. All the other passengers were in cars, so when they tried to leave on foot they were immediately spotted.

'We are Syrians and we want asylum,' Ismail told the officials.

But the official was dismissive and told the boys they were still in the port so were not technically in Italy. Ismail was sure they had reached the point where they could not be turned back, but arguing with the officer was futile. Within minutes he was forced back on board the same ferry and was soon steaming back to Greece, to his disappointed parents, and to a jail cell. The seventeen-year-old spent two days in a men's prison in Greece for illegal exit, and when he was released he was more determined than ever to get himself and his brother out of this country where they had been treated like criminals from the moment they made land.

Now Ismail would join Hanan and Talal every week when they headed to Agios Nikolaos to look for more identification documents and ask around about ways to escape which didn't involve another dangerous sea journey or hiding in a packed truck praying there was enough air to reach the destination without suffocating. One day, they heard about a car going to Austria, and there was room for the two boys. The smuggler was as convincing as they always were when selling an impossible dream to people who had no choice but to believe the lies. The boys would go by car across the Balkans and Central Europe, and after five days driving through Greece, Macedonia, Serbia and Hungary, they would reach Austria.

Ismail made up his mind: this was the only way for him and Riad to get out of Greece, and they had to go. Hanan was shocked by Ismail's proposal at first – she couldn't bear to think of her baby boy, the one who was always by her side, without his parents in a strange land.

'No, I cannot allow this,' she told her eldest son.

'Trust me,' Ismail said. 'I will arrive with Riad. Otherwise he will have to stay in Athens. You can't take him with you. Let him come with me.'

Hanan looked at her strong, proud son, and she believed him. He was only seventeen, but he loved his younger brother and would protect him. So she hugged her boys tight and said goodbye – letting them go was her best chance of giving them a future. Watching them board a train with their sleeping bags and leave Athens without her was painful. Her children's lives were slipping out of her control, and all she could do was trust in Ismail's promise that he would keep Riad safe.

Ismail: Thessaloniki, Greece

The smuggler's lies unravelled almost as soon as Ismail and Riad left their parents. After taking the train to Thessaloniki in northern Greece on 4 January, the boys spent a night in a hotel before the smuggler took them to a station. There was no car to speed them across central Europe as promised, but an abandoned train carriage where they were told to hide for a few days, waiting for a cargo train bound for Macedonia which was going to take them north.

The carriage where they slept was rusting and filthy, but it was no use challenging the smuggler: he was barely able to hold a conversation. Ismail and Riad were not even sure of the Algerian's name. Riad was sure he was giving them a different name every day. At first he asked them to call him Absi, then the next day he was Nadir, then Bakir. Ismail was pretty sure his real name was Absi, but the Algerian was so drunk most of the time that it was hard to know what to believe. Ismail wasn't sure what it was in the bottle that the man kept draining, but he could tell it was strong.

For four nights Riad, Ismail and a handful of other Syrians pulled their sleeping bags around them and tried to get some rest. But when the cargo train finally arrived, it didn't stop for five minutes like Absi promised: it sped through Thessaloniki station and straight to the border.

Absi was unapologetic, but he had another plan. They would walk along the railway tracks to Macedonia and sneak aboard another train before it crossed.

'The train on the border will surely stop for ten minutes,' he said. Some of the other Syrians threw their hands in the air and left, but Ismail had made a promise to get Riad out and he was going to keep his word.

The group set off through the neglected border landscape at 10 p.m. The forest ground had been transformed into a slippery mud slope and the air was thick with a dull grey mist. The trees had long ago shed their leaves, robbing the boys of any shelter as the icy blasts raced over the hills and into the valley. But Ismail and Riad were fit young men. They had layered their clothes, both for warmth and to lessen the load they had to carry, and they were able to walk along the ballast of the railway track rather than on the muddy forest path. But as the hours passed by, the crushed stones under their feet put a terrible strain on their muscles, and pain crept up their legs. Ismail tried walking on the iron rail line, but it didn't help. The three jackets and two pairs of jeans which he thought would insulate them from the cold were instead forming a trap for his body heat, and sweat was pooling in his clothes. Hunger and thirst crept up on him, and would have consumed his thoughts were it not for his constant worries about Riad.

Riad was so much younger, and did not have the strong gym-fit body of his brother. He was softer – fatter, Ismail would have teased him before they left – and had now developed a shooting pain in his knee. For two hours Riad struggled under the weight of his bag, and finally Ismail forced his exhausted brother to hand it over. The younger boy could only carry on with the assistance of another Syrian refugee who helped him hobble along.

Riad shouldn't have come with me, Ismail thought, regretting that he had persuaded his mother to trust him. *He is so tired, he can't carry his bag, he can't walk.*

But there was nothing to be done, so for twelve hours they moved slowly along the tracks, trying to keep their balance, wondering what was in store for them next.

When they reached the border the next morning, there was no time to get clean and dry after the punishing walk: they had to hide in another old carriage and wait for the cargo train to the Macedonian capital, Skopje. For a few hours at least they could sleep. When Ismail awoke, he saw that a train had pulled up beside them. He looked for Absi, but the smuggler was lying passed out in another drunken stupor. Ismail nudged him.

'This is the train!'

Absi barely opened his eyes.

'No, sleep… sleep… it's not the train.'

But Ismail insisted. Absi opened one eye a crack, and leapt up.

'Quick, jump up,' he urged his young charges.

They boys hauled themselves up onto the open-air freight train just before it set off again, and found themselves in a carriage with piles of wet sand filling every corner, caking the walls and streaking the floor. They struggled to find a foot of space between the mounds of filth. The damp in the air soaked the sand and chilled the boys to the bone, their clothes still wet with sweat from the walk, and now encasing them in icy water. No matter how high they pulled their scarves up around their faces and their hoods on their cheap jackets down over their heads, the cold cut right through.

When the train finally pulled into Skopje, the boys were miserable. When dismounting, Ismail had misjudged the distance from the train carriage to the ground and had fallen on his back, and the bruises would ache for days. Riad was still in pain from the walk, and was missing his mother. Ismail could only reassure him that they would all be together again soon.

Their accommodation in Skopje was a filthy refugee shelter where Absi paid the guards and left them for a night. The next morning, he packed them off in the bus to the Serbian border, handing them over to another smuggler for the next leg of their journey. Once again they were expected to walk through the forests and hills into Serbia, but no one seemed to know where they were going. After a few hours, they found themselves in a shelter in the woods. Ismail thought it was part of a farm, but was grateful for the bed and slept through the night.

The next morning, they were finally bundled into the promised car, but had not gone far when they hit a police roadblock. Riad and Ismail were promptly arrested, had their phone taken off them, and were sent to a camp for children. Ismail turned to the gruff police officer who accompanied them to the gate.

'What will happen to us?'

'We will deport you to Macedonia,' the man replied.

He was lying, and they remained at the camp, but they were faced with another problem there: without their phone they could not call their mother to let her know that they were safe. It was there on 19 January that Riad celebrated his fourteenth birthday, far away from the parents who did not even know if he was still alive.

Hanan: Athens, Greece

Hanan was in despair. Of all the hardships she had endured since she was forced to wrench her family from their home in Syria, the week when she heard nothing from her boys was one of the worst. She could not keep still, not for a moment. All she could do was walk and worry: past the boarded-up shopfronts smeared with the graffiti of the disaffected Greek youth; through the Arab areas where smugglers would lord it over the refugee families. Hanan noticed none of these things. She barely noticed the day turning into night as her feet kept going over the uneven pavements, her mind focused only on finding her sons. She called anyone she thought might be of help: staff from the charity Médecins Sans Frontières [Doctors Without Borders] who had already assisted her family; old contacts from her time studying in Budapest nearly thirty years ago; friends of the family scattered throughout Europe.

'Please, I have lost my two sons,' she would say to anyone who would listen. 'Help me.'

She could not believe she had let Ismail and Riad out of her sight and allowed them to set off across five countries without her.

I have made a big mistake, she thought.

But it was too late now. All she could do was trust that Ismail was looking after Riad as he promised, and plunge her resourcefulness into finding her children. The incessant phone calls paid off. A contact at Médecins Sans Frontières managed to track down her children in Serbia. Now all Hanan had to do was get them out. Her mind went back to her youth – her brother had stayed in what was then Yugoslavia on an exchange programme. A few calls later and she had located an old friend.

'Please, my sons are in Serbia, please help them,' she pleaded.

The friend agreed straight away, and told Hanan to send the boys to him.

Ismail: Niš, Serbia

After the week without communication, the camp staff had finally given Ismail his phone back, and Hanan informed her son of the plan. The next day, Ismail told camp staff that he and Riad were going to the shops, and jumped in a taxi to take them the address of their uncle's old friend. Hanan had already put in the calls to a new smuggler, and wired €3,000 to Ismail for payment. Hanan hated burdening him with that responsibility, and tried to make sure he understood that their lives were more important than the cash.

'When you arrive in Hungary give him the money,' she told him. 'But if he makes any problems, if he has a knife or anything, please your mama and give him anything he wants.'

The smuggler did not prove dangerous, just useless. After taking the boys in a taxi to the border, he led them into the woods and straight into the hands of Hungarian police.

'Please, he is only fourteen, he is not going to escape,' Ismail implored as he watched his brother taken away in handcuffs. The policeman shot a glance at the teenager and pulled the cuffs tighter.

Hungary was by 2014 seeing an increase in the number of refugees crossing its territory to reach Austria. This was a sign of how few options were now open to the refugees, for Hungary had a formidable reputation. Men and women were routinely arrested for illegal entry – whether they were legitimately claiming asylum or not – and thrown into detention centres where cockroaches crawled through the cracks of filthy rooms, the hot-water taps didn't work, and the toilets were never cleaned. Many of the detainees were forced to take tranquillizers, the authorities reasoning that a sedated prison population was less likely to cause problems. Some refugees would complain of years of addiction after their experiences in the Hungarian camps. Beatings were common, and any time the prisoners left the centres to go to court or even to visit the post office, they would be handcuffed and put on a leash.

Since his election in 2010, Viktor Orbán, the right-wing Hungarian Prime Minister, had seemed to take pleasure in pushing the European Union's liberal laws to their limit. This provocation may have infuriated the officials at the EU head-quarters in Brussels, but they chose their battles carefully. The European Commission launched infringement proceedings against Hungary in 2012 over changes to the Constitution which lowered the retirement age for judges – a move apparently aimed at weeding out older, less supportive magistrates – and Orbán backed down. But when it came to Hungary's detention and abuse of refugees, the Commission failed to act.

When Ismail and Riad arrived at the centre and found out that they would be locked in, Ismail pleaded with the woman behind the desk.

'I can't stay here because my family are not here and somebody is waiting for me.'

Luckily for the boys, the woman took pity on them. She looked at the two dishevelled and dejected teenagers and then quietly asked, 'Would you really like to leave?'

Ismail nodded.

'OK, after two hours, come back here with your bag,' she said, advising the boys to wait until the other youngsters in the camp were in their rooms: she was breaking the rules helping Riad and Ismail escape, and didn't want anyone to see them leave.

Two hours later the woman opened the door and took them first to a bank to change their euros to Hungarian forint, then to the bus station. Ismail was confused. The last year of his life had been a parade of opportunistic people trying to profit from his family's misery, yet here this stranger was, apparently helping them out of the goodness of her heart.

'Are you doing this for money?' he asked. 'What do you want for doing this?'

She gently reassured him.

'No, I'm just helping you. Goodbye, and be careful,' she urged the boys. Ismail was thankful for her kindness and immediately called his mother.

'Mama, we are now in Hungary, we are going to Budapest.'

Hanan logged on to Facebook and tracked down a man she had known during her studies in Budapest in 1987. Once again she was surprised by kindness – he told Hanan he would help her boys, and together they found another smuggler who would take them into Austria for €750. Once again Riad and Ismail ended up in police custody as soon as they crossed the border. But this time they were happy. The police were kind, and they were in a country with the capacity to treat them like the children that they were, providing them with a warm bed, new clothes and schooling.

They had spent a month on the road, been arrested three times, and their health had suffered. All they had eaten in a month were scraps of bread, cheese and processed meat. Riad had lost eight kilos. All of Ismail's clothes were too big for him. But finally they felt safe, and now they just had to wait for their mother.

Hanan: Athens, Greece

Relief overwhelmed Hanan when she found out her boys were being well looked after in a camp for children in Austria. She was aching to see them again, but she had one more child to get to safety: Bisan. The family had tried over and over again to get their youngest daughter on a flight to join her sister in Norway. Each time, the police would look at her – sometimes with pity, sometimes with hostility – and escort her out of the airport. Often it was bad luck – such as the ID card falling to the floor. But the more she failed, the less likely it seemed that she would ever leave. Each night before a new attempt to board a plane, Bisan would lie awake in bed, worrying. When she finally arrived at the airport, exhaustion would compound her fear and nerves and the airport staff could tell just by looking at her that something was amiss. Her gentle prettiness – just like her mother before life had hardened the edges a little – the vulnerable smile: once you had seen her you would remember her face. After a few failed attempts, security staff would now immediately recognize her the moment she passed through the entrance and ask her to leave.

Similar stories would circulate in the Syrian refugee community. On evenings when they allowed the despair to lift a little, Hanan and Talal could see the humour in some of the tales of thwarted escape. There was the Syrian from the countryside who spoke no English and had never taken an aeroplane, but whose family had money. He paid for the best ID, but he could not understand the instructions of the check-in staff and tried to clamber on the luggage belt when he was asked to weigh his case. One Syrian doctor they knew had been ejected from the airport so many times that he decided to learn Italian and fool the guards, but they laughed in his face.

'Good, your Italian is improving,' a security official told him before asking him to leave.

Hanan and Talal had no choice: they had to trust a smuggler again, or Bisan might never leave. She was getting increasingly despondent, worrying that she was becoming a burden to her family and spending her days alone and lost in regret. Everyone else had left – Rim and Izzat were in Norway, Riad and Ismail were on the road to Austria. Her life was slipping by and she was doing nothing. Hanan could not bear to see her daughter's depression, so she went back to her contacts book and rang an Algerian she trusted called Amin. A few days later, he called back.

'You want your daughter to travel? Tomorrow she will travel.'

The next morning at 5 a.m., Talal took his youngest daughter to a square in Athens, and watched her leave with Amin. Wearily, he returned home. As he closed the door on their small flat he looked at his exhausted wife, who was finally heading to bed. Of all the emotions clouding the air between the couple, hope was a weak one.

'Who will open the door for Bisan when she gets back?' Talal asked.

'No problem,' Hanan replied. 'My cousin is here, she can do it. Let us sleep.'

The couple went to sleep, and slept soundly. There was no point staying awake, as they had done so many times before when Bisan tried to leave. It just meant they would be even more tired if their daughter did return home, dejected and needing the comfort of her parents.

Hanan awoke to the sound of her mobile.

'Your daughter is flying.'

Hanan was still half asleep, and confused.

'Whose daughter?'

'Your daughter – Bisan,' Amin replied. 'I tell you, she is in the plane now, flying.'

Hanan got up and padded round the dark flat. Bisan wasn't there. A few hours later, a photo message arrived: Bisan on the tarmac at Athens airport in front of an Aegean Airlines plane, her arms flung above her head in triumph as she was about to board.

With all her children now in countries with functioning asylum systems, Hanan knew the time had come for her to leave. It had been nearly two years since her family had begun their dangerous migration. Now there was just one thing left to do: get herself across Europe to be with her children again. Talal's darker, traditional Arabian looks made it almost impossible to board a plane on false papers, so he had to remain in Athens and try to find a different way to get to Europe. Hanan, however, knew she could pull it off. She went to an Iraqi smuggler for the last passport she needed, and tried to act casual, even as her insides turned themselves in knots with the need to see her children again. She knew how to play the game now – the family had been cheated so many times.

'I don't care if I get a passport or not, I can wait,' she told him. The nonchalance worked: within an hour he called with two possible passports for her. With her pale skin and brown hair she could just about pass for Western, but she could only haggle so much over the price.

'All I have left is €1,500,' Hanan told the smuggler. He accepted, and Hanan became an Australian woman called Victoria for the final leg of her journey to Vienna.

The smuggler urged her to change her hair and her clothes, but Hanan was back in control. Better to be yourself, because it is the most convincing disguise there is.

'Leave everything to me, I will make it work,' she told him.

'I believe you will travel,' he replied. 'You are a strong woman.'

With those words in her heart, Hanan bade goodbye to Talal and travelled to the airport. But as she approached the first security checkpoint at the airport, she felt her strength ebbing away. After the boys' journey, she knew they needed her. Riad was too young for some of the hardships he had experienced. Now was not the time for the font of emotion and exhaustion that had been building up over all those hard months to spill to the surface. So why were her legs trembling beneath her and her heart thumping so hard against her chest that she could hardly breathe? Retreating to the ladies' toilet at Athens airport, Hanan faced the woman in the mirror.

'I will be strong,' she told herself. 'Why wouldn't I pass? I will pass. I am stronger than the police. I travel all the time, why worry now? I must make them believe me.'

Hanan washed her face in the sink and marshalled her courage.

Now with steady legs, she was ready for the boarding gate and the searching gaze of the police officer.

After passing security successfully, she headed to the gate, and even when she saw the three police officers, she held her nerve. She remembered the smuggler's advice: 'Don't be the first one to board. You must wait. Wait for five people to board, and then go.'

Hanan needed a distraction. Scanning the departure lounge, her eyes alighted on her target: a middle-aged couple. The seat next to them was free, and Hanan joined them and started to make small talk, sharing jokes she would not remember later, making them laugh as she was boiling up with fear inside. She kept up the banter when the flight began boarding, and all the way to the gate, where a police officer looked at her and asked to see her ID.

Hanan remained aloof, rummaging in her handbag to evade the eyes of her interrogator.

'OK, go on,' the officer said casually, unaware of the magnitude of relief her words delivered.

'Thank you.'

When Hanan found her seat on the plane, she was cold from head to toe. She could not believe in her escape until the wheels left the runway and the plane climbed away from Greece, and away from the indignity, the neglect, the prejudice, the hatred, and all the greed.

When I have money I will come back to Athens, she thought. *And when I see one of the smugglers, I will tell them 'fuck you and fuck your mother'*.

Hanan al-Hasan arrived in Vienna on 16 March 2014. There were no passport checks, so she went straight to the taxi rank and gave the driver the address of her sons' refugee centre. When she arrived, she explained that she was Syrian and wanted to claim asylum. Then she held her sons again for the first time in two months, and she held them tight. When she had to leave, she went to a refugee centre for adults and registered herself. Afterwards, she walked onto the bright street outside, looked up at the sky, and her body finally gave up.

There on the outskirts of Vienna, a tiny, fierce Syrian woman crumpled to the ground like burning paper.

17

A Lifeline Cut Off

Majid: Rome, Italy

Every morning when Majid Hussain opened his eyes and stared at the ceiling of his bedroom in a squat in Rome, the same thought played on the edges of his mind.

I am a man without a home.

In the two and a half years since the young Nigerian had walked ashore on Lampedusa, he felt that his identity had been slowly stripped away, until all that was left was a shell, a person known only by the labels he had grown to despise: *refugee, foreigner, immigrant, outsider.*

Majid would pull himself out of bed and try to remember who he was deep inside. He had another day to get through, with all the struggles it entailed: to pay the rent, to find work, to get enough money to eat, to not let anger at the past consume him.

Every memory of his humiliating crawl through Italy's asylum system brought a shudder. First there had been the degrading strip search and the officials snapping at his misery with their mobile phones. Next he was herded into the island's refugee camp, with only a small space on the concrete floor to rest between all the weary bodies. For three days, he followed the orders of nameless camp guards, his somnolent mind barely aware of his surroundings as he lined up for food and queued for the bathroom. On the fourth day, buses arrived and he was back at the Lampedusa dock, boarding a huge cruise liner to a destination he remained ignorant of.

It was the kind of boat which would take middle-class Italians off for a comfortable fortnight at sea, but the refugees did not sleep in the cabins. Their accommodation was the huge hall where paying passengers would have enjoyed balls and banquets. For its temporary guests, there was not even a mattress or blanket. Majid slept on the floor for six nights as the ship slowly made its way up the Italian coast, disgorging its disorientated cargo at various ports. The refugees and migrants were being scattered in camps across the country, most of them straining to provide for the growing numbers of people seeking a safe place.

Majid had disembarked at the port of Civitavecchia just up the coast from Rome, but still no one told him where he was going or what was happening. Ali, his friend and housemate in Tripoli, stayed on the ship as it continued its journey north. Majid did not bother asking anyone if they could stay together. He didn't know who to ask, and he suspected they probably wouldn't care anyway.

His first home in Italy was an abandoned military base in the countryside outside Civitavecchia, where hundreds of men, women and children were living in the barracks designed for young Italian soldiers. Majid looked around as the gates closed behind him – there were no windows, and mosquitoes bothered the air around his head. But on the floor stretched out before him in a hall were beds. After ten days, finally he could get a decent night's sleep. Over the next few years, he would come to look back on that soft mattress as a rare comfort.

The next day, each person was given a white T-shirt and blue shorts, a uniform which made Majid feel like a prisoner. Since his father's death he had tried so hard to hold on to his humanity, but now his identity was threatened too. He could live with the shabby rooms and the bad food and cold water, but he could not bear being treated like a criminal when he had been forced to this country against his will. The Italians had channelled money to Gaddafi when it suited them, and then turned on him and supported the NATO bombing campaign, invoking his spiteful revenge. But why should Majid be punished for the follies of Europe? It made no sense.

A few days after he arrived, a lawyer showed up. But she did not explain what would happen to Majid, or what he was entitled to in Italy. She just told him that they would take his fingerprints again, and asked him to sign a piece of paper. Then she left.

In October, Majid was moved to a refugee centre in a suburb of Rome. Unlike the military camp, the building was designed to house civilians, and the facilities were a little better. But the treatment remained the same. As his application slowly wound its way through the overstretched Italian bureaucratic system, Majid slept in a room with five other people and gave up control over every aspect of his life. His first permit of stay arrived on 17 October 2011, but he could not work or live outside the camp. If he wanted to leave, he had to sign out. When he returned, he had to sign in. He had to sign a piece of paper to eat a meal. Not that the meals were edible – everyone got sick with a stomach bug.

Every aspect of Majid's life was being monitored, day in and day out. It was a system designed to make you feel like a nobody – all these rules for no reason, every piece of paper stamped with a long number.

They always try and let you know you are an immigrant, he thought. *When someone identifies you as a number – not by your name – you know who you are.*

Once, he was called for an interview about his asylum application. A man sat impassively behind a desk and Majid felt powerless, his fate entirely in this stranger's hands.

'Tell me your story,' the man said.

To Majid, the implication was clear: make up what you want to tell me and I will choose whether to believe you, and whether you can stay.

'What story? You need a story? I am not a story,' he replied.

I don't only hate Italians, I hate all Europeans, Majid thought.

He realized that he needed a good lawyer, so he signed out of the camp and found one himself, and in the process discovered some compassion. She never asked him for his story, but listened patiently as he explained everything that had happened to him from that morning of 9 January 2009 when he lost his father. She explained the asylum process, and finally he understood what he had to do. He just did not realize it would take so long. Italy was overwhelmed by the number of people arriving, and there was nothing he could do to speed the process up.

Majid was finally granted asylum in 2013. He left the camp in Rome in July that year, having spent nearly two years in stasis, waiting to find out whether the authorities believed him or not.

Now he was twenty-one years old, and he had to build a life. But there was so little to base it on. There was a reason why people tried to claim asylum anywhere other than Italy. As well as the length of time it could take to process an application, once a person had refugee status they were on their own. There were no social benefits, nor was there any housing allowance for refugees in Italy. There was another camp Majid could have gone to, but he had had enough of being treated like a child, of people trying to control him.

For months Majid travelled between Italian cities, trying to find a job. Nothing worked out, and he returned to Rome, where he came into contact with a collective which offered social assistance to anyone who needed it. There among the excited, politically active young Italians, he finally found people who treated him as an individual, not a number.

In mid-2014 he accepted an invitation from members of the collective to move into an empty townhouse they had occupied in Pigneto, an old working-class neighbourhood which attracted the city's artists and bohemians with its low rents and crumbling charm. The façade of the squat was typical of the area: three floors of faded ochre, bright green shutters and an imposing door under a Roman arch, plastered with posters for socialist gatherings and trade union rallies.

Mattresses and barricades were piled just inside the door, preparation for a potential raid by police trying to reclaim the empty property. But most of the time, the doors were open and people from the neighbourhood were welcome to drop by and use a book exchange. A few times a month, the squat – which they called Point Break – would host drop-in sessions for legal advice.

Majid shared the house with Italians and a Frenchman, and had a cheery room on the ground floor with a red sofa, a shelf full of books, and posters by the American artist Keith Haring on the wall. His housemates were like family and helped him out as much as they could, but he still needed some money for food and clothes, and finding work was difficult in a country where more than forty per cent of young people were unemployed. Jobs would go to the Italians first – unless the company had a motive for hiring someone desperate for work and easily exploitable.

For a few months Majid worked as a security guard at a park, sitting in the cold from 8 p.m. to 8 a.m. watching over a monument under restoration. After a month, no pay cheque arrived.

'Sorry, we are having problems with our bank, we'll pay you in thirty days,' someone at the office told him. A month passed and still the money did not arrive. The lawyers he knew at the collective managed to get him his pay cheque, but that was the end of that job.

Towards the end of 2014, Majid managed to find work as a social worker at a refugee camp on the outskirts of Rome. He liked the job. It made him feel useful, which was not something he had felt very often since arriving in Europe. With the children and young people, he could empathize and help them work through their feelings of alienation and pain. But he kept seeing echoes of the cycle of violence he left behind in Nigeria, especially in the eyes of the Syrian children. That sudden loss of family, of that safe and secure childhood which is meant to be your base for a lifetime's peace. Instead they had been uprooted and seen terrible violence and turmoil at home and on their journey into Europe. What scared Majid was the anger – both in him and in others.

These are children, they have lost their families, they watched their parents die, he thought. *They escaped just like me, but they will grow up, and the anger in them will make them want to take revenge.*

Majid had spoken to a psychologist once to try and understand what had happened to him and its impact. It had helped a little, but in the end he fell back upon his own method. Accept that his past was a part of him, and put everything that happened to him in a box inside himself and lock it away. This helped him get through the day, but it could alienate other people. A few girlfriends came and went, but there was no room in his heart for trust any more. If he had a problem, he would keep it bottled up. But that didn't work in a relationship, so he ended up alone again.

Majid was able to share these experiences with the young refugees at the camp, but he was also bristling at the tasks he was asked to do. All those years he spent in camps, he had felt like the staff were there to control him in a system geared towards financial profit for the management at the expense of the refugee. Now he was part of that system, waking the residents in the morning and asking them to scrub the floors when the allowance from the government should have paid for a cleaner. He tried to be gentle with the refugees, knowing how much they needed kindness and care. His generosity had not gone unnoticed: the manager had already warned him about being too soft, and Majid did not expect his six-month contract to be renewed. He had nothing else lined up.

Now that he had a travel document he could work in another European country, but he was stuck in a catch-22. Italy had no jobs, but to work in another country he would need a permit. To get that permit he first needed a job. So in theory he could go to a country like Germany with more opportunities, search for a job, then return to Italy with the job offer and apply for a work permit at the German embassy. But where would he get the money for the trip? And why would a German company hire someone it could not employ straight away? No wonder some people gave up and took whatever opportunities arose, legal or not.

Soon after Majid had arrived in Rome, an Italian man had approached him on the street.

'Do you have a job?' he asked.

'No, I don't even have my documents,' Majid replied.

The man was unconcerned.

'It doesn't matter, I can give you a job,' he said. 'In a month I will pay you €2,800. You can't find any other job which will give you this money.'

For a moment, Majid was excited.

'What kind of job is this?'

The man told him, and Majid felt deflated again.

'OK, I will think about it.'

For three days the man kept calling Majid, but he did not answer his phone. He had no intention of selling drugs on the street, but he understood why some people might. Majid had no family, no children to feed, no one back home to try and support. If he had, perhaps he would have considered it. It would be better than allowing his family to be on the street.

It's not their fault, Majid thought about those who had no other option.

If the government provided for refugees, or cracked down on the companies exploiting them, people would not be forced to take extreme measures. The foreigners always got the blame. The Italians ran the drugs trade and exploited the refugees and migrants, but it was always the person at the end of the chain who ended up being accused by right-wing politicians of endangering the country.

Majid was so tired of the rhetoric.

'You are here to steal our jobs.'

He heard that so often on the television, in the newspapers. He wanted to speak out, to try and make them understand. His happy, comfortable life had turned upside down in the few minutes it took for his father to bleed to death in front of the chicken coops. Now people were telling him that he left his home to steal their jobs. Why wouldn't they listen? He despaired of the mismanagement, the corruption, the Mafia, the racist words of the far-right politicians.

Majid's frustration found an outlet in the political gatherings he attended with other members of the collective, and in the marches where he would shout for more rights for migrants and refugees. But he was not always convinced by some of his friends' fine words for democracy, and by their criticism of Colonel Muammar Gaddafi.

'Do you know anything about the government there?' he would ask.

Democracy was a nice concept, but the only country where he had felt safe – Libya – had been a dictatorship. Then so many people had died to install democracy there, and it hadn't even worked. Now he was in Europe, the cradle of democracy, and he had never been treated with such contempt in his life.

Here is the democracy that people are dying to have, he thought. *This is democracy where nobody respects you, and you don't even have dignity.*

The European Union could keep their democracy, this democracy they preached far and wide, this respect for human rights which they used as bait for nations wanting to join the bloc, a bargaining chip in trade negotiations, and a stick to beat their foes with.

At the start of the year, the crisis in Ukraine had revived

Cold War battle lines, and when Russia annexed the Black Sea peninsula of Crimea in March, EU officials did not shy away from drawing additional historical parallels with the Second World War and the Nazi invasion of Poland. It was pitched as a battle between the EU's forces of peace and democracy and the Kremlin's authoritarianism and brutality. All the while, a humanitarian disaster and the EU's biggest moral challenge since the Second World War was brewing on its borders, and it was simply letting people die.

There is only one good thing that the Italians have done, Majid thought: *Mare Nostrum.*

By the end of 2014, Italian sailors had pulled more than 100,000 people from their dangerous vessels on the Mediterranean Sea, and taken the men, women and children to safety in Italian ports. The refugees then had to either navigate Italy's overburdened asylum system or dodge border guards on a mission to get further north, but at least they were not drowning. The death toll in 2014 was still immense – a record 3,500 people would die attempting to reach Europe, most perishing in the crossing from Libya – but without Mare Nostrum it would have been much higher.

The operation was costing Italy at least €8 million a month, a significant figure in a country with faltering economic growth. Throughout 2014, the Italians asked again and again for help from the other EU nations, arguing that the people arriving on their shores were hoping to travel to the wealthier northern European countries. Therefore the cost of saving them and the responsibility for re-housing them should be shared across the EU. The Italian navy sent filmmakers on board the rescue vessels, and made glossy videos of Italian sailors lifting bundled babies to safety from the arms of weeping mothers, grateful travellers packed shoulder to shoulder in rubber dinghies clapping in relief as help arrived, families falling to their knees on the decks of frigates.

The films were designed to move even the hardest heart. Politicians' heads, however, were not so easily swayed. As the Italians were out at sea rescuing 270 people a day, leaders across the continent turned away. A British government minister suggested that funding search-and-rescue operations encouraged more people to make the journey, provoking outrage and accusations that Britain was advocating letting people die as a deterrent. The outcry made no difference: there were no funds, there were no pledges of frigates or planes, no serious suggestions that other countries would house some of the refugees arriving in Italy, Greece or Malta.

So the Italians gave up. At the end of October, Mare Nostrum was cancelled. Once again the boats packed to the gunwales with the world's most desperate people set off from Libya and entered choppy waters where there were no vessels to save them. They would travel unseen among the merchant ships, fishing fleets and holiday yachts, sinking away from the eyes of Europe.

In the place of Mare Nostrum, the EU's border agency Frontex launched Operation Triton, named after the mythological sea god with a miraculous conch shell which could calm stormy seas and recall waves and rivers. Legend had it that Triton had also appeared at Lake Tritonis in Libya, and led the lost ship of the Argonauts back safely to the Mediterranean Sea.

The EU maritime operation which borrowed Triton's name and launched on 1 November 2014 had neither sea-calming powers nor the authority to go anywhere near Libya.

Triton operated on less than a third of the budget of Mare Nostrum. It had fewer ships, helicopters and personnel, and was only permitted to venture thirty nautical miles off the Italian coast, leaving huge swathes of the Mediterranean unmonitored. Mare Nostrum had stretched all the way into Libyan waters, covering an area of 73,000 square kilometres. Triton was certainly not the search-and-rescue operation from Cyprus to Spain that had once been promised on the shores of Lampedusa.

UN officials and human rights groups warned that Europe was condemning thousands more people to death. But nothing was having an impact on the political debate – not the videos of the babies saved by the Italian navy; not the statisticians predicting that the numbers of people trying to reach Europe would swell every month; not the Islamic State atrocities; not the warnings from the World Food Programme that refugees were facing a winter of starvation in Turkey and Lebanon; not the booming kidnapping and extortion rackets in Libya; not the horrors of life in Eritrea.

But those escaping the world's horrors were not a passive mass willing to wait until the European Union re-discovered its values. Millions of people had their own powerful drive to get their families to safety, and they would keep moving whether Europe put boats in the water to save them or not. The risk of death was worth taking for the chance that they could live in peace.

In the year to come, the belief that scaling back search-and-rescue operations would stop these people trying to get to Europe would prove to be a misjudgement with tragic consequences.

2015

Number of refugees and migrants entering the EU: 1,004,356
Number of deaths: 3,771

18

Ghosts on the Horizon

Sina: Eritrea–Sudan border

On 1 January 2015, two Orthodox Christians sat eating dinner dressed in Muslim clothing at a small Sudanese restaurant just over the border from Eritrea. Underneath her black hijab, Sina Habte was glowing. *We are free.*

'Thanks to God,' she said to Dani, 'we are safe now – there is no military.'

At midnight the couple had hidden among the New Year's revellers by the main cathedral in Asmara, then slipped unseen into a smuggler's car. Dani knew what a dash on foot over the border meant, and he was not risking the life of his wife and unborn child running that gauntlet of bullets and barricades. His $30-a-month military allowance would not have been enough to pay for safe passage, but his family had been so generous over the years that Dani had been able to put a little aside each time his father pressed some more dollars into his palm. Now, 6,000 of those dollars had paid for a six-hour drive in a Land Cruiser with fake number plates, which allowed the smugglers to get them into Sudan without even having to show their forged documents.

Sitting for an hour quietly enjoying their meal, Sina and Dani shared a rare moment of peace. The road ahead was daunting. They didn't have any plans beyond staying alive and getting their baby as far away from Eritrea as possible. Neither Sina nor Dani had left Eritrea since their abrupt eviction from Ethiopia as children. The only life they knew was the tightly controlled dictatorship which forbade independent choice. To have been released from that dreadful but predictable existence was as frightening as it was empowering. Now their lives were in the hands of a smuggler they had only met a few hours ago, but so far their trust appeared well founded.

Their car had sailed through the border, and the smuggler had supplied the black dress for Sina and the white robes for Dani which would disguise them as Sudanese Muslims for the last part of their two-day journey from Asmara to Khartoum.

When they arrived in the Sudanese capital, Sina bristled at the local custom which dictated that she must stay inside while Dani walked the streets, but it was only a few days before they were on the move again. Another $800 bought them a drive across South Sudan. The country had only declared independence from Sudan in 2011, but was already engulfed in ethnic strife and a power struggle between rebel factions, another of the many civil wars sending yet more refugees on the road. Sina saw nothing of the conflict as the forests and villages passed the window, her thoughts turning inward. The roads were unpaved, and as they bumped over them at 180 kilometres per hour her hand would move protectively to her belly. Even expectant mothers in the safest places in the world feared for the mysterious life growing inside them, and there were moments when the movement within would stop and she would grab Dani's arm.

'What has happened to my baby? Something has happened,' she would say, before the familiar lurch of the tiny body and a heel in her ribcage brought relief.

The bumpy drive would prove to have been relatively comfortable compared with the next stage of their journey. The only way across the border to Uganda was on foot, but Sina didn't complain. All those marches during military service and the hardships of life in the field as a chemical engineer had prepared her well, and she followed Dani and the smuggler through thick forest tracts for two hours. When they reached Uganda, she gratefully sank into the car which would take them to the capital.

Travelling from Asmara to Kampala had taken six days, and now they had time to rest, to gather their thoughts and prepare for their next leap away from everything they knew.

The further the couple took their baby from Eritrea, the better they felt. But such was their fear of the Eritrean regime that they could sense its shadow, even in Uganda. Sina had heard that the intelligence agencies could track people down across sub-Saharan Africa, so they needed to keep moving. And where in Kampala could she give birth? All their savings were going towards their journey, and there was no medical insurance covering her for a room in a comfortable private hospital. Sina and Dani contacted a smuggler called Kibrat. For $14,000, he would prepare everything for their passage to Turkey, but he warned it could take a while.

The weeks passed, and Sina's belly grew. The couple tried not to worry, and Dani did everything he could to reassure his wife. He cleaned and cooked in the small flat they rented, and Sina burst out laughing when he offered to feed her as well.

'I don't want you to do anything with your hands!' he insisted.

At night Dani would trawl the Internet for articles about pregnancy and birth. Sina was relieved. She knew nothing about having a baby and being a mother, so she let Dani take charge.

'Sina, you have to walk for half an hour a day,' he would say, as they set off on a brisk march through Kampala.

'Sina, you must eat this kind of fruit, you must drink milk and drink water,' he told her. So she let him prepare her healthy drinks and drained the glasses he put in front of her.

You can't compare this man to anyone else, she thought, enchanted as always by his energy and enthusiasm. Fatherhood was going to suit him.

After two months, Kibrat called. Their fake passports were

ready, and the couple could continue their journey and fly to Istanbul that coming Sunday – 16 March. His call came just in time: Sina was eight months pregnant and starting to worry that she would never reach a safe place in time to give birth. Then on Saturday, Kibrat called back. There had been a change of plan. Sina would have to fly alone and Dani would follow a few days later.

'You have to go now,' he said. 'You are pregnant, and very pregnant people can't fly.'

His advice seemed to make sense, so on Sunday morning Dani and Sina got into a car to go to the airport. Just before the passenger drop-off point, Kibrat pulled over – Sina had to enter the airport alone. The couple held each other by the roadside.

'Take care of yourself,' Dani said.

Sina just smiled – she would see him again in a few days. Her car was waiting.

She felt no nerves when she showed security staff her fake passport and the hospital certificate incorrectly stating that she was six months pregnant. The airport officials had been paid off too, and soon she was in the air retracing her route back over Uganda, South Sudan, Sudan and Eritrea as she flew towards Istanbul. Her only concern was that the altitude might induce labour or harm her baby, but the little life form carried on kicking, reassuring her that he was there and he was fine.

When she landed, an Eritrean smuggler called Mehari was waiting for her at the airport. For a week, Sina stayed in Mehari's filthy apartment waiting for Dani.

But Dani never came.

Kibrat had stopped answering his phone. After a week, his number was disconnected. He had disappeared with the money, and Dani was left alone and penniless in Kampala, just a voice at the end of the phone promising Sina he was doing everything he could to get back to her.

Within a week, the promise of their new life together which

had begun with such hope on New Year's Day was beginning to collapse.

Sina and Dani were not the only ones whose journey to Europe was running into difficulty. The situation for those already trying to cross by sea was becoming increasingly treacherous. In the first few days of 2015, the Italian coastguard detected a freighter adrift off the Turkish coast. Flying the flag of Sierra Leone, the *Ezadeen* was rusting and old. It had bars along the bulwarks to stop sheep and cattle from leaping into the sea, but the vessel had long ago been decommissioned for livestock. To the smugglers, that made it perfect for human beings. They packed it with 350 migrants and refugees and set the huge vessel on course for the Italian coast without a captain. The *Ezadeen* listed in the rough winter seas as it sailed blindly towards Europe, forcing an Italian coastguard helicopter to make a precarious landing on the deck and seize control. An Icelandic coastguard ship – one of the few vessels donated to the EU's Operation Triton – then towed the freighter to Italy.

It was the second ghost ship approaching Europe's shore that week. A few days earlier, a Moldavian cargo ship, the *Blue Sky M*, was just forty-five minutes from running aground in Corfu with 900 people on board when the Italians took control.

With Mare Nostrum no longer operating in the further reaches of the Mediterranean, the smugglers adopted new tactics: abandon the ships once they were out at sea in the belief that Europe would only pay attention if they sent passengers in extreme peril right to their doorstep. British officials had predicted that demand for the journey would diminish when there was no search-and–rescue mission to pick the boats up. But more people than ever were trying to get to Europe, and for the first time large numbers were risking the journey in winter months when the elements were against them.

Every day now, refugees limped off the leaking fishing vessels coming from North Africa, their feet beaten and their bodies broken by the Libyan smuggling gangs. Some people had been forced on to boats against their will, their protests that the sea was too rough met by the rifle butts of fighters determined to make room for the next wave of people paying around $1,500 a head.

With Mare Nostrum no longer venturing into Libyan waters, boats also had to travel further in freezing conditions before coastguards spotted them. Children disembarked shivering with fever. On 9 February, twenty-nine people died of hypothermia on the deck of a small Italian coastguard vessel. Giusi Nicolini, the mayor of Lampedusa, said the tragedy would never have happened a year ago.

'The small patrol boats were completely swallowed by the waves during the trip back,' he said. 'If Mare Nostrum were still going, the migrants would have been given shelter inside a large ship within an hour.'

Between January and March, arrivals in Europe were up forty-five per cent on the same period in 2014, and at least 480 people had died during the crossing, in comparison with fifty in these same months a year earlier.

Europe's leaders noted the trend, but took little action. Operation Triton was extended until the end of the year, but its resources remained the same – woefully inadequate to deal with the disaster unfolding at sea. How many more people would have to die before the European Union acted? The answer was 800.

At around 11 p.m. on Saturday 18 April, hundreds of people boarded an unusually large fishing vessel in Libya. Just like on every other boat that was setting sail under the grey winter skies, its passengers were filled with a mixture of emotions: hope that their journey away from war would soon be over; fear of the voyage and the sea; denial that tragedy could befall their boat.

When people had been packed into every cranny of the vessel's deck and two floors in the hull, the smugglers locked the doors to stop those fated to make the journey in the dark from trying to make it up to the fresh air on deck.

It took less than a day at sea before the three-storey trawler started to list under the weight of so many bodies, and a smuggler issued a distress call. The only vessel nearby and able to respond was the *King Jacob*, a Portuguese-flagged merchant ship. Without professional search and rescue boats stationed across the Mediterranean, the crews of commercial ships frequently found themselves saving lives, dragging drowning people onto their decks despite being ill equipped for such tasks.

There was not much the crew of the *King Jacob* could do when the inexperienced captain of the fishing trawler accidentally rammed their hull. The impact sent the smaller, overcrowded vessel tipping to one side. The refugees surged to the other side to try and right the craft, and the boat was quickly swallowed by the waves, along with all but twenty-eight of the people on board. It was midnight on 19 April, and by the time the Italian navy arrived there was not much they could do but sift through the discarded clothes in the petrol-soaked sea looking for the bodies of the victims.

With an estimated 800 people dead – no one was sure of the exact toll as there was no passenger manifest and most of the bodies could not be recovered – it was the worst disaster of its kind on the Mediterranean. The UN's High Commissioner for Refugees warned that more blood would be on the hands of EU leaders unless they acted.

'This disaster confirms how urgent it is to restore a robust rescue-at-sea operation and establish credible legal avenues to reach Europe,' António Guterres said. 'Otherwise people seeking safety will continue to perish at sea.'

Between 1 November 2014, when Mare Nostrum stopped running, and the end of April 2015, 1,866 people died trying to cross the Mediterranean. In the same period a year earlier, when the Italian navy boats scoured the sea, the death toll had been 108.

Finally, on 23 April, the European Union's twenty-eight heads of government met in Brussels to discuss ways to respond to prevent further tragedies. They tripled the budget for Operation Triton, expanded its scope to within 138 nautical miles of the Sicilian coast, and fifteen countries, including France and Germany, offered air and sea assets to patrol the waters for vessels in distress. Britain, which had previously only offered one technical expert to Operation Triton, now sent a Royal Navy ship, HMS *Bulwark*, to help save lives which finally seemed to matter.

The brief restoration of Europe's humanitarian spirit came too late for Sina.

Mehari arrived at the apartment in Istanbul and told her to get ready to travel to Greece on the same morning that the 800 bodies locked in the hold of the doomed fishing vessel sank to the bottom of the sea. Sina had no idea about the tragedy unfolding halfway between North Africa and Europe, or about the soul-searching in Brussels and other capitals across the EU. Her own personal tragedy was consuming her: Dani was 3,000 miles away and their baby was coming. Sina had visited a private clinic a few days earlier. Her due date of 15 April had passed, and she was worried that the six-hour flight from Kampala may have harmed her child. The doctor reassured her: he was fine, and ready to come out.

'You will deliver your baby within three days,' the Turkish doctor said on the morning of 17 April, a Friday, telling her how to contact the hospital and how to ask for help.

That night, tears streamed down Sina's face as she spoke to Dani. Everything scared her – the birth, becoming a mother alone, the smuggler, the sea.

'You are so much better than me, I know nothing of these things,' she told him.

But there was nothing Dani could say but promise her once again that he was doing everything in his power to get to her. Since arriving in Istanbul, Sina had pleaded with Mehari to put them in contact with Kibrat, but he claimed not to know where Kibrat was any more than they did. Dani's parents sent some more money, but it wasn't enough to buy another set of documents and a ticket to Turkey.

When Mehari came to the flat on Sunday and told her it was time to go, there was no one to help her make such a huge decision about her life and the life of her unborn child.

'I am waiting to deliver my baby,' she explained. 'The three days the doctor told me are nearly up. Friday has already passed, Saturday has passed – tomorrow I will deliver my baby.'

'If you deliver in the morning, OK,' Mehari replied. 'But if in the morning you seem fine it's better to go because it only takes one hour to reach Greece and the ship is not a small one, it is a big one, so it is safe.'

Sina called Dani again, and once again he told her to follow the doctor's instructions, to stay in Istanbul until the baby came.

But when she took her doubts back to Mehari he brushed them aside and insisted that an hour at sea would do no harm.

'Sina, you have to leave.'

Sina couldn't call Dani again. She had to trust her instinct, so she chose to believe the Eritrean in front of her. Perhaps he was a good man, and he seemed so sure that it was a short, safe trip. And there was one overriding emotion about Turkey clouding all other thoughts.

I hate everything here.

It was the country where she had been separated from Dani, and now she had a chance to escape.

Before she left the apartment, Sina looked at Dani's number on her phone. She did not dial it. He didn't need to know where she was going. She would spare him the worry. Better to call him when she arrived in Greece, safe and settling into a clean European hospital ready to deliver their child. Then the first words he heard from her would be good news, the first good news she'd been able to share since they were separated in Kampala.

Sina gathered her few belongings and boarded a small bus on Sunday evening. Before setting off for the coast, the driver made a tour of the many smuggling houses of Istanbul, stopping at one apartment after another to pick up more passengers. By the time the bus left Istanbul for the ten-hour drive, the windows were steaming up and Sina struggled to breathe. People squeezed between the seats, others stood in the narrow aisle, but the windows had to remain closed: if the police saw how many people were on the bus they would surely stop them.

As the crowded bus trundled on, Sina starting chatting to her fellow Eritrean travellers. Selam, a thirty-seven-year-old house-wife from Asmara, was travelling alone with her six-year-old son Elyud. She too was trying to reach a country where her boy could grow up free from the threat of military service and the fear of arrest. Selam had family in Sweden and Norway, but anywhere safe would do. Just like Sina, she had faced a difficult journey to Turkey. There was not enough money for both Selam and her husband to travel to Europe, so they decided that Selam would take their only child and her husband would follow later – if he was able to escape his military service. Despite her own worries about the journey ahead, Selam took the time to soothe Sina's concerns.

'You don't have to worry, your baby is safe, you will be OK,' she told her.

Sina was also reassured by the presence of another pregnant woman, although Nigisti's belly was considerably smaller than her own. Then there was David, a young man who seemed to have a kind heart. And despite their hardship, the travellers shared moments of humour. After a few hours on the road, a woman near Sina asked to go to the toilet. The driver refused to stop, despite voices of protest rippling through the bus.

'What should we do?' 'She wants to go to the toilet.' 'Stop!'

The bus drove on, so Sina and some others covered the woman with their coats as she relieved herself in a plastic bag. Sina couldn't help laughing, but two hours later, she too had to suffer the indignity of a toilet break on a crowded bus.

When the bus finally pulled up at the side of the road near the Turkish port of Marmaris, its exhausted passengers barely had time to shake the cramp from their legs before they were marched off into the forest. For two hours, Sina struggled over rocks and battled through the tree branches which blocked their path. A cramp seized her belly. She didn't know if it was a contraction or a muscle spasm as the long walk took its toll on her nine-months-pregnant body, but the tears had started to flow and would not stop. She tried to stifle the sobs of regret. How could she have believed Mehari over her own Dani? The Eritreans gathered around her in the dark and tried to comfort her.

'Don't worry, you will be safe, Sina, you will be OK,' David told her. Their support helped a little, and Sina struggled on until finally they pushed aside the last branches and the sea was in front of them. It was 4 a.m. and the ship which would take them to Europe had not arrived yet, so she sank to the sand and waited.

She barely had time to catch her breath when a voice rang out.

'Hey everybody, stand up, stand up, the ship is coming. We are going.'

When Sina looked out to sea, she saw a wooden sailing boat about thirty metres long approach the beach. For a moment, she could not speak – it looked so old, its naked masts reaching into the darkness and rocking the boat back and forth in the low swell. David turned to one of the smugglers.

'She is pregnant – how can we travel with this kind of boat?' he said. 'She can't travel like this. Where is the ship?'

The smuggler shrugged.

'If you want, you can go, if you don't want to go, you can stay here on the beach.'

David and Sina decided to call Mehari.

'You don't have to worry,' Mehari reassured them. 'The large ship can't reach the shore because it is so big. So this small one will take you to the middle of the sea and you will change to the big one. There will be life jackets on there as well.'

Once again, Sina trusted Mehari, and with David's help, she boarded the swaying craft.

We would never reach Greece in this boat, she thought, relieved that a sturdier ship was on the horizon. Sina went down to the hold and retreated to the darkest corner she could find, as they lurched into the waves with ninety-six Syrians and Eritreans on board.

All the deceit became clear when more than an hour had passed – the hour that Mehari said it would take to reach Greece. Instead, the waves seemed to be getting higher, and Sina realized there was no bigger boat, just as there were no life jackets, and just as there was never a passport or a plane ticket for Dani. Perhaps in her heart Sina always knew there was not going to be another ship. She had to believe the lie to get on the boat, as there was no one to accompany her on a two-hour trek back over the hills to the nearest road, to drive her for ten hours back to Istanbul, and to give her a place to stay and to look after her when the child arrived. Her room at Mehari's was probably already taken by another customer paying over the odds for their chance to make this wretched journey. Now that she was in the dark with her thoughts for company, Mehari's actions started to make sense. He told her to leave because he didn't want a room taken up by a woman and a baby when he could pack it with more paying travellers. It was all just money to him. How could she have thought he had the interests of her and her child at heart? The best she could do was to try and remain calm and do nothing that might bring on her labour in the middle of the sea.

Dani would be so afraid if he saw her now. All around Sina people were doubled over and vomiting in response to the violent rocking and the stink of rotten fish. As the boat tipped from side to side, the bodies crammed in the small space would skid in the stagnant water and the sick, and the stench was overwhelming.

Sina put her hands over her face, blocking out the sight, the sounds, the smell.

If I start to vomit, I will deliver my baby here.

When she peered through her fingers she saw Selam retching into her hands. Her little boy Elyud was throwing up too, but Selam was too sick to offer him much comfort. Sina covered her face again. All she could do was focus on keeping her baby inside her for a few hours more. The other pregnant woman, Nigisti, sat nearby. Every so often they would exchange a few words.

'How are you, Sina?'

'I'm fine, Nigisti, how are you?'

'I'm OK.'

Then Sina would retreat back into her dark corner, mentally isolating herself from all the suffering. And it was so hot down there in the hold. Sina was wearing two pairs of trousers, four T-shirts and a jacket. Mehari told her to wear all her clothes and only take a small bag. She needed to be light on her feet if the police chased her in Greece, he reasoned. But now she realized it just created more room on the boat if the passengers wore their clothes rather than lugged heavy bags – more room for a few more bodies and a few more dollars.

Eventually, the flickering bulb which threw ghoulish shadows across the decaying wood went out. Darkness enveloped the hold just as people started to notice the seawater seeping through the planks. Sina put her hand to the floor. Cold water pooled around the tyre where she sat. One after another the passengers realized that calamity was approaching, and cries of terror spread back and forth through the throng of people, an anguished call and response.

The boat inclined steeply to one side, and like on so many other doomed vessels, the panicked passengers hastened their fate by surging to the other side. The vessel rocked with greater ferocity, and a voice rang out in the dark.

'Stop moving! Everything is OK, this has happened because of the waves. Everything is fine. We are near the Greek coastline.'

Sina didn't know who said it – maybe the captain – but it made no difference. The panic intensified when the boat suddenly sped up, and the calm which had possessed Sina until that moment vanished, to be replaced with adrenalin as she braced her body against the wood.

The force of the waves flung the passengers back and forth in the hold, dozens of bodies colliding and shouting and slamming against worn boards. David and two other Eritrean boys held Sina down, trying to protect her and her unborn child from the violent manoeuvres of the boat.

Throughout the journey Sina had tried to ignore the sounds: the small motor churning beside her, the retching, the cries of panic and fear. But the worst sound of all was the sudden and load rattling followed by an almighty crack.

And then the boat stopped.

'We've reached Greece!' Sina heard someone near her shout. 'Bravo!'

But no victorious cries filtered through from the deck above. Some of the boys scrambled out of the hold to see what was happening. The morning light streamed in, along with a panicked voice.

'The boat is sinking! Come outside!'

Sina was confused.

What are they talking about? We've arrived, haven't we?

Then the boat tilted under her, and this time it did not right itself again. The arms of David and the other young Eritreans were around her, pulling her up and into the daylight. Hauled onto the deck, Sina could not believe what she saw.

We are almost dead.

The sailing boat was disintegrating beneath her feet: it had been ripped in two when it had attempted to turn at speed in the rough conditions. Huge waves tore parts of the boat away, and all Sina could hear was the sound of splintering wood – a racking, shuddering sound – and the cries of the people flinging themselves into the water. The coast was in sight, but it didn't matter now. Sina grabbed on to a rope dangling by her hand, and thought of Dani. All she wanted to do was say sorry.

He would have loved to have a child, and his father so wanted a grandchild, she thought. *I have hurt those people. They were praying to have a baby and instead of keeping my baby safe I have done this.*

Sina looked out to sea. Selam was already in the water, holding Elyud in front of her, the red bobble hat she had put on him to try and keep him warm clearly visible in the swell. Selam kicked her legs trying to reach the shore, using all the strength left in her body to get her child to safety. But Sina could see what Selam could not. Each wave sent more water into the terrified six-year-old boy's mouth, as he coughed and choked and thrashed in the sea.

Oh my god, this boy will die, Sina thought. *She can't reach the shore like this.*

Sina willed Selam to stop, to grab on to some wood, to wait for help. But her friend kept on kicking. Then David was beside Sina on the deck.

'Don't worry, we will be safe,' he said. 'We are very close to the beach. We don't have to worry. We will not die, I promise you.'

At that moment Sina felt the wood beneath her feet give way and slide into the water, taking her with it. First she went down, then up again, desperately trying to keep hold of the slippery rope. Then there was nothing to hold on to any more. She was in the water. Sina heard a voice.

'Please help us, we have a nine-month-pregnant woman, help her, she is here.'

Then everything went black.

*

Antonis Deligiorgis, a sergeant in the Greek army, had just dropped his six-year-old son and twelve-year-old daughter off at school and was having a coffee by Zefiros beach on the Greek island of Rhodes. His eyes lazily drifted over the brilliant blue of the Mediterranean, a little rough that day but still beautiful in the early-spring sunshine. He had seen plenty of suffering that year: Antonis had worked night-time rescues, saving people from the fragile inflatable dinghies to which they had entrusted their lives. But on 20 April at 9.30 a.m., he was off duty, and enjoying spending time with his wife.

He didn't see the tall sailing ship that had swerved in a tight turn to avoid the rocks on approach to Zefiros, the force of the manoeuvre snapping the craft in the middle. But by the time the sirens grew louder and crowds had gathered on the port, he was up and ready to do what he could.

'Whoever is a good swimmer can help,' a passing police officer shouted.

Antonis had spent his life by the sea and was built for the trials it could throw at a man. His bear-like shoulders could battle the current, and a generous bulk around his midriff now inured him to the cold. He did not hesitate before removing his shoes and jumping into the swell. As he pulled himself through the high waves, he thought about his children, he thought about his wife, but most of all he thought about getting to the drowning bodies in time.

When Antonis reached the wreck, the water was slick with oil and wood, and all around him screams battled to be heard over the roar of the waves. He saw wild eyes filled with terror; he saw panicked people vomiting into the water, their bodies trying to process the exhaustion, the mouthfuls of seawater, the fear of death. One by one, Antonis grabbed thrashing bodies and dragged them through the water to the shore: children, women, an old man missing a leg.

A heavily pregnant woman clung to a life jacket. She was close to the rocks, and her exhausted eyes darted with fear as she tried to battle the swell dragging her towards sharp crags. The waves had already churned up the wood and glass from the broken boat and ground them into her flesh. Antonis reached Sina just in time, pushing her into the arms of two men on the shore.

'Thank you, thank you,' Sina repeated over and over again, 'you are saving my life.'

Ninety-three Eritreans and Syrians were rescued that day, but Antonis remembered the ones who were lost. The middle-aged Syrian man he dragged all the way to shore repeated 'thank you' like a mantra to keep the panic at bay. But when they finally reached dry land, he grabbed his chest and fell to the ground, and the paramedics were unable to jolt his heart back to life. Antonis watched a small boy walk past as the medics covered the man with a white sheet.

'What happened?' the boy asked.

'He just died,' Antonis replied, shocked that a life could be saved and then lost in minutes.

Most people had survived because the boat broke up in daylight within yards of the Greek coastline, but three people perished: the Syrian man who died of the heart attack, and Selam and Elyud. The mother's battle through the waves to save her son had failed, and they drowned side by side. A Greek fisherman gently carried the limp body of Elyud ashore, the boy's red woollen hat still pulled tightly over his head.

The next day, a photograph of Antonis stripped to the waist and pulling a gasping Eritrean woman from the sea appeared on the front pages of British newspapers, an image of strong and powerful Europe coming to the aid of those in need. But the symbolism proved to be short-lived. The shores of the Greek island would be the year's killing ground. On Rhodes that day, a handful of life jackets were discarded on the beach, where soon there would be mountains of them all across the islands. One boy's body washed up on the shores, when soon dozens of dead children would be marooned on the rocks and sand.

But then there was also life.

Sina was taken straight to the hospital in Rhodes, where she was treated for cuts all over her body. Doctors kept her under observation for a couple of days while her body regained its strength, then took her to the operating theatre for a Caesarean section. On 23 April, Sina gave birth to a healthy baby boy. Andonis Georgis – named for his saviour – was born at 9 p.m. weighing 4.5 kilograms, strong like his mother and destined to keep her going through the days ahead.

19

At the Crossroads of Europe

Hanan: Vienna, Austria

When Hanan al-Hasan had arrived in Vienna more than a year ago, she had been obsessed with finding her sons. Now, even though Riad and Ismail were living with her, she marvelled at how much time she still spent chasing after them. At least she knew exactly where to find them: Platform 1 at Vienna's Westbahnhof. Almost every day she would stand on the concourse, craning her neck past the wall of officers guarding the train to Munich. As always, she was looking for Riad. He was here at all hours, a dedicated member of the team of volunteers working day and night at the station to help the newly arrived refugees. At last, Hanan spotted him. She strained on tiptoes and waved her arm to catch the attention of the teenager. Riad's round, puppyish face broke into a grin when he saw his mother beckoning and calling his name. The fifteen-year-old started walking along the platform towards her, making slow progress as he stopped to talk to all the people who touched his arm and asked him questions.

The platform was alive with activity. Across central Europe, people were on the move, and they had to do it quickly. The men, women and children escaping persecution and marching from Greece to northern Europe had to navigate a continent lurching between welcoming them and casting them aside, never sure whether the police force in the next country would fire tear gas at them or guide them to safety. The refugees were determined to get to their destination before another government sent in the army and put up a steel wall where an open border used to be, as the biggest movement of people across Europe since 1945 sent the continent into meltdown.

But in Vienna on that particular warm evening in early September 2015, the new arrivals found hospitality after the long, hard passage through Hungary. Volunteers rushed through the crowds with foil-wrapped sandwiches. Broad-shouldered police with their sidearms and blue berets kept their distance, their task limited to making sure there was no dangerous surge onto the trains heading west. The German Chancellor, Angela Merkel, had a few weeks ago suspended the Dublin Regulation and welcomed all Syrians seeking asylum, launching a rush of people across the continent towards this promised safe haven, a rare out-stretched hand in a summer of enmity.

Hanan was torn between pride in her son's compassion for the refugees, and motherly concern. The day before she had woken at 6 a.m. to discover that Riad was not in his bed. She had traipsed down to Westbahnhof to bring him home. Ismail was there at all hours as well, but he was a man now, and could make his own decisions. Riad, though, had to sleep. He had school on Monday. Suddenly her youngest son was showing his wilful side, arguing with his parents and disobeying their wishes in his determination to join the volunteers.

It had been the same story when Hanan called Riad that morning.

'Please, just come home and sleep for one hour.'

'I can't come home, Mama, there are too many people, I must help.'

Hanan understood the impulse to help those who were trying to find their feet in Europe. Her first few months in Austria had been so hard. After collapsing on the streets, she had been taken to hospital and diagnosed with low blood pressure. The doctor ordered her to remain there overnight for observation, but how could she stay in the hospital? Her body had been ravaged by the mental toil of getting her four children to safety. Now she was finally with her sons she was not going to spend a moment without them. When the doctor left the room, she took off the hospital gown, put her dress on, and went back to her boys.

For ten nights, Hanan had to stay at Traiskirchen refugee camp just outside Vienna, while Riad and Ismail remained in the children's camp. It was the first time since she and Talal had been married that she had had to sleep alone, and she was frightened. It was a new city, a new culture, a new language, and she was by herself in a dormitory with seven unoccupied beds. Traiskirchen was empty. It would not remain that way for long though: a year and a half later, 1,500 refugees, including babies and pregnant women, would be sleeping in the open air on its grounds. The number of people uprooted from their homes and gathering at Europe's gates had been growing for years, but when they finally started moving, Austria was one of the many rich nations utterly taken aback and incapable of coordinating an adequate response. 'Inhumane' would be how a UNHCR official described the conditions at Traiskirchen, as men and women were forced to take showers in the same blocks without curtains for privacy, and children were separated from their families and left to fend for themselves.

When Hanan stayed there, however, she had a room inside and they gave her bread and marmalade and made her feel welcome. She spoke to other refugees who passed through, and was shocked by some of their stories. One woman had been forced to leave her two small children in the care of her brother, but he had been arrested and she had no idea where her babies were now.

Hanan's heart ached for her own daughters, Rim and Bisan, so far away in Norway, in a strange new culture without their mother. But she knew she was lucky.

Thank God my sons are OK, and my daughters are healthy, she would think to herself.

On 24 March 2014, the Austrian authorities had moved Hanan, Riad and Ismail into a hostel for families in Vienna. By August, a charity had helped the family find a small flat, and the three of them had received their refugee passports by early June.

It would be another seven months before Hanan was reunited with her husband. Talal had to stay in Athens. Smuggling him out of Greece would have cost another €5,000, which the family did not have, so they applied for family reunion. Most European nations grant visas to allow families separated by war to reunite, but it could be a lengthy and difficult process. First a person had to have their own refugee status granted, then they had to prove their kinship to the husband, wife or child they wanted by their side. There were forms, interviews, piles of documents to submit – it was a daunting web of bureaucracy in an unfamiliar language and culture, especially for the thousands of refugees who had lost their paperwork in dangerous journeys over sea and land. A trade in fake identification documents was thriving. Given increasing public hostility to refugees over the years, the asylum systems in most European countries were designed to reject people wherever possible. So the Syrians who had lost their passports were desperate to get their hands on something which proved their nationality, while people from other countries – both those genuinely fleeing war and others entering Europe for work – were also in the market for the fake documents.

Talal had a genuine Syrian passport, but that wasn't much use until he was able to reach Austria. The Austrian embassy in Athens told him to go to the Greek Council for Refugees, a non-governmental organization. Hanan, meanwhile, was lobbying the charities who had helped her in Vienna. She was not the kind of person to be daunted by bureaucracy, and approached the process the same way she approached every obstacle in her life – as a challenge to which she could systematically and logically apply her intellect until she got the desired result.

Finally, on 1 December 2014, their perseverance paid off and

Talal arrived in Vienna. But Hanan could not go to the airport to welcome him. First Talal had to be processed through the system, and it was only after he had spent three days in an immigration centre and four days at Traiskirchen that Hanan was able to go to a café and see her husband for the first time in nine months. It was a reunion tinged with sadness: Hanan was pleased to see him, but the married life they had built together didn't exist any more. They were in their early fifties, and she didn't know what lay ahead, or how they would cope now they had been robbed of their independence and their livelihood.

Her dream of bringing the whole family together was also fading. Rim and Bisan had been able to get a bus down from Norway and visit their mother and brothers, but they had started their asylum applications in Norway and were now bound to stay there until they had permanent residence. This process would take three years. The young women were so miserable. Rim had completed four years of her degree in information systems in Damascus and was just one semester from graduating. But the Norwegians would not recognize all the work she had done, and now the twenty-four-year-old was back at high school for the certificate she needed to start her degree all over again. Bisan was in the same situation, and wasn't even sure if she could bear to repeat the three years of architecture. But there was little else for her to do with her days: the Norwegian refugee service had assigned them to a house on the outskirts of the city of Levanger, about 260 miles north of Oslo. It was too cold to go outside most of the time, and there were no buses into town anyway. Bisan desperately wanted to go and live with her mother in Austria, but there was no legal way for the family to reunite.

At least Riad and Ismail were able to go to school. Their cosseted existence in Syria was far behind them. The spoilt teenagers who would step out of their dirty clothes and leave them for the maid had grown into industrious young men who had washed the dishes and helped clean the refugee centre where they had stayed in exchange for a little extra pocket money. Ismail felt immense respect for what his parents had put themselves through, and was as determined as ever to help turn the family's fortunes around. He had started looking for work, all the while keeping a protective eye on the little brother he had safely brought across Europe. Each day, he would sit Riad down and together they would learn fifty new German words.

'You must learn something new every day,' he would instruct Riad.

And when the refugees started streaming through Vienna's Westbahnhof on their way to Germany, both the boys knew they could not stay at home and do nothing, not when they knew every facet of fear and anxiety which accompanies a person on the journey they themselves had made more than a year earlier.

The scale of the movement of people arriving in Greece in 2015 then setting off for northern Europe had taken the EU's leaders completely by surprise. It shouldn't have: the UN's World Food Programme had warned them that there was no money left to feed the refugees in Turkey, Lebanon and Jordan – nations where people had also become increasingly hostile to their Syrian guests. Air strikes by a US-led coalition against Islamic State targets in Syria and Iraq had made life even more difficult at home. People had no choice but to leave and try and find the safest way to Europe.

The EU had at least stemmed the tide of death in the stretch of water between Libya and Italy, with a bulked-up Operation Triton pulling more people from the water. For years migration experts had argued that a comprehensive search-and-rescue effort would save many lives, and sure enough fatalities fell from an all-time monthly high of 1,308 people in April to 68 in May.

Such unity of purpose around a humanitarian goal would be short-lived. EU governments were already considering drastic action against the smuggling networks that Fortress Europe had helped create. The EU's foreign service proposed a military campaign to destroy the smuggling boats at sea. But both of Libya's rival governments – by early 2015 there were two warring administrations pulling the country apart – said they would not tolerate such a campaign in their waters. The UN Secretary-General Ban Ki-moon was also unconvinced. How would the European navies be able to tell a smuggling boat from a fishing boat, when most of the time they were one and the same? The Libyan fishermen recovering from the war did not need their livelihoods destroyed. Refugees could also be caught in the crossfire, either travelling in the boats when they were attacked, or left in the hands of the brutal kidnapping and extortion gangs thriving along the Libyan coast with no means of escape.

It was a re-run of the old EU policies: lock down the borders and keep people out, no matter what the human cost may be. But without permission from the Libyan government or the United Nations, military action in the waters of a sovereign nation would break international law, so instead a scaled-down operation dedicated to surveillance began in June.

But by late spring, the crisis had already shifted away from North Africa. The promise of making land in Italy no longer outweighed the risks of the treacherous journey from Libya. The transit routes to Libya were also being shut off as North African nations introduced visa requirements for Syrians, while the risk of kidnapping and extortion also soared as chaos engulfed the country and the rival militia saw only profit in the world refugee crisis. While in previous years it was mostly men braving the sea with the intention of bringing wives and children over later, the situation in Syria and in the neighbouring countries had become so dire that whole families had to make the voyage together. The distance between Turkey and Greece was much shorter, and the beaches of the Greek islands became the new epicentre of the crisis while the EU's leaders were still scratching their heads about how to sink smuggling boats leaving Libya.

In the whole of 2014, 43,500 people had made the journey from Turkey. By the end of September 2015, nearly 400,000 people – seventy per cent from Syria and all but three per cent from countries blighted by war – had arrived in Greece. Boat after boat ran aground on the sand or rocks, some people falling to their knees in gratitude at making it to Europe alive, others consumed by fear and scrambling to keep their children out of the water as they dragged themselves ashore. They began arriving in large numbers just as Greece's holiday season began. Many tourists rushed to help, handing out water bottles and food. Others stood dumbly by, cursing a ruined holiday as they watched the dazed men and women come ashore on the islands of Lesbos, Samos, Chios, Kos and others.

The new arrivals were greeted with squalor and mayhem. All facilities for housing the refugees on the islands were full, and with the toilets overflowing many people chose to sleep outside rather than bear the stench and the squalor. Greece provided little else beyond a limited number of beds: no soap, no food, no clothes, no medicine. New arrivals strung nets from the olive groves, trying to create some shelter from the fierce Mediterranean sun. Tented camps sprang up in car parks, as local officials tried to help the best they could. Charity workers and volunteers cleaned the makeshift camps, handed out water bottles, tried to coordinate transport so the refugees did not have to endure long walks in the searing heat to towns where the Greek authorities could register new arrivals and try and arrange onward transport.

Lesbos was seeing 3,300 people arriving each day, and more than 10,000 refugees would regularly be trapped on an island with beds for only 2,800 people. Just 10 kilometres of sea separated Lesbos from Turkey, but that did not mean it was a safe crossing. When autumn arrived and brought rough seas, dozens of people would die in the space of a few weeks. So heavy were the casualties over the years that there was no room left in the paupers' section of the main cemetery to bury the victims in unmarked graves. Some residents would head to the beaches and do everything they could to prevent more deaths, but others marched on the streets to demand the removal of the refugees. On the island of Kos further south, 2,500 refugees were locked in a football stadium in the August heat for twenty-four hours with no water or shade. The Greek authorities did not know what to do with them, and dozens fainted in the heat. By September, tension among local citizens had peaked and the refugees had to hide from small gangs of thugs wielding bats.

Boats which were meant to take the new arrivals to Athens were delayed for weeks, and the holiday islands became the refugees' purgatory, where they were unable to get enough food or water to keep living with any semblance of normality, unable to return home, unable to move forward.

When ferries finally arrived and people were able to travel to Athens, they would begin their slow migration out of Greece by bus, foot, train, even bicycle. When Riad and Ismail had made the journey, there were just seven in their group traversing a continent, and they only came across others undertaking the same journey behind the bars of various European police stations. Now crowds all moved along the same paths, queuing at the same border crossings. Couples held the hands of small children as they struggled through fields; relatives of the infirm pushed them in wheelchairs; mothers and fathers hauled babies in slings and carriers.

Europe's leaders panicked at sight of tens of thousands on the march, and Riad and Ismail watched with horror as each border they had crossed became the site of more suffering. In June, Hungary's Prime Minister Viktor Orbán closed the border with Serbia and ordered work to begin on the EU's newest fortification – a four-metre-high and 175-kilometre-long steel barricade sealing off the most direct route into the Schengen zone.

Macedonia closed its border with Greece on 20 August and

sent the army to two crossing points, trapping thousands of refugees behind barbed wire with nowhere to go. The authorities treated them not like victims of war, but as unruly rioters to be brought in line by truncheon-wielding policemen whose wall of plastic shields faced men and women falling to the ground from exhaustion and shock. Toddlers clung to their parents as their faces contorted with terror; children crouched on the ground and sobbed uncontrollably. When a group of men tried to push their way past the razor wire, special forces fired stun grenades into the crowd.

On 27 August, police found the decomposing bodies of seventy-one people including Syrians and Iraqis in the back of a grocery truck parked in a lay-by in Austria just over the Hungarian border. The refugees had escaped the barrel bombs and chemical weapons of Assad and the medieval horrors of the Islamic State, only to slowly suffocate in Europe.

By September, Europeans were waking up to images of children being tear-gassed on EU soil. Orbán had almost completed his fence on the Hungarian–Serbian border, and when a group of frustrated young men tried to cross it anyway and hurled stones and water bottles, his forces responded with tear gas and water cannons. Parents covered the faces of their babies with rags, but the gas seeped through.

Hanan watched each development with growing disgust. She could not bear what was happening to her people, both in Syria and now across Europe. She would think of her grandmother, Watfah, and wonder if her children would ask her why she had uprooted them from their charmed existence in Syria and dragged them to a continent which treated them with such contempt. No, she decided, the children understood.

Every day, every hour, someone we know is killed in Syria and we see the photos, so they say thank god we left.

But it was hard for Hanan. She wanted to be a proper mother for her children, and Rim and Bisan could not even live in the same country. Even if they could, Hanan had no local knowledge she could pass on. In Damascus she knew every street corner, every neighbourhood, she could guide her children while they were young, steer them away from danger and towards opportunity. Vienna was an alien city to her and she had to rely on Riad and Ismail to help her find her way. Talal could not work until he learnt German, and the family were forced into the humiliating position of relying on state handouts.

'We don't *want* to ask for charity,' she would tell anyone who questioned their motives in doing so. 'It's difficult for a man who has worked for thirty years, who has given his children absolutely everything they need, to take money like that.'

But they had no choice.

I don't see anything sweet in life any more, she thought. *For us, it is too late – a new city, a new language, it's too late.*

Ismail tried to reassure his mother. At times he had to steel himself against the hostile stares on the metro, but overall he felt welcome in Austria. He would start an information technology degree in a few months, was speaking German well and had made Austrian friends.

'The war will end soon and our house hasn't been destroyed,' he would tell Hanan. But he wasn't even sure if he believed his own words.

Hanan was convinced that there would be no Syria to return to. Perhaps it would split into three or four separate states, but her home was long gone. Now they lived in a cramped flat in a block in a run-down suburb of Vienna. Instead of the smell of jasmine and camellias that had wafted down from her balcony in Damascus, the corridors here occasionally smelt of marijuana, but most of the time of cement dust and cooking fumes. Their front door opened straight onto a small kitchen with room for only one person to man the pots and pans. The family lived in three rooms – two small bedrooms and a living room with exposed wires around the light sockets and cracks in the greying plaster.

Only two photographs adorned the walls. One was of Hanan's four children in their glamorous dresses and smart suits at Rim and Izzat's engagement party in Beirut. The other showed Rim on her wedding day on 29 December 2014. The whole family had gathered in Vienna for the wedding, with Hanan's brother and sisters travelling from around the world to celebrate the rare moment of happiness in her life in Europe.

Now I will just live for my children, Hanah decided. *I just want to take care of my family.*

They made her proud, now more than ever. Rim and Bisan, beautiful and clever and trying to make a life for themselves in Norway. Rim had a job at a kindergarten, and in their spare time the young women had joined a choir. Hanan beamed when she read an interview Rim gave a Norwegian newspaper about her life in Syria.

'When I came here I lost my good life,' she told the journalist. 'I had everything that any girl could wish for.'

Then there was Ismail: he had been strong for Riad and now he was strong for the other young Syrians arriving in Vienna. And while Hanan would scold her youngest child for neglecting his studies, she marvelled at Riad's ability to see the good in people. Her faith in humanity had been shaken by their experiences as refugees, but Riad's was undiminished. If someone acted selfishly or spitefully, her boy would try and find a reason.

'Maybe he has his own problems and this is why he acts like this,' Riad would say.

Still, Hanan wished he could come home, just for a few hours in bed. But Riad knew that the people at Westbahnhof needed him more he more than he needed an extra hour of sleep. And so Hanan would head down to the station herself, notionally to get her son back, but she liked to help too. The sight of women nursing their babies on the station concourse, children too young to be so well behaved sitting silently at their parents' feet, men so exhausted that they lay on the hard ground and stared blankly at the sky – it filled her with so much sadness. Why were they being forced to make these journeys, and to risk their lives over and over again?

Norway, it's a big land, Germany, it's a big land. Denmark, Holland, they need people, she thought. *Why not let these people go to a ministry and apply there? In Lebanon, in Turkey, and also in Syria. Why? If you arrive, they say 'welcome'. If you die in the sea, they say 'never mind'. Why? Thousands of people die, and after that, they cry.*

Hanan didn't even believe the promises she kept hearing from EU leaders to crack down on the people smugglers. They had operated in plain sight in Agios Nikolaos, the square in Athens, and she saw no police there. Now she heard that Rami – Talal's nephew who had cheated them – was in the Netherlands, so Hanan went to the Austrian police and gave them a detailed report of what he had done. She never heard anything back about her complaint.

The army of volunteers had restored some of her faith in Europe, though. While governments bickered over relocating the hundreds of thousands of refugees arriving in Greece, ordinary people in Greece, Serbia, Hungary, Austria and Germany went to the railway stations and to roadsides to hand out drinks and food. Many people offered their homes to families in need, just as she had done back in Damascus.

At Westbahnhof, smiling young Austrian women wheeled trolleys full of bananas and thrust food into the hands of travellers. The packets were taken gratefully, but not effusively. The refugees were focused on their mission. It was not desperation written on their faces, but a determination to win this battle of survival. Hanan picked up a couple of bottles of water which rolled away from a family, and tutted. She had cleaned the square in front of the station a few days ago, but with thousands of people passing through, it could not stay clean.

Vienna had always been at the crossroads of Europe – divided between the Allied Powers after the Second World War, a gateway from east to west during the Cold War – and so it became again for those few weeks in the summer of 2015. It was a no man's land which most refugees wanted to transit through as they tried to shrug off the hostility of many central European countries and head towards the hope offered by nations like Germany and Sweden.

Riad did not dwell on the symbolism of the place. He was busy advising people which trains were going where, how to access the toilets, where to get food and medical help for their families. His name was written in marker pen on a tag pinned to his chest under the logo for the Catholic charity Caritas. Finally he was more to Europe than just a number scrawled on a wrist.

20

Dark Thoughts

Sina: Rhodes, Greece

Sina knew the first words she wanted Dani to hear when she finally picked up the phone.

'I have a healthy baby and I am in a good condition.'

It did not quite work out as planned. Heavily sedated after the shipwreck, and before the Caesarean section which delivered Andonis, Sina had woken up confused and frightened. Trauma had erased the accident from her memory, and she didn't know where she was.

Have I delivered my baby? Am I in a hospital in Istanbul?

She placed her hand on her belly. No, her baby was still inside her. Memories of the sea, the rocks, and the terror stirred.

Am I dead? Am I alive?

Sina looked around her – monitors, a television, hospital equipment. She must be alive.

A social worker rushed in.

'You were in a shipwreck,' she said, explaining how the doctors had cleaned all her wounds and were monitoring her baby. After reassurance that her child was fine, Sina asked for a phone. Dani must have been trying to call her Turkish mobile, now at the bottom of the sea, and would be wild with worry. As his phone rang, Sina decided he didn't need to know the truth – not just yet. She would spare him that.

'I am in Greece and I am safe,' was all she told her husband.

Sina reassured Dani that the baby was fine, and said she was planning on checking herself into a hospital soon for the labour.

Within hours, Dani called back.

'What happened, Sina?'

'Nothing.'

'I heard something about Rhodes. You are in Rhodes. I looked on Facebook. Some accident happened with someone called David and David was with you.'

'No, he is lying,' Sina protested from her hospital bed. Her deception was met with silence. 'OK, there was a small accident, but it was OK.'

Sina explained the shipwreck as gently as possible, but as she feared, Dani flew into a panic.

'This accident must have done something to the baby,' he said. 'Don't think about the baby. You don't have to worry, even if something happens, we will have another one.'

No amount of reassurance from her could convince Dani that their baby was fine, so Sina found a doctor and handed him the phone. He was used to the anxiety and feeling of helplessness that can consume expectant fathers, and talked Dani through all the scans and explained how they were going to deliver his baby. When Sina was finally ready to go up to surgery, Dani had calmed down a little, but he did not stop looking at his phone – not for a second – until it finally pinged with a photo message.

There was his son, with his sweep of velvet black hair, cheeks already so chubby and rounded, staring up through puffy, thoughtful eyes. Dani rang the doctor straight away. He couldn't believe that such a beautiful and healthy baby could be born from such an ordeal.

'How is he? Is he healthy? Tell me the truth,' he asked over and over again.

The doctor laughed, and the nurses snapped more photos to send to the proud father.

Dani raced into Kampala and spent some of his precious savings on a laptop. Staff from the Red Cross in Rhodes were going to set up a video chat with Sina the next day, and he needed to see his wife and his baby, and to speak to Sina face to face for the first time in months. When they finally connected, they couldn't stop smiling at the tiny life in Sina's arms.

'That's our baby!' each would say in turn, their euphoria infecting the nurses, the doctors, the Red Cross staff who jostled to get in front of the camera and congratulate Dani.

Sina and Dani conferred about the name. They had planned to call him Delina, but he may not have even made it into the world without the bravery of the off-duty army sergeant, Antonis Deligiorgis. The parents agreed that they should honour his bravery and call their son Andonis. Word of the baby who had survived the shipwreck and was named after his Greek saviour spread around Rhodes, and visitors lined up at Sina's door with flowers, pushchairs, baby clothes, nappies, toys. In her four-bedroom ward, three of the beds were covered in gifts. Antonis Deligiorgis came too, brimming with pride at his tiny namesake. He was hoping to be the child's godfather, but the mayor of Rhodes had already staked that claim on the tiny local celebrity.

Sina knew who she wanted as godmother: Despina, the president of the Red Cross of Rhodes, a formidable woman in her late seventies who barely spoke a word of English but who had been by Sina's side since she had arrived. When Sina and Andonis left the hospital, Despina found her a house. Most refugees arriving on the Greek islands were only meant to stay a few days before being shipped to Athens for processing, but Despina insisted that the baby was too small to move, and that both mother and child needed looking after. The authorities agreed, and each day Despina would come to the house and cook and clean so that Sina could focus only on her baby.

Like every new mother, Sina had a lot to learn. Breastfeeding came easily, but there were so many other tasks she had to master to protect the tiny life she had created, and she worried all the time that she was not doing a very good job. But anyone who saw how tenderly she washed Andonis – so many more times a day than most parents – and how she strived to keep him warm would tell her that she was an inspiration, and that Andonis had the best mother in the world.

As well as giving her moral support, the citizens of Rhodes met all Sina's material needs. The Orthodox Church on Rhodes gave her a generous donation. Despina took her on trips to the neighbouring islands, and her convalescence felt a little like a holiday. But what Sina really longed for was her husband back by her side. Every time she looked at their son, he was there. As the weeks passed Andonis was growing to look so much like his father, the huge soulful eyes, high forehead and charming smile.

In Kampala, Dani was getting increasingly desperate – he was consumed by the need to see his wife and hold his child, but every broker he asked seemed to raise the price for the trip to Europe: $15,000, $16,000, $17,000. He called his family and all his friends and they gave everything they could, but it was not enough.

'Sina, I will come. I am trying to find a passport, I miss Andonis and I want to see him now,' he would say.

Sina tried to reassure him.

'You don't have to worry,' she said. But she could tell that he would not be satisfied until he was with them. He had to find a way to get to Europe, but he was now just one of many Eritreans hoping to make the crossing and facing more and more barriers to safety.

By the end of the year, Eritreans would comprise the fourth largest nationality arriving in Europe via the Mediterranean, after Syrians – who accounted for fifty-two per cent – Afghans and Iraqis. The situation in Eritrea was as dire as ever, but the European Union saw an opportunity: perhaps it could pay the dictatorship to stop people leaving. By late summer, plans were being drawn up to give €200 million in development aid to the country. In theory the money would bypass the government and go directly to projects which would help create jobs, foster prosperity and entice people to stay. But it was unclear how that would happen when the government had such tight control over every aspect of life in Eritrea. Britain, meanwhile, had in March started applying its new guidelines for Eritreans seeking refuge, based on the disputed Danish report, and sixty-six per cent of asylum applications had been refused in the second quarter of the year. All the while, the refugees kept coming and Europe still didn't have a plan for how to accommodate them and make life bearable.

But if the leaders struggled with the idea of accommodating a group of refugees, when it came to the welfare of just one woman and one baby – whose family shared the religion of their host country – it seemed that hearts could be kind and obstacles overcome. The people of Rhodes began to mobilize to get the young family back together. The mayor of Rhodes had decided to intervene on Dani's behalf, and prepared a letter of invitation which was to be sent to a Greek embassy to allow him to apply for a visa. Then Dani would just have to pay the plane fare, and he could arrive in Athens safely and legally – which was all any of the refugees wanted.

Sina herself hadn't even considered trying to organize an official family reunion – she hadn't started the process of applying for asylum in Greece, and even if she did it would take months. But Andonis needed his father straight away, and even with this help from the mayor, it was still not going to be easy. When Sina saw the letter, she was dismayed to read that it incorrectly stated Dani's nationality as Ethiopian, rather than Eritrean. And there was only an honorary consulate in Kampala, whereas Dani would need to find a full embassy. But it was a lifeline, and Dani was determined to grasp it and hope it would lead him to his family. The nearest Greek embassy was in Khartoum, so first he needed to find a smuggler to take him back there in order for him to set the visa process in motion.

Sina was also on the move again. Her months under the care of the people of Rhodes were coming to an end. While she had been recovering from her journey and the birth, she had been allowed a brief respite from the gruelling process of applying for asylum, but now that she and Andonis were stronger, she had to begin the application. Her ticket to Athens was booked, and a bed in a shelter run by a charity arranged. Sina didn't mind too much: she knew she had to keep moving forward and getting on with her life. She was a chemical engineer – there wasn't really anything for her to do on Rhodes, no matter how beautiful it was or how kind its people were. An encouraging letter had also recently arrived – a scholarship she had applied for to study a master's degree in chemical engineering at Münster University in Germany had been approved. If she could make it to Germany, then the promise of a new life in Europe might be realized.

So Sina bade farewell to Despina, and in early July she and Andonis travelled to Athens, where they found themselves sharing a room in a dingy shelter where the staff only provided one meal a day. It wasn't enough for a nursing mother, and when her champions back in Rhodes heard about the conditions, Despina and her granddaughter Debbie Karnachoriti – a young woman who worked north of Athens helping refugees access state services – contacted a charity in the capital and asked for its help. Within days, the charity transferred Sina to a business hotel in a nice suburb of Athens, where the room was adapted for a baby bed and all available space filled with plush toys. Sina finally headed to the immigration offices. Unlike most of the hundreds of thousands of people arriving in Greece and planning to register for asylum elsewhere in Europe, she was going to apply in Greece itself and then look into transferring to continue her studies in Germany. Best to try and follow Europe's laws, Debbie and other friends advised her.

Wherever Sina went, the bubbly personality which had first caught Dani's eye back in her university days won her friends, and now people were charmed by her baby as well. Soon, Athens was beginning to feel as welcoming as Rhodes. However, the confident, exuberant man she had fallen in love with was not faring so well. Dani had become consumed by paranoia, convinced that Sina was hiding something. He texted a woman on Rhodes whom Sina had befriended.

'Please tell me whether Andonis is OK or not,' he wrote. 'I have a dream all the time that someone wants to take him. When I ask Sina she says everything is OK, but these dreams repeatedly come into my mind. Please tell me the truth.'

When her friend forwarded the texts, they laughed at first. Dani missed his baby so much, and just needed some reassurance. Sina called her husband.

'Please, no one will take Andonis,' she said. 'I am his mother and I am OK, I am healthy, nobody will take him, you don't have to worry about this.'

But he would not be placated.

'No Sina, last night I saw in my dream that someone stole my Andonis. Please, tell me the truth, does someone want to take my Andonis? I can't sleep, please. These dreams keep repeating. What should I do? Please tell me what is happening there.'

It must be the stress of the separation, she thought. Getting on the road again and moving towards his son would help. On 20 July Dani finally left Kampala and went with a smuggler back through South Sudan and into Sudan, renting a hotel room in Khartoum. He called the next day from the Sudanese capital, and told Sina that he had an appointment with the Greek embassy there in a few days' time.

Soon they would be together again, and he would be able to hold his son in his arms for the first time.

21

A Moral Emergency

Nart: Garmisch, Germany

'Mama Merkel.'

Nart Bajoi had heard other Syrians utter those words so many times since arriving in Munich. For years Chancellor Angela Merkel had been *Mutti* to the German population. Now she was becoming a mother figure to the growing number of people arriving in a country that was determined to learn from its dark history and not let the forces of racism and xenophobia triumph ever again. The memory of trains leaving Germany packed with terrified souls fleeing the Nazis would be replaced with images of crowds welcoming the refugees at stations across the country. Berlin's old Tempelhof airport built by Hitler on the site of a prototype concentration camp would be transformed into a vast temporary shelter for some of the hundreds of thousands of new arrivals.

But the European Union's founding values of tolerance and equality for all were in short supply elsewhere. If you asked Hungary's Prime Minister Orbán, the columns of Syrians, Afghans, Iraqis, Eritreans and others arriving on the shores of Greece then wearily moving north were not there because of President Assad's barrel bombs, Taliban suicide bombers, Islamic State brutality, or slavery in Eritrea. They were there because of Mama Merkel and her generosity.

'The problem is not a European problem, but a German

problem,' Orbán told reporters in Brussels in mid-September as EU officials tried in vain to bridge the chasms which had appeared in the union. As the refugees carried on piling out of the boats in Greece then dragging their exhausted families through the muddy fields and dark forests, trying to avoid the razor wire and the tear gas and the water cannons, European unity disintegrated.

On 24 August, Germany had quietly stopped returning Syrians to their place of entry under the Dublin Regulation. Merkel spelled out Germany's policy a few days later, after the bodies of the seventy-one suffocated Syrians were found in the truck in Austria.

'If Europe fails on the question of refugees, then it won't be the Europe we wished for,' she said. Germany would welcome more than one million people seeking asylum in 2015, and Merkel expected all members of the EU to work together to meet its most urgent moral challenge since the Second World War.

Unfortunately, Nart had arrived in Germany before Merkel's moral awakening, and after a few months in a refugee hostel in Munich he was told that he would be going back to Bulgaria. The deportation order arrived in July 2014, but by then he could barely walk. His old footballing injury – aggravated first by the hike over the mountains to Bulgaria and then by the cold European winter – was causing him constant pain. The German immigration service agreed not to deport him until he had had medical treatment, and his first experience of Germany was of being in a legal limbo, unsure where he would end up as he launched a series of appeals against his deportation.

After a few months the immigration office transferred Nart to Garmisch, a Bavarian mountain resort south of Munich which had a lake at its centre and spectacular views of Germany's highest peak. It was pretty, but there was not much to do during his convalescence apart from dwell on his bleak existence. And despite two operations for patellar tendonitis, his knee still hurt.

Nart had read that the Portuguese footballer Cristiano Ronaldo had had the same problem and was back on the field within six months. After fifteen months, Nart had still not recovered and asked his doctor why.

'You are not Ronaldo,' the doctor replied.

When he complained that the pain got worse in the cold, the doctor had a solution.

'Why don't you go to a warm country?'

Nart tried to fill his days usefully, with German lessons and volunteer work. For a while, he taught computer skills to German children, but his knee pain intensified in the winter and he no longer had the strength to peddle his bike to the school. He was still waiting for the appeal against his deportation order when Merkel decided to suspend the Dublin Regulation. On 24 September 2015, Nart had an interview with immigration, and was told that he could stay after all. But he wasn't getting residence: he had a status known as *Duldung*, which meant temporary suspension of the deportation order but without any certainty about the future. It meant he could be returned to Syria or back to Bulgaria at any time the German authorities deemed it safe. He could work, but needed to secure a job offer first, apply for a work permit, then wait twenty days.

Why would someone hire me? he thought. *Why would they make a contract with me when perhaps tomorrow or the day after tomorrow I would be sent back?*

Eventually he managed to get some work at a US Army base doling out food in the canteen for the minimum wage of €8.50. He thought the American soldiers would be interesting to talk to, but the only interactions allowed were questions about whether they wanted peas or carrots. After a few months, the American base administrators asked to see his passport. When he showed them his *Duldung* papers, they shook their heads and let him go.

The rules seemed to be changing every month, and Nart had no idea what to do or how to try and build a life. He had known that Bulgaria was a poor country, so when he was arrested, prosecuted, assaulted and then left to fend for himself there, he could understand. But this was Germany – the promised land for refugees – and even here all he could do was eat and sleep and try and pass the empty days watching the news as Syria fell apart. Now Russia had launched air strikes, but all Nart could see were countries focused on protecting themselves, not the Syrian people.

ISIS had made an explicit threat to the West on 15 February, slaughtering twenty-one Egyptian Christians on the Libyan shores of the Mediterranean – the same coastline where each week hundreds of people set sail for Europe. One of the militants pointed across the sea at the heart of Europe: 'We will conquer Rome, by the will of Allah.'

The raising of the black flag of the Islamic State over parts of the Middle East had further confused the Western world's response to the refugee crisis. Muslims were overwhelmingly the victims of the militant group, but the fact that many of the people arriving in Europe were fleeing the Islamic State didn't seem to matter. With each beheading of a British aid worker or an American journalist, hate crimes against Muslims would rise in Europe, and opportunistic politicians would draw a link between the religious extremists and their Muslim victims. Equating the refugees with terrorists was an easy way for politicians to get headlines and boost support.

It was not only the fringe right-wing groups stoking religious prejudices. In August the Slovakian interior minister said the country would only accept Christian refugees. In Hungary, Prime Minister Orbán took a similar line, portraying himself as the defender of Europe's Christian values and arguing that the Ottoman occupation of Hungary and other parts of Europe in the sixteenth century was reason to deny shelter to Muslims. The former Soviet states were generally poorer and had little experience with multiculturalism, which went some way to explaining their hostility. But even rich countries with diverse populations bitterly fought against welcoming the refugees.

Britain loudly campaigned against any imposed relocation of refugees from inside or outside the EU's borders, arguing that bringing peace to the Middle East was a better solution. No one disagreed that ending the war in Syria would help, but that seemed a very distant prospect. The refugee boats carried on sinking as the politicians argued, and hundreds of lives were lost every month. Even when the UNCHR confirmed that eighty-five per cent of the people arriving in Europe were from the world's top refugee-producing nations, British government ministers carried on implying that they were economic migrants. Rather than challenging the rhetoric of the populist right, mainstream politicians found it easier to hijack their message and repackage it as policy.

In Germany, Merkel was facing the same determined core of xenophobia that coloured the debate in Hungary, Greece, Britain, France, Denmark, the Netherlands and other European countries. At the end of 2014 and the beginning of 2015, tens of thousands of supporters of a radical group called Patriotic Europeans Against the Islamization of the West, or Pegida, rallied to protest against Germany's refugee policy and what they claimed was the dilution of their culture. Pegida was one of many movements to emerge from the ashes of the financial crisis, as nationalistic leaders exploited a depressed population, a lack of trust in the political establishment, and diminishing moral direction from governments. In parts of Germany, gangs attacked refugee shelters and set centres on fire.

But in contrast to her European counterparts, Merkel chose loud defiance, rather than silence and quiet shifts towards more restrictive policies. There was also an element of pragmatism in Merkel's choice. Germany's population had been shrinking for years, and the nation relied on foreign labour to keep the economy growing. The middle-class Syrians and Iraqis with their engineering degrees and computing skills were exactly the kind of industrious people who could keep Germany booming. Most other leaders, however, did not dare suggest that the refugees might be able to bring something positive to their host countries, despite similar problems with declining birth rates and labour shortages across much of the EU. Sealing the borders and keeping people out remained the priority. By the middle of 2015, the EU had only agreed to resettle 32,256 refugees from Greece, Italy and Hungary, when a million people were expected to arrive that year.

Instead of the solidarity and 'ever closer union' which some nations had been pleading for for years, countries in the bloc began to turn on each other and nations became consumed by the same self-interest that had allowed the continent to fall into conflict a generation earlier. Orbán blamed Merkel for the migration crisis, saying her decision to suspend the Dublin Regulation was encouraging more people to traipse across his country. So he built his fence along Hungary's border with non-EU member Serbia. The day after it was completed only eleven people managed to get across. But the rest of the refugees did not give up and return to Greece – they just had to walk for longer. That same day, 5,932 people entered Hungary from Croatia, so Orbán began building another fence, this time on the border with another EU nation. When the Hungary–Croatia fence was completed, the government in Zagreb decided to bus the thousands of people trapped in Croatia to Slovenia, where politicians angrily accused their southern neighbour of dumping people on their doorstep. In late October, as the weather turned cold and icy rain transformed borderlands into mud pools, Slovenia started restricting movement over its border into Austria. Once again, it was the weakest who suffered most: children slept in plastic bags as their parents tried to keep them dry. Refugees lit fires to try and stay warm, but nothing would help get the mud out of their clothes.

There was no coordination, just recriminations as governments blamed each other for the crisis. Over the course of one summer, the arrival of less than one million people in a rich region of 500 million had started to unpick the stitches which were meant to hold Europe together. The Schengen Area was one of the central principles of the dream of a united continent, but now trains were being stopped as they crossed between countries. Austria would start a fence on the Slovenian border. Even Germany – the cheerleader of a closer European Union – started reinstating passport checks when the authorities realized they had nowhere to put all the new arrivals.

When Merkel called for solidarity in Europe, she was met by a wall of silence.

Arguments failed to persuade, and moral appeals left people unmoved. In the end, what it took to change minds was the tiny body of three-year-old Aylan Kurdi washed up on the shore of a Turkish beach, still in the red T-shirt and blue Velcro shorts that his parents had dressed him in for his final journey.

Mohammed: Msida, Malta

Mohammed Kazkji could hardly bear to look at the pictures of little Aylan. The Syrian boy had set sail from the Turkish coast with his mother, father and brother Ghalib on 2 September, headed for the Greek island of Kos. They had only been at sea for a few hours when the waves toppled their inflatable dinghy. Aylan's father tried to hold on to his family, but they slipped out of his arms one by one and vanished under the water. Aylan washed back up on the beach they had set sail from, and a Turkish photographer saw the small child, the white foam of the surf rising around his bluing face, and snapped a picture. The next day, Aylan's lonely death was on the front pages of newspapers around the world. He was not the first child to die trying to reach Europe, but his prone position on the beach – head to one side and his bottom in the air like a child sleeping in his crib – touched a nerve.

Finally, the refugees had a face.

That little angel, Mohammed thought, *maybe people will start to understand what the refugees have to do to reach Europe.*

Since his deportation back to Malta in March 2014, Mohammed had been doing everything he could to try and discourage others from repeating his mistake.

I was crazy, I had a water phobia and I put myself in the middle of the sea, he thought. *I want to tell my story, to say please don't try to get to Europe like I did. Maybe someone will read about October 11, 2013, and they won't get on a boat.*

Mohammed had seen how quickly so much life could be extinguished, and how those lost lives seemed to mean so little to anyone apart from the husbands, wives, fathers and mothers who mourned for bodies which were rarely recovered. The young electrician spoke to any journalists who came to Malta asking about the shipwreck. He took part in a report which Amnesty International put together on the accident and its aftermath. And most importantly of all, he spoke to his brothers who had fled to Turkey, and told them to stay where they were.

The sea still haunted Mohammed, but slowly he had managed to build a life. He had wanted to flee Malta from the moment he found himself in the bowels of a government building shivering from the shipwreck and being asked for his fingerprints before he even had a pair of trousers to wear. But the bitterness which peaked as he slept rough in a Valletta park had melted away, and his innate hope and optimism had risen once more. Within days of leaving the chapel at the refugee camp and moving in with other Syrian refugees, Mohammed was back at work. Every morning he walked to a roundabout where Malta's residents headed to pick up cheap labour for a day's work. It was all illegal of course, but no one seemed to care. It was an arrangement which suited all parties on an island where there was always another expatriate building a pool, a family looking for an extension to their beachside home, or a businessperson investing in a new resort.

Mohammed was happy to take the wages, even if they were lower than locals would get. He would much rather work than queue at the immigration centre for the €130 he was entitled to each month. At first he was busy with manual labour and plastering and cleaning – whatever he could do to keep busy and earn money to send back to his family. Then when he casually mentioned that he was studying to become the world's best electrician, a few people hired him to do their wiring. Just like in Libya, the work mounted up as news of his skill spread. One company told him that as soon as his papers were in order, there would be plenty of jobs for such a gifted young man.

He had a home now too. Omar was out of jail, and the pair had moved in with two other young Syrians. Their ground-floor flat was on a busy thoroughfare of pale sun-baked houses not unlike those found in parts of the Middle East. The area just a few blocks from the port of Msida was slightly run down, with the wooden doors splintering and losing their paint and for-sale signs hanging above long-empty shopfronts. The further away you were from the water in Malta, the less people tended to look after the façades. But Mohammed didn't want to be near the sea, the waves lapping at the shores still reminding him of how close he came to death. Water was difficult to avoid in Malta, however. In the winter their road would flood and he would have to wade to get to the small local grocery shop with a few moulding fruits in the window and a sign reminding customers not to ask for credit. In the summer, the moisture would come off the sea and fill the air with a humidity that could soak you through in a few minutes. But slowly Mohammed had been able to come to terms with his trauma, and the nightmares were abating. It helped that he now had a mobile phone which he could charge, and the money to pay for credit. Every night at 11 p.m., he would call his mother. She would wish him goodnight, and that would help him sleep soundly.

Mohammed grabbed every opportunity he could to learn and to become a better person, and rather than dwelling on what he had lost, he marvelled at the new world which was opening up for him.

When I was in Syria, I spoke Arabic, I knew two or three areas in Syria, I was never thinking about leaving Syria. Now I speak English and have different friends from another country.

He spoke to a friend in Germany, who was almost in tears explaining his efforts to master the German language. But Maltese was so close to Arabic and Mohammed was already speaking it well. When he finally got his refugee papers and a passport in the spring of 2015, the work was pouring in and Mohammed started to feel real affection for his second home. He wanted to give something back to the island which saved his life, so when he heard that children in the cancer ward were in need of wigs, he shaved his head and donated his long dark locks.

Such acts of generosity would be wasted on some Maltese. A man living a few floors up from the Syrians' flat would tell anyone who asked that the refugees were responsible for all the crime on Malta and that he was afraid for the safety of his daughter. But such hatred could not poison Mohammed's spirit. The only time his thoughts darkened was when he worried about his family. While his two brothers had fled, his mother, father and sisters were still in Damascus, and he desperately wanted to get them to safety. But where was this elusive safety? Not in Syria, not in neighbouring countries, and not in Europe while the journey to get there was so perilous.

Then of course there was the sadness Mohammed felt for the lost little children like Aylan.

But as it had taken the loss of 800 lives for the European Union to put boats in the water in the stretch of the Mediterranean separating Libya from Italy, so it took the life of a child for politicians to examine their consciences. In the face of a public outcry, British Prime Minister David Cameron backtracked on his earlier statement and said Britain would resettle 20,000 Syrians directly from the camps in Lebanon. France's President François Hollande ended his opposition to quotas and backed Merkel's plan, announcing that France would take 24,000 refugees over two years. The European Commission finally launched infringement proceedings against nineteen EU countries for not implementing the bloc's asylum laws. Then on 22 September, the European Union pushed through a plan to take 160,000 refugees from Greece and Italy and relocate them across other EU nations by quotas based on population, size and GDP. The plan was approved despite continued opposition from Hungary, the Czech Republic, Romania and Slovenia. The newer EU members protested that they had been bullied by the West, and the continent settled into an animosity which would fester for the rest of the year.

Some progress had been made, but new battle lines were drawn in Europe and most of the refugees would still have to fight their way through a hostile bloc of countries more determined than ever to keep them out. The political will of the rest of the European Union would also be tested in the coming months by terrorist attacks which once again forced Europe's deepest prejudices to the surface.

Aylan would not be the last child to die trying to reach Europe's shores.

So Mohammed still had a job to do, and at the end of September he went on a tour organized by Amnesty International to speak to the press, public and officials in Austria, Belgium, the Czech Republic and Hungary. He hoped it would help with his guilt. There were hundreds of thousands of people still risking their lives at sea, despite his warnings.

The shipwreck of 11 October – maybe no one heard about it, maybe no one wanted to listen, or maybe I just did not do enough, he thought.

But walking down the platform at Westbahnhof when the Amnesty tour took him to Vienna, he began to realize that nothing would stop the flow while war still raged around the world.

'Why are you putting your family in this situation?' Mohammed asked a Syrian man sitting on the floor of the station.

'All you hear are bombs and explosions,' the man explained. 'Hearing it is worse than seeing it because you just don't know if the next bomb will hit you. I didn't know if I would reach Europe alive or not, and I didn't care because I am dead already in Syria.'

Mohammed walked away, trying to keep the tears at bay. Finally he understood.

As he ambled between the trains thinking about his own family, his path may have crossed that of another young refugee – a slight Eritrean woman with the pockets of her jacket filled with nappies and her arms wrapped tightly around the tiny baby strapped to her chest in a cheap sling.

22

Lockdown

Sina: Athens, Greece

On the morning of Sunday, 26 July, Sina got up, fed Andonis and went for breakfast in the hotel restaurant. Just like they did every other morning, many of the regular guests asked after Dani. They were so used to seeing this cheerful young woman tending her baby with one hand and clutching her mobile phone in the other, chatting away to her husband as if he were right there beside her. Since Andonis's birth, she and Dani had spoken on the phone every few hours, sharing all the new developments and delighting in each facial expression, movement and sound. Photographs flashed back and forth over continents. Sina would send image after image of their son, although it was never enough for Dani, who pored over every picture of the chubby little boy who was growing to look so much like him. Dani would send photos of himself burying his head in Sina's clothes, and anyone who overheard their conversations could tell this was a couple deeply in love.

But that morning, Sina was not her usual sunny self. She had not spoken to Dani in five days. The last news she had had from him was on 21 July, when he had arrived in Khartoum and called to say he had an appointment at the Greek embassy. Then there was silence. His phone just rang and rang.

'I don't know what's going on,' Sina said over the phone to Despina's granddaughter Debbie Karnachoriti, who had just left after a visit to Athens.

'Maybe he can't call you because he doesn't have any credit,' Debbie suggested.

Sina was not convinced. Dani would always find a way to speak to her and Andonis.

When Sina returned to her room, she tried Dani's number again. The couple used Viber, a free online messaging application. Each user had a profile and a photograph, and it was the lifeline which allowed Sina and Dani to talk, send messages and exchange pictures without having to pay for long-distance phone calls. But when Sina opened the application that morning, it was not an image of Dani staring back at her. His handsome face had disappeared. In his place was another man whom Sina had never seen before in her life, his arms covered with tattoos. She called anyway. A stranger answered.

'Who is this?' the voice said.

Confused, Sina asked him to put Dani on the phone, or to tell her where her husband was, but the man laughed and hung up. She tried to call back, but there was no answer.

What is going on? Where is Dani?

Sina did not sleep that night. Every scenario possible ran though her head, but she forced herself to stay positive. Andonis slept soundly beside her, and she had to stay strong for him.

Debbie Karnachoriti was still in bed the next morning at 10.30 when her mobile phone rang. Groggily, she answered. At first she could not understand who was calling or what they were saying. All she could hear were sobs and gasps and someone trying to catch their breath. Then she made out the voice of her friend in Athens, Sina Habte.

'He's dead, he's dead, he's dead.'

Shock pulled Debbie out of her daze. Who was dead? Had something happened to Andonis? Her blood ran cold, but she forced herself to remain calm. Slowly, she managed to piece together the events of Sina's morning. Sina's mother-in-law had phoned, beside herself with worry. She had just received a call – she did not know who from – and the voice brought heartbreaking news.

'Dani is dead,' a man told her, then hung up.

Now Sina was all alone in a hotel room shaking with shock, confusion and disbelief and Debbie didn't know what to do. Sina managed to force out a few more words.

'I have this number – please call them and ask them what happened.'

It was the telephone number of the smuggler who had brought Dani from Kampala to Khartoum. Debbie braced herself and dialled the number. Someone picked up, but the signal was terrible and the line crackled. Debbie explained who she was and why she was calling, but the man did not speak English well and it was difficult to make herself understood.

'Tell me about Dani,' she said, speaking slowly and clearly.

'He is dead of malaria, the disease of Africa,' the man finally replied.

Debbie tried to keep him on the line, to find out as much as she could, but it was no use.

'Nobody knows, nobody knows,' the man repeated.

The call was over.

If he was sick, I would have known.

Nothing made sense to Sina. Dani had been fine when they spoke on the phone. Malaria could not kill someone that quickly, could it? Surely Dani would have called her to warn her if he was seriously ill. Other scenarios played over in her mind. He had all that cash on him for a plane ticket. Could he have been killed in a robbery? Then she thought about the rumours of the long reach of the Eritrean intelligence services. Was she safe? Was Andonis safe? Debbie urged Sina to give the Red Cross in Sudan a chance to investigate the smuggler's claims.

'Maybe it's not true, we should search better,' Debbie said.

'No, this must be true,' Sina replied, 'because otherwise he would have called me.'

Debbie and Despina did everything they could, sending counsellors to Sina's hotel and trying day and night to find out more about Dani's death. But Sina retreated into her grief. She would not answer her phone for days, and her friends resorted to putting in desperate calls to the hotel reception staff to try and find out what was happening. Sina threw all her energy into Andonis, feeding him, holding him tight, making sure he knew nothing of this wretched limbo she found herself in. Life had never felt so desperate, she had never felt so alone, even surrounded by people who were trying to help.

The guests in the hotel who had cheerily asked after Dani every morning now looked at Sina with pity in their eyes, and Sina turned away from their sympathetic glances. Hatred welled up in her heart: all she wanted was to be alone with her son and her loss, not listening to other people cry and tell her how sorry they were. When she tried to escape and went out on the streets, she was sure the Greek people in the neighbourhood had the same sorry look in their eyes. The only way to come to terms with Dani's death was to keep busy, but what was there for her to do in a hotel room in Athens beyond look after Andonis, her little copy of her husband?

Once again, she was unable to separate the place from the anguish inside, and just like Istanbul, Athens became another city which meant only one thing: separation from Dani.

I hate my life in Greece, she thought, *because everybody reminds me of Dani. I can't ever forget him, but sometimes you need to forget a little because it hurts all the time, and he is gone.*

Find something positive – that would be the best way to distract her anguished mind. Sina logged onto her email account and looked at the acceptance letter from Münster University. The term began in September. Yes, that was the best thing she could do – take Andonis to Germany and continue her education. She called the German embassy and made an appointment with their visa section for 17 August, but a lawyer at a local charity warned her to prepare for the worst. The Red Cross had not been able to get a death certificate for Dani and the lawyer advised her that without permission from both parents – or proof of the father's death – Andonis would not be granted a visa. If Sina was so keen to study, the lawyer suggested, she could leave the baby behind with the charity.

Sina was appalled. She and Dani had endured all the suffering and hardship of the past year for one reason: so that they could be together with their baby in a safe place. Now someone was suggesting she abandon him. Sina panicked. She would not go to the German embassy – she never even tried to call them to confirm the lawyer's advice. Instead, she phoned David, the young Eritrean man who had been by her side when their ship was swallowed by the sea.

It was Sunday morning, and he was in the Netherlands.

'How did you get there?' Sina wanted to know.

'Sina, it is difficult,' David replied. 'If you know someone who can help you, you can try. But alone by yourself – you can't do this. Even for me it was very difficult.'

Eventually he gave her a smuggler's number, on one condition.

'Ask him to find someone who can help you,' he said.

She dialled the number straight away.

'I am a friend of David and I want to know the payment to travel out of Greece.'

The man on the other end of the phone asked for €400, and told her to pack. Borders were closing every day, so unless she moved soon, she could be stuck in Athens.

'Today I am ready and I have a place for you,' he said. 'Are you ready?'

Sina looked around her hotel room – she looked the baby carriers, the prams, the toys, the mounds of stuffed animals and the piles of tiny clothes, and she decided to leave it all behind.

'Yes,' she replied, 'I am ready.'

Mother and son packed light. Sina selected one of the baby carriers that the good people of Rhodes had donated, pulled on a pair of white shorts and training shoes, and slung an extra pair of trousers in a bag along with two outfits for Andonis and a blanket to keep him warm.

Within hours of deciding to leave, Sina was on a coach, Andonis sleeping in her lap, heading away from Athens towards the border with Macedonia. It was Sunday, 16 August, and as they drove across the country where her first experience had been the wrath of its sea, then the kindness of its people, then the pall of death, she felt relief. For so long she had looked to others to guide her through her life, and she had not realized how strong she could be.

If you want to do something, you can do it, she told herself.

The coach arrived at the Macedonian border at dawn on Monday, two days before riot police and the army sealed off the frontier. The blockade would only last a few days – the government in Skopje quickly realized that it was impossible to block the path of so many determined souls without more people getting hurt. But that would come after Sina and Andonis had passed. Getting down from the coach, Sina faced a two-hour walk through the sunflower fields to the border. Andonis snuggled close to his mother's chest, the sound of her heartbeat and the rhythm of her walking soothing him to sleep. He knew nothing of the pain in her hips and back, nothing of her constant worries about how to give him his next feed, how to change his nappy, how to keep him clean and warm and safe.

After crossing into Macedonia, Sina followed the crowd to a police station which was issuing permits to transit through the country. Night had fallen, but there were no beds. Sina sat on the pavement and drifted in and out of sleep as she cradled Andonis. When her papers were ready, she shook the sleep from her eyes and walked up to a Sudanese man who was touting rides north. Another €150 of the Greek Orthodox Church's donation bought Sina a seat in a taxi all the way to the Serbian border.

Summer rain had started to fall on the Balkan states, and when their driver left Sina, Andonis and two young Somali men in a shopping mall car park at 3 a.m., there was nowhere to go as the skies opened. Rain soaked through Sina's cotton jacket. A plastic bag and a blanket were not enough to keep Andonis dry and all she could do was try and shelter him with her body. Three hours later, another taxi arrived with two Eritrean men, and the driver offered to guide them by foot into Serbia.

Sina steeled herself for another long walk, this time in the pouring rain through muddy fields where each footstep had to be carefully placed to stop herself and her baby tumbling to the ground. After a few miles of forest path, their group of seven travellers first encountered dozens and then hundreds of other people heading north towards the European Union.

Andonis wasn't sleeping quietly any more. With Sina's hair and jacket soaked through there was no way to keep him dry, and he cried as he clung to her. Breastfeeding calmed him, but it was difficult when no one in the group would wait. At some points early on in the journey, other mothers and fathers had tried to help, but people now were looking out for their own. Sina understood: she only thought of Andonis, her head down towards the wind, trying to move forward silently to safety and warmth. If only Dani were with her. But Sina tried not to let memories of her husband consume her. So each time Andonis needed a feed, Sina had to run ahead, sit on a damp patch of ground and allow her baby five minutes of nursing, then race to catch up with the group. She did the same every time she changed his nappy. Her belongings had been sacrificed to make room for the supplies to keep him clean. One jacket pocket was stuffed with nappies, the other with baby wipes, and the stock would be replenished in each town they crossed.

But it would be another six hours of marching through the rain and mud before the forest path turned into a road and they were finally in a small Serbian town. Sina dug into her wallet and bought a set of dry clothes for herself and Andonis, before following the crowds for a few more hours along asphalt roads to a Serbian police station. There was food and shelter, which Sina took gratefully, sleeping well enough to regain her strength.

The government in Belgrade had taken a pragmatic approach to the tens of thousands of people heading across its territory. When the trickle began in 2014, the state responded with a heavy hand to try and scare people away from its borders, forcing some people back to Macedonia and refusing to offer shelter to others. When the trickle became a flood and up to 4,000 arrived every day in the summer of 2015, it seemed easier to help them on their way, and the government put on buses and provided food to help smooth their transit to the country they really wanted to reach: Hungary, and the start of the passport-free Schengen zone.

One of those buses took Sina further north the next day, to a town just outside Belgrade where other refugees had told her she could find a smuggler – a Sudanese man named Ahmed – who could help her get to Hungary.

'Please help us,' Sina begged Ahmed, exhausted from the walk and desperate to find a safe place, 'we can pay whatever you want, but we need help.'

With the Hungarian Prime Minister, Orbán, unrelenting in his efforts to force refugees out of his territory, the Hungarian border was the hardest to cross. Ahmed asked for €1,500 for the trip all the way to Austria, and Sina agreed. An Ethiopian woman called Jasmine – six months pregnant and travelling alone – was also waiting to make the same journey, and the pair settled into a hotel together. After a week's wait, Ahmed told them to gather a small bag with food and water. Their transport was ready. For their €1,500, the women would be driven to the border, have a half-an-hour walk into Hungary, then rendezvous with another smuggler who would drive them to Austria.

After a few hours on the road, the driver slowed down as they approached the border.

'When the car stops,' he told his passengers, 'you have to get out and run very fast.'

A pregnant woman and a mother carrying a baby could only run so fast, but they tried to move as deftly as possible in the direction of the forest when the car pulled over. Sure enough, another smuggler was hiding there, beckoning them into the trees, where more fleeing refugees were gathered.

'Come on, come on, this way into the forest, cover yourselves.'

Sina and Jasmine ducked down and ran under the cover of the trees.

'Now we have to walk for eight hours,' the smuggler said.

Once again, Sina had believed the lies and she had been forced to put her child in jeopardy thanks to a combination of the European Union's policy and the ruthlessness of the smugglers. As the group set off, Sina fought back the tears and pleaded with their guide – an Afghan man whose name she did not know – to give her some time to feed Andonis. She worried about her milk supply. Her small bag of food and water was not enough for an eight-hour walk, so she was grateful when they stopped in a clearing in the middle of the forest and the smuggler gave her some biscuits and water.

'We have to wait here for four hours,' he said, 'then we will cross the border.'

At 8 p.m. they were on the move again, crossing bumpy forest paths with only the light of the moon to guide them.

'Just follow the feet of the person in front of you,' the smuggler told them.

Then another light appeared through the trees – the beam of a torch searching through the darkness.

The urgent voice of the smuggler rang out.

'Down, down, get down on the floor!'

'Why? Why? What is happening?' someone asked.

'Police!'

Sina locked her arms around Andonis and dropped to the forest floor.

The torch beam continued to move through the canopy, searching for the refugees who crouched still and silent, willing the police to move on. Finally, the light and the shuffling of the leaves seemed to pass: safe again. The smugglers were not so sure, and decided to keep their human consignment hidden for a little longer. They could not risk anyone giving them away. One of the smugglers approached Sina, holding something in his hand.

'We have medicine for the children,' he told her. 'You must give this medicine to your child. Then he will sleep very well. But if he cries the policemen will come to catch us.'

Sina stared aghast at the syringe, and hugged Andonis to her chest.

'He is three months old!'

'No problem,' the smuggler replied, 'this is OK for him.'

'You are not a medical professional – you cannot give medicine to a baby.'

The others who were huddled in the dark cast anxious glances in Sina's direction. She was getting no sympathy, not even from Jasmine. The group were so terrified of the Hungarian police that they urged the young mother to drug her newborn baby into silence.

'If he cries the policemen will catch us and they will return us to Serbia,' one man said.

Sina had to gather all her mental strength to stand up to the smugglers, to the other refugees, to the voice in her own head telling her that maybe it would be easier just to use the syringe.

I have to do what I want to do, and that's it.

She faced the group.

'I will not give these things to my son.'

For a moment, Sina wondered if they would try and force the medicine into Andonis, and if she would have to get up and run. But they backed down. Andonis did not make a sound, and a short while later the group was on the move again through the dark forests. At around midnight, their walk across the border was finally over, and a van was waiting for Sina, Andonis, Jasmine and a few others. Sina could barely stand up, her feet covered in blisters, her ankles swollen, and her small body aching under the weight of her baby and the gruelling walk. They spent six hours in the back of the van with eight other people. Sina couldn't sit down properly – she had to just crouch on the van floor – but at least she was not walking any more. Then the van stopped.

'Hey, come on out, this is Austria,' the driver shouted.

Sina jumped down and looked around her. She was on a wide road, there was forest all around, and not a house in sight.

'Where are we going? Why don't you take us to the hotel?' she asked.

'This is Austria,' the man replied, and drove off.

Sina looked up and down the road, and realized that they would simply have to guess which way to go. A despondency fell over the group. They could be heading back to Hungary, they could be walking into a forest, they just did not know. Their exhaustion was so complete that they were like sleepwalkers moving aimlessly through the night. Then the police came. Through the fog of tiredness, the Austrians seemed kind. They gave Sina a hot drink and a blanket, offered her a bed to sleep in at the police station, and asked her if she would like to claim asylum.

When Sina said no – she was determined to get to Germany – they put her in a police car and took her back to Hungary. The Austrian police left Sina, Andonis and Jasmine at a Hungarian police station at the border, where they were registered and put on a train to Budapest. They arrived in the Hungarian capital just as the authorities decided to close the city's main Budapest Keleti station, stranding up to 3,000 people on the streets outside without adequate food or medicine.

It was chaos. All Sina could see was rubbish, filth, crowds of hot and panicked people shouting and jostling to try and get back into the station to board their train.

'Germany, Germany, Germany,' some young men chanted. Others held placards over their head: 'Please Open the Station', 'We Want To Go To Germany – Please Help Us'.

Prime Minister Orbán was making a point. Germany had suspended the Dublin rules, so Hungary was going to try and enforce EU's asylum rules by stopping people from travelling north. His tantrum would only last a few days and then the station reopened, but in the meantime thousands of people were left sleeping on the pavement in the forty-degree heat.

Sina and Jasmine needed somewhere to stay, and went to three hotels to ask for a room. They had papers from the Hungarian police and money to pay, but that was not enough to convince hoteliers to take in the mother, baby and pregnant woman.

'You don't have a passport so you can't stay,' one unsmiling receptionist explained.

The women returned to the train station and sat on the pavement outside. It had been eighteen days since Sina had bundled Andonis in her arms and left the hotel room in Athens where she had experienced such extremes of joy and pain. She had barely slept or eaten. She was suddenly overwhelmed, and she wept.

A man – a Syrian refugee – approached her.

'Why are you crying?' he asked. 'You are a refugee, so are all of the people here.'

Sina looked at him though her tears, and gestured to the baby on her lap.

'No, please, I have a baby, I can't keep carrying him like this, we need a house,' she said, but the man couldn't help and walked on.

A journalist approached Sina.

'Why are you crying?' she asked.

The reporter took notes when Sina answered.

'I need a room for my baby, I can't stay here like this. There are so many people and it is not good for my baby. Please help me – if you can find a house for me or a hotel, please, I can pay whatever you want.'

The journalist gave Sina a bottle of water and walked away.

Then a Nigerian man approached. He didn't ask Sina why she was crying, but told her she and Jasmine could have a bed to sleep in for €15 a night. Sina didn't ask any questions, but pulled herself onto her aching feet and followed him to a run-down apartment were thirteen other people were sleeping on the floor of a small room. The man pointed to a mattress where two people were already lying down on their sides, pressed up against each other. Sina didn't complain. She wedged herself and Andonis onto the small space, and closed her eyes and slept.

A few days later, on 3 September, Budapest Keleti station re-opened, and Sina bought an open ticket to Munich. She decided not to travel right away. It was chaos, and she wanted to keep Andonis away from the crowds. She spent another week on the filthy mattress, then returned to the station. By then German officials had also started to panic at the surge in people coming over the border, and on 13 September they temporarily stopped trains from Austria entering their territory. The furthest Sina could go was Vienna, and she asked a police officer at the station for advice. He asked her where she was trying to get to, then gestured to a platform.

'That train, it will go on to Munich,' he said. 'Don't tell anyone. But you have a baby, and you have a ticket to Germany, so you should be able to go all the way.'

Sina settled on the train with Andonis. After a few hours, it pulled in to Vienna. Sina got off and asked a railway official for help. Sure enough, the final destination of her train had changed to Munich, so she got back on and was soon pulling away from Platform 1 at Vienna's Westbahnhof.

Sina knew by then that her odyssey was not going to end in Germany. To register for her master's degree course, she needed her original degree certificate from Eritrea, but she had given that to a smuggler for safekeeping in Uganda. At the time, it had seemed like a good idea, as it would not be safe to take her most important documents on a sea voyage. But when she contacted the smuggler and asked for them back, he was evasive. He would send her certificate to someone in Sweden, and she needed to go there to collect it. So in Munich, Sina transferred to a train bound for Malmö, where she changed once again and travelled to Gothenburg.

She had gone as far she could. It was 16 September. Sina had carried Andonis across eight countries and covered more than 1,500 miles. It was time to rest. She walked into a police station in Gothenburg and told them she was a refugee. She had arrived in a country with a long tradition of offering sanctuary to those in need, and Sweden was one of the few EU states which was now honouring its historical promises to help the downtrodden. More than 170,000 refugees were expected to arrive before the end of the year, and they were ready for Sina and Andonis.

After a few days at a shelter in Gothenburg, mother and baby were transferred to the campsite at Borås, a small textiles town an hour's drive west of the city. Home was a small wooden cabin designed for hikers to take a day's rest before setting off into the surrounding forests, but there were two single beds and a small stove for making tea. Sina still had a lot on her mind – she needed to defer her master's course while she applied for asylum in Sweden, and she was waiting for Dani's death certificate. But the longer she spent in Borås, the more she liked it. There was a library with free Internet access, the air was so clean, and a team of friendly doctors had started Andonis on his vaccinations. In the centre of town, on a small island in the middle of a man-made lake, stood an adventure playground with slides and climbing nets and swings in bright primary colours.

It was the childhood she and Dani had hoped they could offer their baby when they had begun searching for a new life at the beginning of the year.

Yes, thought Sina, *this could be home.*

Epilogue

No Direction Home

The year 2015 ended with terror and fear. France suffered an unprecedented attack on its soil as ISIS extremists opened fire and detonated explosives at bars, restaurants and a club in Paris on Friday, 13 November, killing 130 people. The following week the Belgian capital Brussels came to a standstill, with schools, shopping centres, nurseries and public transport shut down for days as the authorities warned of a similar attack. The centre of the city that hosts the European Union institutions resembled a ghost town, with armoured vehicles blocking pavements and soldiers watching over the wary few who ventured downtown. On 31 December, as Europe prepared to bid farewell to a tumultuous year and cautiously welcome 2016, Brussels cancelled its municipal fireworks display after another terror alert. In Munich, German authorities acted on a tip-off that militants were planning an imminent attack and shut down two train stations an hour before midnight. Fears of an attack in Belgium were realised a few months later when, on 22 March, a cell of Islamists detonated bombs at Brussels Airport and on the city's Metro, killing thirty-two people.

Europe was meant to be a safe place, free from war, but suddenly everything seemed different and frightening. And as fear often does when mismanaged and exploited, it turned into hatred and mistrust. The photograph of three-year-old Aylan

Kurdi's lifeless body on a Turkish beach was now forgotten and once again the Syrian refugees who were fleeing the same kind of violence inflicted by zealots on Paris became a target of anger and suspicion.

Hanan al-Hasan's two daughters, Rim and Bisan, were still living in the remote city of Levanger in Norway, and found they had to explain themselves to every person they met.

'No, I'm not a terrorist,' Rim would say. 'I'm not here to harm you, I'm just here for a short time until I can live back in my country. I had everything in Syria and I lost it. I was just like one of you living a normal life, but war is very ugly.'

Fighters from ISIS had now overrun the Yarmouk neighbourhood where they had lived in Damascus, and Rim was sure that the bottles of wine the family kept in the house would have provoked the religious fanatics into destroying their property.

In Malta, Mohammed Kazkji was also forced to explain his religious and personal beliefs to people who he thought were friends and colleagues. Now they were asking him if he was with ISIS and if he knew who carried out the Paris attacks.

'I am so sorry about Paris,' Mohammed would tell them, even though he had nothing to apologise for. 'I want to be an electrical engineer, not a terrorist.'

He didn't blame people, though. When he watched the news and saw reports suggesting Syrian refugees carried out the attacks, he understood their questions and tried to be patient. Within a couple of weeks, seven of the ten key suspects in the Paris attacks had been identified. They were all French or Belgian, born and radicalized in Europe. Like thousands of other disaffected Europeans, they had travelled to Syria to fight alongside ISIS, and were the kinds of people Mohammed, Rim and Bisan had left Syria to escape – foreigners coming to their country and making their lives even more unbearable. The problem was the Syrian passport found near one of the suicide bombers. Reports quickly spread that a Syrian refugee was one of the attackers, apparently confirming the scaremongering of right-wing politicians who had been warning that the destitute new arrivals were little more than a ticking time bomb, potential terrorists waiting for their chance to attack Europe. Further investigations proved that the passport was fake and the attacker could well have been a European citizen on a watch list who used the EU's chaotic response to the refugee crisis to buy a cheap fake passport and slip in unnoticed along the Balkan migration route. Investigations by the BBC suggested that a second attacker had entered Europe in a similar way. As of the end of 2015, not one of the attackers had been confirmed as a Syrian national, and it was actually European governments' insistence on measures to keep people out which had created the roaring trade in forged documents that the attackers had exploited.

But the truth never seemed to matter when it came to refugees. In Poland, a new right-wing government had taken power in October 2015, and its Minister for European Affairs, Konrad Szymański, said the Paris attacks meant Poland would no longer take part in the EU-wide resettlement scheme for 160,000 of the refugees staying in Greece and Italy. The Hungarian and Slovakian governments launched lawsuits at the European Court of Justice to challenge the relocation scheme, with Hungary's President Viktor Orbán saying the plan posed a 'serious threat'.

Nowhere was the toxic link between electioneering and fearmongering clearer than in the United States, where the personalities battling to become the Republican candidate in the 2016 presidential election decided that insulting Syrian refugees would be a good way to boost support. One hopeful, Ben Carson, compared the refugees to rabid dogs. The businessman Donald Trump said he would return all Syrians to the war zone if he took power and would temporarily ban Muslims from entering the country. US President Barack Obama accused his political rivals of being afraid of 'widows and three-year-old orphans' and insisted he would go ahead with plans to welcome at least 10,000 more Syrian refugees in the coming year. But the governors of thirty-one states said they would refuse to house them.

Alienating entire communities does not create conditions for a peaceful and stable future, neither in the United States nor in Europe. History has shown that divided societies where communities feel unwelcome tend to fuel feelings of marginalization. The one million people who arrived in the EU in 2015 and the hundreds of thousands who came before them are seeking peace, not more war and terror. But the danger is that the policies promoted by the right-wing governments and politicians end up creating the very extremism they fear. Governments need policies that will welcome and integrate those in need of refuge because while conflicts continue around the globe, their victims will keep finding their way to Europe's shores, desperation forcing them around whatever barriers are put in their way.

Keeping the refugees out, however, remained the EU's priority well into 2016. In March, the EU signed a deal with Turkey. They promised Ankara €6 billion and other sweeteners including visa-free travel for Turkish citizens and the acceleration of Turkey's EU membership talks on the condition that Turkey take back people arriving in Greece who had not applied for asylum or who had had their asylum applications rejected. For every Syrian returned, the EU pledged to resettle another Syrian staying at a refugee camp in Turkey. UN experts warned that the deal could be in breach of various international laws and treaties, but the EU went ahead regardless. At the start of April, despite reports that Turkey was sending people back to Syria against their will and firing in the direction of families trying to cross the Syria–Turkey border, the returns began. Once again the EU found itself compromising its most cherished ideals to further its own self-interest. It had not been long before this deal that EU leaders had been condemning the authoritarian tendencies of the government of

Turkish President Recep Erdoğan, which had over the years taken measures to curb an independent press and judiciary. Journalists and academics were being locked up, and more than 2,000 legal cases of insulting the president had been opened. But those concerns were pushed aside. European leaders enthusiastically embraced the deal, even as Turkish officials threated to send more refugees to Europe if all their demands were not met, echoing the rhetoric of Colonel Gaddafi back in 2010.

Improving the lives of refugees in Syria's neighbouring countries is an admirable aim and it could remove the motivation for many people to risk death to reach Europe. Had Nart been able to find paid work rather than exploitative labour in Istanbul, he would have stayed. Turkey is meant to spend the EU's €6 billion on such projects as Arabic-language schools, and there needs to be strict monitoring to ensure the money is well spent. Allowing the refugees to work would provide the greatest incentive for them to stay. But if the only goal is reducing the numbers of people leaving the Turkish coastline for EU soil, then the incentive for Turkey is to keep Syrians out of the country in the first place, risking more push-backs and other abuses. The EU must also look further afield than Turkey. Lebanon and Jordan need help with their huge refugee populations and incentives to improve the lives of their guests. If Hanan had been able to place Ismail, Riad, Rim and Bisan in schools and universities in Beirut, the family could have remained in Lebanon, comforted by the thought of their home just an hour's drive away. Simply spending millions building vast tented refugee camps in the desert where no one wants to live will not work. Nor will paternalistic handouts to developing nations stop the flow of economic migrants, as EU leaders found out at a summit with their sub-Saharan African counterparts in the Maltese capital Valletta in November 2015. On the table was €1.8 billion in aid, to be distributed among those African countries on the condition that the leaders implement measures to stop people leaving and agree to take back failed asylum seekers. Most of the leaders were dismissive: the sum was tiny for a whole continent, and fairer trade policies and investment were the tools which would actually help alleviate the poverty people had fled from.

'What Africa needs today is not charity, but investment,' said Somalia's Prime Minister Omar Abdirashid Ali Sharmarke.

Economic migrants from across the developing world will continue to attempt the dangerous journey to Europe while there is extreme poverty in their own countries and no way to try and better their lives. There are, however, plenty of entry-level jobs for the newcomers in Europe on farms, on construction sites, in restaurants and in care facilities for the sick and elderly. Right now those posts are often filled by black-market migrant labour, and governments need to combat this exploitation and open up legal channels for people to apply for work visas from their home countries.

The crisis of 2015, however, was fuelled not by economic migrants but by genuine refugees, and finding safe homes and opportunities for work – be they in the Middle East and Turkey, or in Europe and other rich regions – must be the priority. Relocating refugees already arrived in Greece and Italy is a start, but allowing people to apply for resettlement from outside the EU would offer an avenue of hope where none exists right now and stop many people getting into the boats in the first place. Syrians and other people coming from the Middle East and Asia should be able to apply for asylum in Europe from centres in Turkey, Lebanon, Jordan or Libya. A similar system could be established for Eritreans in a sub-Saharan nation where they felt safe from the reach of Eritrean intelligence services. Sina and Dani were forced to entrust their lives to ruthless smugglers who persuaded them to go to Europe because there were no other options available. Had there been hope that Dani could legally apply to reunite with Sina and Andonis from Kampala, he may not have decided to pay the smuggler for his final, fatal journey back to Sudan.

The current resettlement scheme for 160,000 Syrians and Eritreans staying in Greece and Italy allocates the refugees among the participating EU states depending on the host's size, population, economic prosperity and unemployment. A similar matrix can be used for resettling people from outside the union. The scheme is far from perfect: many refugees don't want to go to countries like Slovakia or Romania, where there are fewer jobs and no Syrian communities. It is true that many might then take advantage of the Schengen zone's open borders and simply get on a train to France or Germany. But if the European Union believes that the free movement of people for labour is in the economic interest of the bloc, then refugees too must be able to follow the labour market. Moreover, the poorer, less populous nations are being asked to take such small numbers of people that if a portion of, say, the 802 refugees allocated to Slovakia decide to move on elsewhere, it would not have a significant impact. The larger, richer nations, however, need to do more. Britain, with its population of 65 million and one of the healthiest economies in the EU, can do better than the 20,000 Syrians it has agreed to re-house over five years. The European Commission also needs punitive measures to enforce the quotas it introduces, otherwise they will simply be ignored.

A large-scale relocation of people has been done before: between 1975 and 1995, 1.3 million refugees from Indochina were resettled across the West, with no discernible impact on the cultural fabric of the host nations. The difference between then and now, however, is the religion of most of the new refugees and the unpalatable fact that Islamophobia overshadows much of the debate about re-housing victims of war from the Middle East. Since the attacks on the United States on 11 September 2001, Muslims have been a target of suspicion, hatred and often outright abuse. Members of no other group are so frequently blamed for the actions of a few, as the reaction to sexual assault allegations against a group of North Africans and Syrians in

Germany on New Year's Eve 2015 once again proved. Politicians need to acknowledge this prejudice and provide the moral leadership to counter it, rather than quietly kowtowing to the forces of hatred. It was a moral imperative which led to the creation of the European Union, and to its founding vow never to return to the dark, divided days of the past. The conviction was that Europe would be stronger and safer if its countries' economies were interdependent, its borders fluid, its people part of something bigger than one nation. Those beliefs have fractured, and the EU needs to re-discover its unity if it is to meet its current responsibilities.

So, how would this work in practice? Most of the refugees are arriving in Greece, but the government in Athens is absolutely right to say that the war-weary are simply using Greece as a springboard to the richer North, and therefore the burden needs to be shared to ensure the refugees' safe arrival and smooth onward passage. First, lives need to be saved in the Aegean Sea, then there needs to be safe and clean accommodation for refugees in Greece. If there were more resources – more funding, staff and equipment pledged from other EU nations – initial asylum claims could be processed in Greece, and the EU law enforcement agencies could run any background security checks there. Then those deemed to be in genuine need of protection could be sent onwards to the nation which will offer them a home and the opportunity to work until it is safe for them to return home again.

But in the early months of 2016, there was little sign of the political will or unity needed to properly implement such measures. While the Turkey deal notionally allowed for asylum applications to be processed in Greece, authorities were overwhelmed and other nations did not step forward to help. Macedonia closed their border in March, trapping 50,000 people in Greece. More than 10,000 of them were forced to live in dire conditions in a makeshift camp near the village of Idomeni. Others were detained in official camps but with so few resources that they were forced to burn trash to keep warm. Putative measures – returning people to an unknown fate in Turkey – had been implemented well before any of the other policies were in place to ensure the new arrivals were treated humanely. Of the 160,000 people the EU agreed to re-locate in late summer, less than 1,000 had left for their new homes by the end of March. As the year began, photographers came across the bodies of more dead children washed up on the Greek and Turkish coastlines, but the pictures didn't make the front pages any more. Children fell out of boats into the cold sea, dying from hypothermia, with only one doctor in a shack to try and save them. Bodies were pulled from the water by groups of volunteers who had travelled to Greece from all over the world, not by coordinated search-and-rescue teams or European coastguard vessels.

'There was no sign of the European Union and people were asking when the EU would come, when will you help us,' the European Health Commissioner Vytenis Andriukaitis wrote after visiting the Greek island of Lesbos in November.

Countries continued to shirk their responsibilities and the more generous nations were overwhelmed. With thousands of people arriving in Sweden every day, the government ran out of shelters. When official reception centres filled up, they started using places like the Borås campsite where Sina lived in a small wooden hut with Andonis. But with 170,000 people arriving in a year in a nation of 9.5 million, soon there were no more huts left, and in mid-November the government announced that it would reintroduce border checks in an attempt to limit the flow of people into the country. The iconic five-mile bridge linking Denmark and Sweden – a symbol of united Europe – would now be policed, with ID checks for everyone crossing. Germany too was forced to reintroduce border checks, and as domestic opposition to the open-door policy grew, the government began to send refugees back over the border to Austria and tightened their asylum rules.

Hostile policies proliferated across Europe: Denmark passed a law to seize jewellery and valuables from arriving refugees to pay for their housing, brushing off concerns about the parallels with the Nazi seizure of Jewish property. In the Czech Republic, President Miloš Zeman addressed an anti-refugee rally organised by the Bloc Against Islam on the anniversary of the Velvet Revolution. Hungary introduced emergency laws, including three-year jail terms for people trying to cross its recently completed fence with Serbia.

Hungary's determination to keep refugees out had an unintended consequence for Nart Bajoi: it prevented him from going home. Since his arrival, Nart had struggled to adapt to life in Germany. The cold weather made his knee ache all the time, he could not find work, and he was never sure if he would be allowed to stay or if he would be sent back to Bulgaria.

Nart was thirty-four years old and had neither the youthful energy which propelled Mohammed to see only opportunity in his misfortune, nor the parental commitment that kept both Sina and Hanan going during their darkest hours.

All roads are closed, I cannot work, I cannot go to school, I can't do anything – just eat and drink, he thought. It's better to go back to Syria. At least that is my country.

On 12 October 2015, preferring the uncertainty of a country at war to staying on in Europe, where he had felt hated, rejected and useless ever since he had arrived, Nart took a bus to the Austrian border. After taking a train through Vienna, he found himself in a village near the Hungarian border. When he crept out at night to try and cross the frontier, he saw police on every road. Nart knew he could face years in jail if he was caught, and he had seen enough of the inside of Europe's prison cells. So he trudged back to Germany.

Perhaps I can try again on New Year's Eve, Nart thought. On that night, everyone will be drunk, and I will be able to cross.

Within a few months, however, the thousands of emails Nart had sent to prospective employers paid off. In December, he was offered a job in a petrol station, and the German government gave him permission to take it. He would stay in Europe – for now.

When the conflicts end, many of Europe's recent arrivals will, like Nart, choose to go back to their home countries, provided there is somewhere left to go back to and some assistance in returning and rebuilding their shattered lives. But if home is where your family are, there are those like Majid Hussain who have no home to go back to. His surrogate family are his friends in Rome, but as 2016 began, Majid still had found no employer willing to give a smart young Nigerian a chance, and each day it became harder to find the money to buy food and get by. Mohammed Kazkji did not think about going home either. The teenager who never dreamed of leaving his Damascus neighbourhood was now an impassioned young man who spoke three languages and travelled throughout Europe to talk about refugees' rights. He had grown into his strong features and his rugged looks and infectious enthusiasm for life attracted the attention of a Hungarian woman working in Malta's film industry. Mohammed was astonished by the speed with which they fell in love, and soon they were planning a wedding and looking forward to a life together. Mohammed was still troubled at night by visions of his family in peril and desperately wanted to get them out of Syria, but he made the most of the circumstances which had brought him to Europe. He would be an asset to any community he lived in: intelligent and hard-working, caring and charitable, exactly the kind of young person many of Europe's faltering economies needed.

Hanan al-Hasan's four children also had a lot to offer Europe, and she and Talal were trying to focus on their futures, rather than dwell on the life they had lost. Although Hanan struggled to keep the depression at bay, she and her husband got up every morning to go to their German classes, tried to find work, and watched as their sons and daughters adapted to their new lives with hope in their hearts. Now that the flow of refugees through Westbahnhof had slowed, Riad was able to devote his energy to his studies, much to his mother's relief. Ismail was looking forward to starting a course in information technology at the University of Vienna in February. Bisan just wanted to leave Norway and be with her mother and father in Austria, and was waiting until she got Norwegian residency to decide where to continue her studies. Rim remained the most optimistic about going home to Syria, and had faith that the war would end soon and she would resume the perfect life she had left behind.

Unlike in Syria, where at least Western politicians were working to forge a political solution, no country seemed interested in Eritrea, and Sina Habte couldn't imagine it ever being safe for her to take Andonis home. So she applied for asylum in Sweden, and just like everywhere else she went, Sina found friends and champions there who were happy to help out the extraordinary woman and her baby. Back in Athens, Andonis had not been able to be baptized without a death certificate for Dani. But the Red Cross finally managed to confirm his death from malaria in Sudan. So on a snowy December morning, Sina pulled a warm coat and boots over a traditional white Eritrean robe and took Andonis to an Orthodox church. There, in front of new friends and old ones who had travelled from across Europe, Andonis was immersed in water, a young life starting anew.

Author's Note on the Text

This book is the story of Majid, Nart, Mohammed, Sina and Hanan and her family, and the primary source material consists of extensive interviews with those individuals, as well as supplementary materials they provided, including photographs and video footage of their journeys. Where possible, I have attempted to corroborate their accounts, and all their experiences closely match similar and extensive accounts given to human rights organizations and the media. Quoted speech is reported as recalled by one or more of the protagonists. Italicized text denotes direct quotes of the protagonists in their interviews with me. At times they were describing their general feelings about an issue and I chose where in the narrative to insert those quotes, and other times they were recalling their specific feelings at the moment described. These quotes have occasionally been paraphrased for clarity in English. Two of the protagonists decided not to use their real names as they have family back home whose security could be compromised by their participation in this book. They chose to go by names with personal resonance to them, and other minor biographical details have been changed to cloak their identities. Everyone else gave their real name.

Cast Away is the culmination of a career-long interest in migration and refugee policy, and I have reported extensively on the issue from Cambodia, Thailand, Myanmar, Pakistan and

Afghanistan, and from 2011 from the Middle East and Europe too. The text draws heavily upon my reporting and editing work from January 2011 when I joined *The Independent* foreign desk just as the Arab Spring began. Most of all it draws on my work since moving to Brussels in March 2013 to cover the European Union, and on many reporting trips following the fate of people trying to reach Europe. For countries I have not been able to visit personally – notably, Libya and Eritrea – I relied on the descriptions given to me by the protagonists, as well as photographs, reports from NGOs and the excellent reporting of fellow journalists. Please see the Sources section for specific details.

And a final a note on the terminology, a controversial issue when writing about the movement of people into Europe, given that it is a mix of those seeking to illegally enter the continent for work and people fleeing war with a legal right to cross a border with no paperwork. Where possible, I have simply referred to them as *people*, but in the interests of variation I also use the term *refugees*. The term *migrant* is widely used in the media as it is perceived as being the most neutral, but it does imply an element of choice in the decision of a person to leave their home, when most of the people entering Europe have been forced out. The UNHCR states that eighty-four per cent of the people who arrived in Europe in 2015 came from the top refugee-producing nations. The protagonists of the book all had their refugee claims accepted, and were mostly travelling with people of the same nationality who would also be granted asylum. As the people on the journeys have not yet had their refugee applications approved, the most accurate term would be *asylum seeker*. But such is the tone of the debate over the last few decades that the two words to describe a person pursuing a universal human right have become loaded with negative connotations. So I go back to the origin of the term *refugee* as described in the *Oxford English Dictionary* – a person gone in search of refuge. Even the minority who will not be officially recognized as refugees are seeking refuge from extreme poverty – no one puts their lives at such acute risk simply for pleasure.

Glossary

Dublin Regulation: *An EU law adopted in 2003 which stipulates which nation is responsible for examining an asylum application. The rules state that a person should claim asylum in the first EU country they arrive in, and must stay there until their application is either approved or declined. Should they travel elsewhere in the EU while their application is being processed, they can be returned to the country where they made their claim.*

European Commission: *The executive arm of the European Union, the Commission proposes EU legislation and policy, and is responsible for upholding EU law.*

European Commissioners: *The College of Commissioners consists of 28 politicians – one from each EU member state – who oversee different policy areas.*

European Convention on Human Rights: *Separate to EU law, the Convention has been in force since 1953, and as of January 2016 there were 47 signatories. The European Court of Human Rights oversees the Convention. Both the Convention and the Court are part of the Council of Europe, an organization founded after the Second World War to ensure human rights were placed at the heart of the continent. While the Council of Europe is independent of the EU, all EU members must be signatories to the Convention.*

European Council: *The grouping of the leaders of the 28 countries making up the European Union, the European Council meets regularly to discuss policy and approve the most important pieces of legislation proposed by the European Commission. Most legislation must also be approved by the European Parliament.*

European Parliament: *The EU's 751-seat legislature, with Members of the European Parliament (MEPs) elected from each of the 28 EU member states every five years. The parliament debates and approves most legislation proposed by the European Commission.*

European Union: *The EU began life as the European Coal and Steel Community, established in 1952 by France, Germany, Belgium, Luxembourg, Italy and the Netherlands to bind together the economies of the European powers in the hope that such financial and political interdependence would prevent a return to war. It became known as the European Union in 1993, and had expanded to encompass 28 countries as of January 2016.*

Eurozone: *The grouping of the nations that use the euro single currency, established in January 1999. As of January 2016, there were 19 countries in the eurozone.*

Frontex: *The EU agency responsible for managing security at the EU's external borders.*

International Organization for Migration (IOM): *An intergovernmental organization established in 1951 and tasked with promoting the rights of migrants and assisting in the operational challenges of migration.*

Mare Nostrum: *Latin for 'Our Sea', Mare Nostrum was the naval search-and-rescue operation launched by the Italian government after the two migrant shipwrecks near the Italian coastline in October 2013. It ran until 1 November 2014.*

Pegida: *Patriotic Europeans Against the Islamization of the Occident, an anti-Islam protest movement originating in Germany.*

Push-backs: *An informal term used to describe the forced return of an asylum seeker to the country they have come from without registering and examining their claim for refuge. The practice is illegal under various international laws and conventions.*

Schengen Agreement: *In 1985, Belgium, France, Luxembourg, Germany and the Netherlands abolished internal border controls, another step towards creating a genuine single market where people, goods and services can move freely. The deal was signed in the Luxembourg village of Schengen, and the Schengen Zone has since expanded to 26 countries. Of the 28 EU nations, the United Kingdom and Ireland opted out of joining Schengen, while (as of January 2016) Bulgaria, Croatia, Romania and Cyprus are waiting to join. Four non-EU nations – Iceland, Norway, Switzerland and Lichtenstein – are also Schengen members.*

Shabiha: *The private militia of Syria's President Bashar al-Assad, made up of members of the Alawite community, the sect of Shia Islam of which the Assad family are members.*

Triton: *The EU-funded mission in the Mediterranean which began operating when Mare Nostrum ended.*

UNHCR: *The Office of the United Nations High Commissioner for Refugees, established in 1950 to assist Europeans displaced by the Second World War. The UNHCR is the UN agency tasked with protecting the rights of refugees in the world.*

Sources

The primary sources for *Cast Away* are author interviews with Majid Hussain, Nart Bajoi, Mohammed Kazkji, Sina Habte, Hanan al-Hasan, Talal Al-Hamzah, Ismail Hamzah, Riad Hamzah, Rim Hamzah and Bisan Hamzah. Additional sources and suggested further reading are indicated below. Incidents which were widely reported by numerous media outlets are not sourced, but where I have relied on one specific article to describe an event I have given full details. Figures at the start of each section on the numbers arriving in Europe and the death tolls are from the EU's border agency Frontex, the UNHCR and the International Organization for Migration (IOM).

Introduction

Details of the length of the fence barricading Europe comes from Amnesty International's report, 'Fear and Fences: Europe's Approach to Keeping Migrants at Bay', published on 17 November 2015.

The IOM released a report – 'Fatal Journeys: Tracking Lives Lost During Migration' – on 29 September 2014. It showed that the migration over the Mediterranean to Europe was the most dangerous in the world, with 3,072 deaths in the time scale it looked at, compared with 230 deaths on the US–Mexico border. It estimated that at that point, 22,000 people had lost their lives trying to reach Europe since 2000.

The IOM's spokesperson in Rome, Flavio di Giacomo, gave the figures for unidentified shipwreck victims in an interview with the author.

1. A Dictator's Revenge

Journalists in Libya at the time reported extensively on the retribution attacks against sub-Saharan Africans, and on 26 August 2011 the UNHCR put out a statement urging all sides to show restraint amid reports of several hundred black migrants trapped in the capital.

Drew Hinshaw and Joe Parkinson of the *Wall Street Journal* wrote an excellent report on the history of the smuggling trade out of Agadez, 'Migrant Boom is Saharan Boon: Agadez Traffickers Profit from Movement through Niger to Libya', which was published in July 2015.

The figures on the number of migrant workers in Libya come from an EU-financed report by the Migration Policy Centre, which cites IOM and Libyan government data.

Gaddafi made his threats about 'chaos, Bin Laden, armed factions' in an interview with France's *Le Journal du Dimanche*, published on 5 March 2011.

Details of Gaddafi's complicity in the migrant trade and reports of him dumping migrants in the desert come from author interviews with IOM's Flavio di Giacomo, and various reports by NGOs.

Details of the Italian push-backs to Libya come from a report on *TIME* online – 'Italy's Troubling Immigration Deal with Gaddafi', by Stephan Faris, published on 5 April 2011 – and the Human Rights

Watch Report 'Pushed Back, Pushed Around', published in September 2009. On 23 February 2012 the European Court of Human Rights ruled that Italy had violated the European Convention on Human Rights' article on *non-refoulement*, which prohibits returning migrants to countries where they may face persecution or inhuman or degrading treatment.

The figures for clandestine arrivals come from the Frontex 2014 Annual Risk Analysis.

The European Commission announced its deal with Gaddafi in a press release on 5 October 2010, entitled 'European Commission and Libya agree a Migration Cooperation agenda during high level visit to boost EU–Libya relations'.

2. Into the Storm

The colour and description of the clandestine aid networks and protests in Damascus are based on interviews with Nart Bajoi, and on interviews conducted during the author's February 2012 reporting trip to Damascus. See 'Inside Damascus: The Poor Get By, The Rich Find a Way to Make Money', 9 February 2012; 'Assad, Wake Up! We're with Homs to the Death!', 11 February 2012; 'Inside the Torture Chamber of Assad's Inquisition Squads', 19 February 2012; 'Syria's Wounded Lay Blame on Mossad or MI6 – but Never Assad', 14 February 2012, all published in *The Independent*.

The Amnesty International report 'I Wanted to Die: Syria's Torture Survivors Speak Out', published on 14 March 2012, goes into great detail about the regime's torture methods.

3. Welcome to Europe

The figures for arrivals on Lampedusa and the reception conditions for the refugees come from the UNHCR, in particular their briefing notes from 22 March 2011.

The figure of the EU resettling just 400 refugees from the Arab Spring was given by the European Commissioner for Home Affairs at the time, Cecilia Malmström, in an editorial in the *Times of Malta* entitled 'Refugees: How Europe Failed', published on 19 January 2012.

The European Court of Human Rights on 1 September 2015 ruled that the reception conditions on Lampedusa diminished the human dignity of the arrivals, their detention was unlawful, and Italy breached the European Convention of Human Rights by not adequately assessing each individual claim for asylum, once again contravening the crucial principle of *non-refoulement*.

4. Married to the Military

For a fascinating history and context to the current situation in Eritrea, see Michela Wrong's excellent book, *I Didn't Do It for You: How the World Used and Abused a Small African Nation*.

The Eritrean government largely bars access to foreign journalists, but Matina Stevis of the *Wall Street Journal* was granted entry in 2015, and her report – 'African Dictatorship Fuels Migrant Crisis: Thousands Flee Isolated Eritrea to Escape Life of Conscription and Poverty' – gives a valuable insight into the government's justification for national service.

Most of the accounts of life in Eritrea come from exiles. Apart from interviews with Sina Habte, the primary source for Chapter 4 was the

'United Nations Office of the High Commissioner for Human Rights – Report of the Detailed Findings of the Commission of Inquiry on Human Rights in Eritrea', published on 5 June 2015, which was based on the interviews of over 550 witnesses. To quote the report in full on national service: 'National service in Eritrea is based on conditions and measures that are not proportionate, reasonable or necessary in the interest of national defence. National service as implemented by the Eritrean authorities involves the systematic violation of an array of human rights on a scope and scale seldom witnessed elsewhere in the world. In particular, the commission finds that national service violates the rights of Eritreans to life; to liberty and security; not to be tortured or subject to cruel, inhumane or degrading treatment; to be treated with humanity and inherent dignity of the human person while deprived of liberty; to be recognized everywhere as a person before the law; to enjoy freedom of thought, conscience, religion, expression and movement; to privacy and family life; to education; to the highest attainable standard of physical and mental health; not to be subjected to forced labour; and to gain one's life by work freely chosen or accepted.' The Eritrean government has denied and denounced the findings of the report.

Details of Ethiopia's expulsion of ethnic Eritreans and the toll of the Ethiopia–Eritrea war come from a Human Rights Watch report from January 2003, 'The Horn of Africa: Mass Expulsions and the Nationality Issue'.

A vivid description of life at the Sawa military academy can be found in a US diplomatic cable from November 2006, published by WikiLeaks.

Details of the number of people fleeing Eritrea come from the Human Rights Watch country report of 2013, and the Frontex 2013 Annual Risk Analysis.

5. Sleeping on the Roofs of Police Stations

The description of the protests at the Arab International University comes from interviews with Hanan al-Hasan, Rim Hamzah and Bisan Hamzah, and from a number of clips of the protests uploaded by students to YouTube. Hanan also shared video clips of the shelling of the family's neighbourhood in Yarmouk.

Details of the first chemical weapons attack in Syria in December 2012 came from a leaked cable from the US State Department.

6. Three Friends

For figures on the Syrian refugee crisis, the UNHCR keeps a detailed interactive tally at data.unhcr.org/syrianrefugees

General observations about life in refugee camps are based on my reporting from camps in Asia. Specific details about the situation for Syrian refugees are from a Médecins Sans Frontières report from 8 October 2013 about the mental health of Syrian refugees in camps in Iraq, and a World Health Organisation-funded report, 'Assessment of Mental Health and Psychosocial Support Needs of Displaced Syrians in Jordan', published in October 2014.

The figure for the numbers of Syrians trying to enter Europe in 2012 is from the Frontex 2015 Annual Risk Analysis.

There are two books which provide an excellent account of the developed world's deteriorating treatment of refugees, and they are Caroline Morehead's *Human Cargo: A Journey Among Refugees*, and *Border Vigils: Keeping Migrants out of the Rich World* by Jeremy Harding. An unparalleled book on the Europe that emerged from the Second World War and the formation of the European Union is *Postwar: A History of Europe since 1945* by Tony Judt.

Another source for the background to Europe's treatment of refugees was author interviews with Jeff Crisp, a former UNHCR official who now consults for the Refugee Studies Centre at the University of Oxford.

The figures on arrivals in Europe are from the Frontex 2015 Annual Risk Analysis.

7. A Family Betrayal

Figures of Syrian refugees in Lebanon come from the UNHCR data portal. The estimate of the $2.5 billion cost to the Lebanese economy is a World Bank estimate contained in a UNHCR briefing from 3 April 2014, which also details the strain on the Lebanese state. Jeff Crisp, the visiting fellow at the Refugee Studies Centre at the University of Oxford, also visited the Lebanese refugee settlement during his time at the UNHCR, and further details are from interviews with him.

Push-backs by the Greek authorities have been detailed by a number of journalists and human rights organizations, based on interviews with the people returned to Turkey. See 'Greece: Frontier of Hope and Fear', the 29 April 2014 report by Amnesty International.

Push-backs are considered illegal under a number of EU laws and international conventions, notably the European Convention on Human Rights, which prohibits the collective expulsion of people, and Article 33 of the 1951 UN Refugee Convention, which prohibits the return of a refugee to a place where their life or freedom would be threatened. In an interview with the author in May 2014, the then-European Commissioner for Home Affairs, Cecilia Malmström, said she was 'convinced' push-backs were happening, but defended the lack of infringement proceedings, saying it was difficult for the European Commission to gather evidence against nations as they had no investigative powers.

8. An Indefinable Suffering

The primary source for the accounts of the prison network and torture by the regime was the 'United Nations Office of the High Commissioner for Human Rights – Report of the Detailed Findings of the Commission of Inquiry on Human Rights in Eritrea', published on 5 June 2015. Also the 2009 Human Rights Watch report 'Service For Life: State Repression and Indefinite Conscription in Eritrea'. Details about the intelligence networks came from the report and author interviews with Meron Estefanos, the director of the Eritrean Initiative on Refugee Rights.

Accounts of the Bedouin kidnapping rings are also from Meron Estefanos, who has co-authored a report on the phenomenon, 'Human Trafficking in the Sinai: Refugees between Life and Death', published in September 2012. The UN report also corroborates the accounts.

The description of conditions around the fence separating Morocco from the Spanish enclave of Melilla is from the author's reporting trip to Melilla and Morocco in August 2013. See 'The Chairman of Melilla: Misery at the Gates of Fortress Europe', published by *Roads & Kingdoms* on 14 October 2013, and 'As Syria Implodes, Europe Braces for a Spiralling Refugee Crisis', published on *TIME* online on 5 September 2013.

Accounts of mistreatment came from author interviews with migrants in Morocco, from the March 2013 report by Médecins Sans Frontières, 'Trapped at the Gates of Europe', and from the February 2014 Human Rights Watch report, 'Abused and Expelled: Ill-treatment of Sub-Saharan African Migrants in Morocco'.

Details of the current Morocco–EU cooperation agreement can be found in a European Commission fact sheet dated 6 October 2015, 'Funding of Migration-related Activities in the Southern Neighbourhood Region'.

The figures on Eritrean arrivals in Europe are from the Frontex 2015 Annual Risk Analysis.

Descriptions of the Lampedusa shipwreck of 3 October 2013 come from four sources: underwater photographs taken by Francesco Zizola published on *TIME* online in November 2014 of the sunken vessel at the bottom of the sea, and accounts of survivors in the following articles: 'Aren't We Human Beings? One Year After the Lampedusa Refugee Tragedy', by Juliane von Mittelstaedt and Maximilian Popp, published on *Spiegel Online International* on 9 October 2014;'Lampedusa Boat Tragedy: A Survivor's Story', by Zed Nelson published by the *Guardian* on 22 March 2014; and 'Thousands of Eritreans Face Torture and Death as They Flee Despotic Rule', by Samuel Oakford, published by *Vice News* on 3 October 2014.

Details on the final death toll from the Lampedusa tragedy and efforts to recover the bodies come from author interviews with Tareke Brhane, president of the 3 October Committee founded in the aftermath of the sinking.

9. Never Again

Details of the value of smuggling operations come from author interviews with Rob Wainwright, the Director of the EU law enforcement body EUROPOL. He estimated that human smugglers made a profit of between $3 billion and $6 billion in 2015.

Insights into how the EU's closed borders fuel the smuggling trade come from author interviews with François Crépeau, the UN Special Rapporteur on the Human Rights of Migrants.

For a fascinating look at how different nationalities are treated at various points in the journey, see 'How Money, Race and Religion

Determine the Fate of Europe-bound Migrants', by Matina Stevis and Manuela Mesco, published in the *Wall Street Journal* on 16 August 2015.

The primary sources for the details of the 11 October 2013 voyage are accounts given to the author by Mohammed Kazkji and Omar, who declined to give his surname. Another crucial source is the 30 September 2014 report by Amnesty International, 'Lives Adrift: Refugees and Migrants in Peril in the Central Mediterranean'. The report has a detailed time line of attempts by the refugees to contact the Italian and Maltese coastguard, based on interviews with the refugees on the boat and officials in Malta and Italy. Mohanad Jammo, the doctor who made the calls for help, also gave a detailed interview to the Italian magazine *L'Espresso*, published on 7 November 2013.

10. Fortress Europe

Figures of Syrian refugees in Turkey come from the UNHCR data portal.

For descriptions of conditions for refugees in Turkey, see the 20 November 2014 Amnesty International report, 'Struggling to Survive: Refugees from Syria in Turkey'. Figures on the amount Turkey is spending on refugees and how much they received from the international community come from the same report.

Figures on the numbers crossing the Greece–Turkey border come from the Frontex 2015 Annual Risk Analysis.

Human Rights Watch put out a report on the effects of Greece's Operation Xenios Zeus on 12 June 2013, entitled 'Unwelcome Guests: Greek Police Abuses of Migrants in Athens'.

The portion of Chapter Ten dealing with the numbers of arrivals and the reception conditions in Sofia draws heavily on the author's reporting trip to Bulgaria in October 2013. See 'Bulgaria's Human Timebomb: Syria's Crisis Hits EU's Poorest Nation', published in *The Independent* on 3 November 2013, and 'Refugees Find Discomfort and Unrest in Bulgaria', published on *TIME* online on 16 November 2013.

Regarding the detention of asylum seekers, Article 31 of the United Nations' 1951 Refugee Convention states that states 'shall not impose penalties, on account of their illegal entry of presence, on refugees who, coming directly from a territory where their life or freedom was threatened in the sense of article 1, enter or are present in their territory without authorization, provided they present themselves without delay to the authorities and show good cause for their illegal entry of presence'. The same article also addresses detention of refugees, stating that states 'shall not apply to the movement of such refugees restrictions other than those which are necessary'. On 21 September 2012 the UNHCR released new guidelines on detention of people seeking refugee status, with its spokesperson Alice Edwards clarifying that 'seeking asylum is not a criminal act, and that indefinite and mandatory forms of detention are prohibited under international law'. EU law and the European Convention on Human Rights also prohibit the routine detention of asylum-seekers, listing a limited number of exceptions.

For details about push-backs along the Bulgaria–Turkey border, see the Human Rights Watch report 'Containment Plan: Bulgaria's Pushbacks and Detention of Syrian and Other Asylum Seekers and Migrants', published on 4 April 2014. The Bulgarian government denies the reports of push-backs.

The description of conditions at Harmanli comes from the photographs and text on a blog by the Agence-France Presse correspondent Diana Simeonova, published on 3 December 2013.

11. Our Sea

Interviews with Mohammed and Omar provide the primary source for the descriptions of the sinking and the rescue. The exceptions are the detail about Hasan Yousef Wahid and his family, which comes from the 30 September 2014 report by Amnesty International, 'Lives Adrift: Refugees and Migrants in Peril in the Central Mediterranean', and the detail about the father watching his son drown, which is from a report on the BBC on 12 October 2013, headlined 'Mediterranean "A Cemetery" – Maltese PM Muscat'.

Another crucial source was a video of the immediate aftermath of the sinking and the rescue published on YouTube by the Armed Forces of Malta on 23 October 2013, with the title: 'AFM Release – Search & Rescue 118NM off Malta 11th October 2013'.

Regarding the Italian and Maltese response to the sinking, Martin Xuereb, head of the Maltese Armed Forces at the time, told the *Malta Independent* that Italian boats which were closer to the sinking vessel should have gone to assistance of the dying Syrians. See the 22 December 2013 article in the *Malta Independent* entitled '11 October Lampedusa Tragedy: Documentation Remains Unpublished'. Both Italy and Malta say they acted with full compliance of their international obligations at sea.

For Malta's history of detaining migrants and refugees, see the 18 July 2012 Human Rights Watch report, 'Boat Ride to Detention: Adult and Child Migrants in Malta'.

12. Europe Turns Ugly

The Médecins Sans Frontières report of 1 April 2014, 'Invisible Suffering: Prolonged and Systematic Detention of Migrants and Asylum

Seekers in Substandard Conditions in Greece', contains descriptions of the conditions and medical complaints of people detained in Greece.

The figures for the amount the European Commission gave Greece for improving its reception conditions and for border security measures come from the Amnesty International report, 'Greece: Frontier of Hope and Fear', published on 29 April 2014.

For the effects of Operation Xenios Zeus, see the Human Rights Watch report from 12 June 2013, 'Unwelcome Guests: Greek Police Abuses of Migrants in Athens'.

The estimate for Bulgaria's shrinking population was contained in a 2013 report by the National Strategy for Demographic Development of Bulgaria.

On the attacks on ethnic minorities in Bulgaria, see the author's 'Refugees Find Discomfort and Unrest in Bulgaria', published on *TIME* online on 16 November 2013. Also, on the political situation in Bulgaria at the time, see the author's article published in *The Independent* on 8 November 2013, 'Students Invoke Spirit of '68 in Fight to Rid Bulgaria of Corruption'.

13. Escaping 13V105

For the conditions on the Maltese naval frigate, see the video published on YouTube by the Armed Forces of Malta on 23 October 2013, entitled 'AFM Release – Search & Rescue 118NM off Malta 11th October 2013'.

For details of Prime Minister Joseph Muscat's hard line on the arriving refugees, see the 6 August 2013 story on the BBC headlined 'Malta Refuses European Demand to Accept African Migrants'.

14. Hunted

The extensive UN report of 5 June 2015 – 'United Nations Office of the High Commissioner for Human Rights – Report of the Detailed Findings of the Commission of Inquiry on Human Rights in Eritrea' – gives this account of the conditions for pregnant women in prisons in Eritrea: 'Of the few cases the Commission received about pregnant women in detention, none were permitted to give birth in a hospital outside of the prison. The Commission is also deeply concerned about reports received of pregnant women miscarrying and being forced into premature labour as a result of beatings. In one case, a Christian woman detained for her religious beliefs was given the choice to give birth in a hospital on the condition she relinquish her faith, or give birth in the prison: "If you want to go to the hospital, you have to stop the Christianity" she was told. A man described seeing a pregnant woman beaten: "It is called the butchery because there is blood everywhere. I saw one pregnant girl (three to four months) lose her baby from the beating. She was caught trying to go to Sudan. I was in the queue after her to be punished. I could see her getting hit with a thin sleek stick all over her body by four men. She began bleeding. She was taken to the nurse. I don't know what happened there, but I heard they took the baby out."'

The figure of 5,000 Eritreans leaving each month is from the UNHCR.

On 18 June 2015, the UNHCR put out a statement confirming that worldwide displacement had in 2014 hit an all-time high. The figures are contained in its report, 'Global Trends Report: World at War'.

Details of the number of resettlement places offered at the Geneva conference come from a UNHCR press release, 'New Resettlement Places Offered for Syrian Refugees', dated 27 June 2014.

The figure of 3.2 million Syrian refugees is from the UNHCR data portal.

The figure of only 14 EU nations offering homes to Syrian refugees was given to the author during a May 2014 interview with the European Commissioner for Home Affairs at the time, Cecilia Malmström, who called the figure 'pathetically low'. The figure of less than 45,000 places found in 2014 is from a UNHCR statement dated 9 December 2014, and entitled 'UNHCR Calls on International Community to Resettle 130,000 Syrian Refugees'.

The figures on the arrivals in Europe from January to April come from a Frontex briefing attended by the author in April 2014.

The Danish report is called 'Eritrea – Drivers and Root Causes of Emigration, National Service and the Possibility of Return' and was published in November 2014. Soon after, the UNHCR put out a statement raising its concerns about the methodology. The revised British guidelines on Eritrean asylum applications came into force in March 2015.

Transparency International ranks Eritrea as the tenth most corrupt nation in the world, while the Reporters Without Borders 2015 World Press Freedom Index has Eritrea at the bottom, just below North Korea.

15. All Alone

Description and detail of the situation at Milan Central Station are from a reporting trip by the author to Milan in February 2015.

Data on returns through the Dublin Regulation are published by the EU's statistics agency, Eurostat. One report looking in detail at the problems with the Dublin Regulation and its effect on families is

'Dublin II Regulation: Lives on Hold' by the European Council on Refugees and Exiles, published in February 2013.

Details of Turkey's increasingly tough approach towards Syrians crossing the border are contained in the 20 November 2014 Amnesty International report, 'Struggling to Survive: Refugees from Syria in Turkey'. The Turkish government has denied forcing Syrians back over the border.

Human rights abuses by the Islamic State in Iraq are detailed in a report by the Office of the United Nations High Commissioner for Human Rights dated 19 March 2015. Abuses by the Islamic State in Syria are documented in an Amnesty International briefing paper dated 19 December 2013 entitled 'Rule of Fear: ISIS Abuses in Detention in Northern Syria'.

The World Food Programme put out numerous statements throughout 2014 warning of the consequences if their funding drives were not met. See specifically 'Funding Shortfall Forces WFP to Announce Cutbacks to Syrian Food Assistance Operation', dated 18 September 2014, and 'WFP Forced to Suspend Syrian Refugee Food Assistance, Warns of Terrible Impact as Winter Nears', published on 1 December 2014.

The word 'swarm' was used by British Prime Minister David Cameron in July 2015 to describe people coming across the Mediterranean. His foreign secretary, Philip Hammond, referred to people waiting in Calais to try and cross the Channel as 'marauding'.

16. A Very Long Transit

The figure of one in every sixty people who cross the Mediterranean dying is calculated using data on crossings and deaths from the IOM and the UNHCR.

Figures for the numbers of people arriving in Italy and Malta compared with the numbers arriving in Greece in 2014 are from the Frontex 2015 Annual Risk Analysis.

Hungary's treatment of people arriving on its soil claiming asylum and the conditions in the detention centres are documented in the UNHCR's report, 'Hungary as a Country of Asylum: Observations on the Situation of Asylum-Seekers and Refugees in Hungary', dated 24 April 2012.

17. A Lifeline Cut Off

The European Union has guidelines for a minimum level of provision for the people arriving in its member countries seeking asylum, including offering food, shelter and medical treatment. Each country can interpret those rules, and in many nations if a refugee chooses not to stay in an official shelter they lose access to those basic rights. Reuters news agency collated a summary of benefits offered to refugees and asylum seekers in the twenty-eight EU states and Norway and Switzerland, entitled 'Factbox: Benefits Offered to Asylum Seekers in European Countries' and published on 16 September 2015.

The figures on the number of people rescued by Mare Nostrum and the cost of the operation are from the Italian navy, while details of the campaign by the Italians to convince other EU nations to help pay for the search-and-rescue operation are from a visit by the author to the Mare Nostrum control room in Rome in July 2014. See 'Italian Navy Pleads for Help Saving Migrant Boats, Saying it "Does Not Want a Sea of Death"', published in *The Independent* on 8 July 2014.

Baroness Anelay, at the time Britain's Minister of State with responsibility for the Foreign & Commonwealth Office, provided a written answer to the House of Lords stating that search and rescue creates 'an unintended "pull factor", encouraging more migrants to attempt the dangerous sea crossing and thereby leading to more tragic and unnecessary deaths'. See 'UK Axes Support for Mediterranean Migrant Rescue Operation', by Alan Travis, published in the *Guardian* on 27 October 2014.

The UN Special Rapporteur on the Human Rights of Migrants, François Crépeau, told the author in an interview in November 2014: 'When politicians are saying, "We should not do search and rescue because it encourages other people to come", to me this is an extremely cynical way of putting it. Not supporting search–and–rescue operations means letting them die. This is what happens, if you don't search and rescue them; they die. If we accept that, I think we go well beyond the moral boundaries of our political system.'

18. Ghosts on the Horizon

A description of the *Ezadeen* was contained in a report published in the *Guardian* on 3 January 2015 by John Hooper, headlined 'Refugees Give Thanks after "Ghost Ship" Ezadeen Rescued in Mediterranean'.

Details of the gruelling winter journeys over the Mediterranean were given to the author by refugees and NGO staff on a reporting trip to Milan in February 2015. See 'Migrants Risk Death to Escape War and Get to Europe', published on *TIME* online on 3 March 2015.

The figures of the increase in deaths in the first quarter of 2015 are from IOM.

For survivors' accounts of the sinking of 19 April 2015, see 'Mediterranean Migrants Crisis: What Happened on the Sinking Boat?', published on the BBC on 23 April 2015.

The figures on deaths between November 2013 and April 2014 and deaths in the same period the following year are from IOM. They are believed to be conservative estimates.

Details about Selam and her son Elyud were given by Selam's uncle, Futsum Isaak, in interviews with the author. Other details came from a photograph and an account of the family's journey published on 1 May 2015 in the Norwegian newspaper *Adressa*, headlined, 'The Tragedy in the Mediterranean: Elyud (6) Died Trying to Get to Europe'.

Interviews with Sina Habte and Antonis Deligiorgis are the primary sources for the description of the shipwreck near the shores of Rhodes. There are also videos uploaded to YouTube and photographs of the boat nearing the shores and of the rescue.

19. At the Crossroads of Europe

Descriptions of the situation at Vienna's Westbahnhof are based on observations by the author during a visit to the station with Hanan al-Hasan in September 2015.

Amnesty International put out a report in German on the conditions at Traiskirchen on 13 August entitled 'Quo Vadis Austria? Die Situation in Traiskirchen darf nicht die Zukunft der Flüchtlingsbetreuung in Österreich werden'.

For the difficulties with family reunion, see the report 'Not So Straightforward: The Need for Qualified Legal Support in Refugee Family Reunion', published by the British Red Cross in 2015.

The UNHCR put out a press release on 1 July 2015 detailing the drop in deaths on the central Mediterranean route, entitled 'Mediterranean Crisis 2015 at Six Months: Refugee and Migrant Numbers Highest on Record'. The figure for the dramatic increase in people arriving in Greece is from a UNHCR press release on 2 October 2015, 'Refugee Sea Arrivals in Greece This Year Approach 400,000'. For a detailed breakdown of arrivals in Europe in 2015, see the UNHCR's interactive data portal at http://data.unhcr.org/mediterranean.

Many journalists and NGOs have reported on the dire conditions for people arriving in Greece in 2015. Specifically, see the descriptions in the Amnesty International statement of 24 August 2015, 'Greece: Chaos and Squalid Conditions Face Record Number of Refugees on Lesvos'. Figures for the arrivals on Lesbos are from the UNHCR.

'Greek Island Struggles to Bury Drowned Migrants', about the lack of space in cemeteries on Lesbos, was published on EurActiv.com on 9 October 2015. The incident of 2,500 refugees in the football stadium in Kos was widely reported. The details about a bat-wielding gang are from an Amnesty International statement on 4 September 2015, 'Refugees Attacked and in "Hellish Conditions" on Kos'.

Descriptions of the situation when the Macedonian border was shut down come from a video published on the *Guardian* website on 23 August 2015.

20. Dark Thoughts

A breakdown of nationalities arriving in Europe can be found on the UNHCR data portal.

Plans by the European Commission to give Eritrea development aid were announced by the European Commissioner for International Cooperation and Development, Neven Mimica, during a visit to Nairobi in September 2015.

Details of refused Eritrean asylum applications come from an Amnesty International report from 2 December 2015, 'Just Deserters: Why Indefinite National Service in Eritrea has Created a Generation of Refugees'. The BBC also ran Home Office statistics on 2 December 2015 showing an increase in rejections after the new guidelines came into force.

Additional detail of Sina's stay in Athens comes from author interviews with Debbie Karnachoriti.

21. A Moral Emergency

Regarding an increase in Islamophobic attacks, see 'The Rise of ISIS and Islamophobia in the UK', a report published by the Al Jazeera Centre for Studies on 24 August 2015.

The economic and cultural benefits which migrant workers, including refugees, can bring to European nations – especially in light of declining population growth – have been documented in a number of reports. For further reading, the book *Immigrants: Your Country Needs Them*, by Philippe Legrain, offers thoroughly researched arguments on this controversial issue.

The European Union agreed to resettle 32,256 refugees from Greece, Italy and Hungary at a meeting on 26 June 2015.

The figures for the number of people crossing the Hungary–Serbia border and the Hungary–Croatia border come from Amnesty International's report 'Fear and Fences: Europe's Approach to Keeping Migrants at Bay', published on 17 November 2015.

22: Lockdown

Additional details of the telephone call confirming Dani's death came from author interviews with Debbie Karnachoriti.

For details on Serbia's initial reaction to refugees trying to cross its territory, see the 15 April 2015 statement by Human Rights Watch, 'Serbia: Police Abusing Migrants, Asylum Seekers'.

Epilogue. No Direction Home

Amnesty International put out a report, 'Europe's Gatekeeper: Unlawful Detention and Deportation of Refugees from Turkey', on 16 December 2015. The Turkish government denied its findings.

For the folly of spending millions on tented refugee camps which no one wants to live in, see 'The £100 million ghost camp for refugees that YOU pay for: It was built with UK foreign aid for 130,000 fleeing war in Syria – but is so grim that only 15,000 live there', by Ian Birrell, published in the *Daily Mail* on 19 December 2015.

Somalia's Prime Minister Omar Abdirashid Ali Sharmarke made his remarks in an interview with the BBC.

The European Commission keeps a running tally of the number of refugees relocated from Greece and Italy, and as of 7 January 2016, 272 refugees had been moved.

In December 2015, the UNCHR reported 103,338 people arriving in Greece, compared with 2,056 in December 2014.

European Health and Food Safety Commissioner Vytenis Andriu-kaitis's letter was leaked and published in the Belgian newspaper *Le Soir* on 1 December 2015.

Acknowledgements

First and foremost, my deepest gratitude to Majid, Nart, Mohammed, Sina, Hanan, Talal, Ismail, Riad, Rim and Bisan, who were
all so generous with their time and had so much patience with
my seemingly endless rounds of questions. They did this when
they had so much other turmoil and hardship in their lives and I
will be forever grateful for the opportunity they gave me to share
their experiences. Their commitment to the book is a reflection
of their desire to help others in similar situations to them, and to
foster understanding between refugees and the communities they
find themselves in. Each went above and beyond just answering
my questions, and I thank them all again for their kindness and
understanding towards me and my family. A portion of the profits
of this book will go to charities which have directly helped the
people featured in its pages. Hanan would like to nominate
Diakonie in Austria, Sina and Andonis were assisted in Athens by
Smile of a Child, and Majid would like to recognize the support
of the Rome organization ESC Infomigrante.

There are many people and organizations doing invaluable
work with refugees, and many of them helped me in various
ways with the research for *Cast Away*. In particular I would like
to thank Maeve Patterson – then of Amnesty International and
now of the UNHCR – who was a great help from the earliest
research stages. My thanks also to her Amnesty colleagues Matteo

de Bellis, Carmen Dupont and Eliza Goroya. From Médecins Sans Frontières, I would like to thank Christof Godderis and Aurelie Ponthieu. In Greece, thanks to Ketty Kehayioylou of the UNHCR and Pepy Papapaulou. Thank you also to Josefin Henrysson in Borås, Sweden. In my general reporting on the refugee issue, Ben Ward, Judith Sunderland and Lydia Gall of Human Rights Watch have been a great help, as have Christopher Catrambone, Regina Catrambone and Christian Peregin of the Migrant Offshore Aid Station. Thanks also to Andrew Cutting of the Council of Europe and Jeff Crisp of the Refugee Studies Centre. Over the years of reporting there are so many people – translators, fixers, interviewees – who have made my stories possible, but there are a few who stood out in helping me get a unique angle and amazing access. They are José Palazón and Sergi Cámara in Melilla, and the group of Cameroonians they helped me find on the other side of the fence in Morocco. And in Syria, I can't stop thinking about the young family with the newborn baby – I never knew their real names – who drove me round Damascus at night and allowed me rare access to the protests and opposition networks. Thank you so much, wherever you are now.

Thanks to my agent Charlie Viney, for having faith in a very early draft of my proposal and for his passion for the subject matter. I have been delighted by the support, encouragement and enthusiasm from everyone I have come into contact with at Portobello Books. Laura Barber has been an incredibly patient and encouraging editor, and her comments have helped make *Cast Away* a much more fluid, readable book. In polishing, producing and publicizing the book, thanks to Mandy Woods, Christine Lo, Lamorna Elmer, Iain Chapple and Pru Rowlandson. I would also like to thank the editors of *The Independent* and *The Independent on Sunday* for their commitment to covering the refugee crisis, and my editors at *TIME* for giving my stories a wider global audience.

The support of friends and family has been invaluable. Thanks to Patrick Falby for his sofa in Milan and for the Eritrean connection; Loveday Morris for reading over the Lebanon chapter; Kim Sengupta for his feedback on the Libya background; Katerina Kongika for being not only the best nanny on the planet but also an excellent research assistant; Now family: thanks to Erika Gardner, Steve Gardner and Jamie McDonald-Gibson for their insights on the first draft and all their encouraging words, not just with this book but over many years; to Sonja Haefelfinger for her invaluable help and marvellous company in Vienna; to Tara Kaikini and Nick McDonald-Gibson for moral support. Thanks also to Violet Kemp, who at age twelve picked up my copy of Barbara Demick's excellent book about life in North Korea, *Nothing to Envy*, and read it from cover to cover in a day, giving me hope in the book-reading public of the future.

There are two people without whom this book would not exist. The first is Danny Kemp, who encouraged me and helped with everything from transcription to edits, from the earliest proposals to the final manuscript. He remains my most trusted editor, as well as everything else. The second person is our son together, Nathaniel Kemp. The project emerged from a deeply misguided idea that I would have lots of free time on my hands after he was born, and that I should use that time to write the book I had had in my head for years. Of course when Nathaniel arrived on 7 April 2015 he was a lot more time consuming than I had imagined. But what an asset he turned out to be, accompanying me on research trips across Europe and delighting everyone he met with his charm and enthusiasm. This book would not be the book it is without him.

About the Author

Charlotte McDonald-Gibson has reported from three continents for the international media, including serving as the deputy foreign editor of *The Independent*. She is now based in Brussels covering the European Union for *The Independent* and *TIME*.

Publishing in the Public Interest

Thank you for reading this book published by The New Press. The New Press is a nonprofit, public interest publisher. New Press books and authors play a crucial role in sparking conversations about the key political and social issues of our day.

We hope you enjoyed this book and that you will stay in touch with The New Press. Here are a few ways to stay up to date with our books, events, and the issues we cover:

- Sign up at www.thenewpress.com/subscribe to receive updates on New Press authors and issues and to be notified about local events
- Like us on Facebook: www.facebook.com/newpress books
- Follow us on Twitter: www.twitter.com/thenewpress

Please consider buying New Press books for yourself; for friends and family; or to donate to schools, libraries, community centers, prison libraries, and other organizations involved with the issues our authors write about.

The New Press is a 501(c)(3) nonprofit organization. You can also support our work with a tax-deductible gift by visiting www.thenewpress.com/donate.